FAMILY-CENTERED MATERNITY CARE

Implementation Strategies

Susan McKay, R.N., Ph.D.

Health, Education, and Psychology Services
Laramie, Wyoming

Celeste R. Phillips, R.N., Ed.D.

Director of Nursing Education
Cabrillo College
Aptos, California

AN ASPEN PUBLICATION ®

Aspen Systems Corporation
Rockville, Maryland
Royal Tunbridge Wells
1984

Library of Congress Cataloging in Publication Data

McKay, Susan, 1942-

Family-centered maternity care.
"An Aspen publication."

Includes bibliographical references and index.
1. Maternal health services. 2. Childbirth.
3. Pregnant women—Family relationships. 4. Hospitals,
Gynecologic and obstetric.
I. Phillips, Celeste R., 1933-   II. Title.
[DNLM: 1. Family—Nursing texts.
2. Hospital departments—Organization—Nursing texts.
3. Infant care—Nursing texts. 4. Nurseries, Hospital—
Organization—Nursing texts. 5. Obstetrical nursing.
WY 157.3 M478]
RG940.M39   1984   362.1'982   83-17141
ISBN: 0-89443-892-1

Publisher: John Marozsan
Editorial Director: Darlene Como
Executive Managing Editor: Margot Raphael
Editorial Services: Jane Coyle
Printing and Manufacturing: Debbie Collins

Library of Congress Catalog Card Number: 83-17141
ISBN: 0-89443-892-1

Printed in the United States of America

2 3 4 5

Dedicated to Doris and John Haire, to whom family-centered maternity care owes so much.

Table of Contents

Forewords

If *Family-Centered Maternity Care: Implementation Strategies* had been written two decades ago, it would have been a much different book. Its philosophy would not as yet have been conceptualized. Its goals would necessarily have focused on consciousness-raising rather than on reinforcement of accepted values. Its specific objectives would have been modest: perhaps to make it a common practice for husbands to remain with their wives during early labor or for breastfeeding babies to be brought to their mothers for a night feeding. It would have been a "why to" rather than a "how to" book. Its strategy would have been to search continuously for tiny cracks in a monolithic system, to plant seeds in those cracks, and to hope almost against hope that those seeds might find a bit of fertile soil in which to grow.

Superficially, the picture today is far different. The philosophy of family-centered maternity care is openly accepted, at least in principle. There is a consensus about its goals, and there seems to be no limit to the specific objectives that can be achieved. The need for change in many current maternity practices is widely recognized, and the forces striving for change are stronger than ever before. Nevertheless, the forces resisting change still appear overwhelming at times. Sometimes that resistance is blunt and obvious; more often, it is subtly expressed. Practices that, in themselves, are completely compatible with

family-centered care become co-opted into a new professional orthodoxy.

This resistance to change is quite understandable in light of the hierarchical nature of hospital care and the enormous professional stake in the maintenance of the status quo. Despite sometimes carefully fostered illusions, the interests of the care-giver and the care-receiver are not always congruent. When, as is so often the case, their aims are in opposition to each other, the result is conflict and immobility. When, however, their interests can be shown to coincide, unparalleled progress can and does occur.

Professional organizations are increasingly sensitive to the clearly expressed desires of their clients. The demands for family-centered maternity care in the 1980s are loud and explicit. They are being heard. Numerous superb maternity programs can be found in North America today. Some find their strengths in overall concepts; others, in particular areas, such as preconceptional or prenatal care, intrapartum or postpartum care, or preparation for parenthood. They can learn from each other, and we can learn from all of them.

The authors have searched out and documented these examples of excellence. They have shown how we can build on what has already been demonstrated to be effective and feasible. Their book is a comprehensive reference source for those who wish to be agents of change in maternity care. It is a book written now, about now, and for now. It is a book to be read, to be enjoyed, and to be appreciated, but, above all, it is a book to be used.

Murray Enkin, M.D.
Professor of Obstetrics and Gynecology,
Epidemiology and Biostatistics
McMaster University
Hamilton, Ontario, Canada

Susan McKay and Celeste Phillips have succeeded in their enormous task of analyzing and describing the many approaches used by innovative health care providers to develop family-centered maternity care programs in their respective facilities. The fact that the book deals with a wide range of problems and solutions in a variety of facilities demonstrates that there is more than one route to a family-centered maternity program that will meet the needs of today's childbearing families.

It is hoped that, in the not too distant future, there will be no need for such guidelines, because family-centered maternity care will be provided for all childbearing couples, not just those knowledgeable enough to seek it out. For the time being, however, while maternity care is in a state of transition, the many patterns of care and facility design set forth in this book will help smooth the way to the development of a program of maternity care in which the lifelong implications of the experience of birth are recognized.

The authors are to be commended for their accomplishments.

Doris Haire
President
American Foundation
for Maternal and
Child Health

Acknowledgments

All over the United States, dedicated people are working at the grass-roots level to improve maternity services for families. In our visits to various facilities, it became clear that the energy being exerted to make childbearing a positive experience for families is unbounded. Most of these people will never be recognized; yet, they continue their work with quiet persistence because they believe in its importance. To all those people who welcomed us, helped us, and shared their experiences, thank you.

The love and encouragement we felt from our families as we traveled and wrote enabled us to complete this project. To John, Julie, and Sharon McKay, and to Roger, Duncan, and Catherine Phillips, we give our heartfelt thanks.

We especially wish to acknowledge the Borning Corporation in Spokane, Washington, and the ICEA Virginia Larsen Research Fund for their interest in our project and their financial support.

Introduction

In our involvement with childbirth education through the International Childbirth Education Association (ICEA), it came to our attention that there was a need for an updated manual on implementation strategies for family-centered maternity care. We set ourselves the task of researching and writing about the state of the art. We began with a review of the literature on family-centered care and then developed a questionnaire to obtain information about family-centered maternity care practices (Appendix A). This questionnaire was mailed to 155 facilities identified as "excellent" by ICEA workers in 42 states, the District of Columbia, and Ontario, Canada. Seventy-eight (53%) were returned. Of these 78, responses were received from 64 hospitals and from 14 free-standing birth centers (Appendixes B, C, and D).

After the questionnaire returns had been analyzed, 29 facilities were selected for site visits (Appendix B). These facilities were located in 19 states, representing each region of the continental United States and Hawaii. Figure 1 illustrates the geographical distribution of site visits. During site visits by the authors, practices and procedures were detailed and facility philosophies identified. Photographs were taken; protocols, policies, and procedures were obtained.

This handbook, developed over a two-year period, is a composite of the work of many pioneers in family-centered maternity care. Our purpose in compiling this information is to provide practical assistance in developing or upgrading family-centered maternity care programs.* As authors, we have combined professional experience in hospital maternity nursing, childbirth education, nursing education, consultation, and the implementation of family-centered maternity care in our own communities and elsewhere. Because we know the "insider's view" of the special challenges and problems involved in the change process and because we are aware of the needs of consumers of maternity services, we feel we bring a unique and realistic perspective to the writing of this handbook. We welcome suggestions and comments from readers and will use the information we receive in future revisions of this handbook.

Susan McKay
Celeste Phillips

---

*The authors suggest Diony Young's book, *Changing Childbirth, Family Birth in the Hospital* (Rochester, New York: Childbirth Graphics) as another helpful reference book.

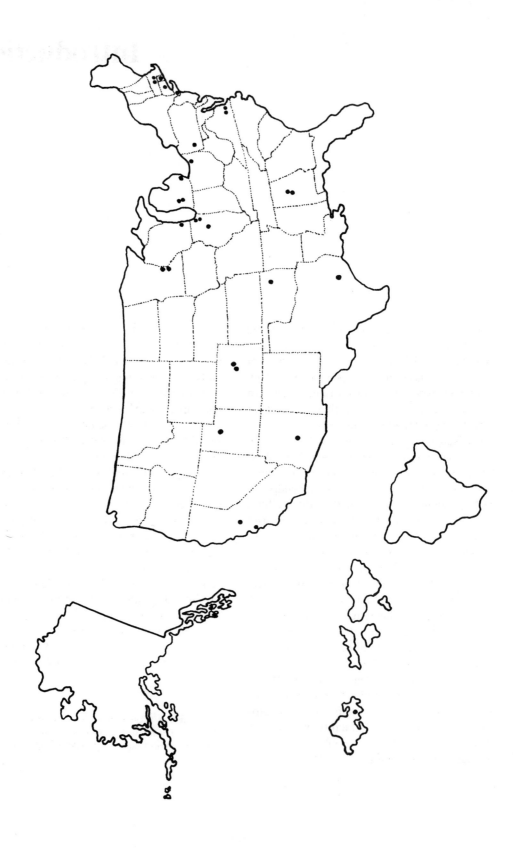

Figure 1 Map of Site Visits

Chapter 1

Family-Centered Care

(photo © Alison E. Wachstein)

1

Family-centered maternity care (FCMC) is a flexible concept of individualized maternity care that focuses on the physical, social, and psychological needs of the total family unit. The Interprofessional Task Force on Health Care of Women and Children, which is composed of the American Academy of Pediatrics, American College of Nurse-Midwives, American College of Obstetricians and Gynecologists, American Nurses' Association, and the Nurses Association of the American College of Obstetricians and Gynecologists, defined family-centered maternity/newborn care as ''the delivery of safe quality health care while recognizing, focusing on, and adapting to both the physical and psychosocial needs of the client-patient, the family and the newly born. The emphasis is on the provision of maternity/newborn care which fosters family unity while maintaining physical safety'' (1978, p. 3). The following family-centered childbirth policies are basic components of FCMC (Interprofessional Task Force, 1978):

1. Hospitals should offer childbirth preparation classes for both mothers and fathers, including education on the role of men at birth.
2. Fathers should be included during the entire birth process.
3. Hospitals should provide homelike birthing rooms that can be used instead of standard delivery rooms, if the family so chooses. Birthing rooms should contain informal furnishings and bear little resemblance to a surgical facility.
4. Hospitals should consider an end to restrictions (some spelled out by state law or health department regulations) on young children visiting their mothers and newborn siblings in the hospital.
5. Hospitals should develop programs for discharge of mothers as soon after birth as possible so that the family can quickly return to the more psychologically secure atmosphere of the home.

The position statement of the Interprofessional Task Force (Appendix E) emphasizes that the major change needed in maternity care to make family-centered care viable is *attitudinal*. In other words, FCMC is a feasible means of implementing a philosophy about childbearing families and the childbearing experience. To attract the childbearing population in a competitive market, many hospitals advertise pretty birthing rooms and alternative birth centers. Comprehensive FCMC is not well-decorated birthing rooms with flowered wallpaper, however, nor is it birthing chairs or birthing beds. Furthermore, when the primary motivation for providing FCMC is financial, restrictive policies and protocols often dominate care. In such settings,

3

parents are "allowed" to hold their baby, and siblings are "permitted" to touch their new brother or sister only with physicians' orders and only during certain time periods. Such restrictions make it very obvious to the family just who is in charge, i.e., the professional staff. As a result, the childbearing family is made to feel dependent on the "experts" in an environment over which they have little or no control— even though the setting is homelike.

In contrast, those who provide FCMC treat each family with dignity, as individuals. Their philosophy is expansive and inclusive, and its foundation is the concept that informed families can make wise decisions about their own care. All policies are designed to promote the maximum health, safety, and welfare of mother, baby, and other family members, while enhancing their childbearing experience. Care-giving and parenting skills are taught to mothers and fathers so that they gain confidence in their ability to care for their new baby. Strengthening their inner resources enables them to parent, and that is what childbirth is: the beginning of parenting, the beginning of a family.

RATIONALE FOR FCMC

Serious inquiry into human behavior at birth is relatively new, and many questions remain unanswered. Published evaluative studies of FCMC have been criticized for failure to use appropriate control groups or for other methodological flaws. Given the limits of predictive science and the large number of events that influence a person's personality and behavior, it is difficult to establish a cause-and-effect relationship between a birth experience and later life events. It is possible, however, to find much evidence that families are pleased with FCMC.

Interviews with families who have received FCMC disclose that they felt increased personal satisfaction from the childbirth experience (Sumner & Phillips, 1981). Informal evaluations of FCMC programs indicate that the programs are popular with parents (Bishop, 1980; Joy, Davidson, Williams, & Painter, 1980). In a comparison of FCMC with traditional maternity care, Jordan (1973) found that parents who experienced FCMC approached infant care with greater self-confidence. Research has indicated that such confidence is related to the development of maternal attachment and adjustment to the maternal role (Williams, 1979). After evaluating the FCMC program at University of Minnesota Hospitals, Sonstegard and Egan reported that "under a system that affords each individual family member recognition and consideration, parenting develops with less difficulty" (1976, p. 249). There is little to lose by promoting maternity practices that enhance feelings of self-confidence. Common sense suggests that there is much to be gained by reestablishing birth as a meaningful, joyous, healthy family event.

PARENT-INFANT RELATIONSHIPS

The term *bonding* describes the beginning of a parent-infant love relationship. Klaus and Kennell (1981) define this relationship as a unique parent-infant attachment that is specific and endures over time. They use behaviors such as eye-to-eye contact, caressing, breastfeeding, and tone of voice as operational measures of parent-infant attachment. It has been proposed that the establishment of a strong parent-to-infant bond immediately after birth facilitates the development of this attachment (Klaus & Kennell, 1981), which is the very foundation of caring and loving.

Numerous studies (de Chateau, 1979; Hales, Logaff, Sosa, & Kennell, 1977; Klaus & Kennell, 1976; O'Connor, Vietze, Sherrod, Sandler, & Altemeier, 1980) appear to support the hypothesis that mothers and newborns will have considerably closer relationships if given "extra" contact immediately following birth. Greenberg and Morris (1974) stated that fathers begin developing a bond with their newborns within the first 3 days after birth. In this research, the term *engrossment* was coined to describe the characteristics of this bond, observable in clinic interviews. These characteristics include a feeling of preoccupation, absorption, and interest in the newborn, along with a desire to look at, hold, and touch the newborn. According to Greenberg, early contact of the father with the newborn seems to encourage engrossment.

Restrictive maternity care practices may well modify the effects of early parent-infant contacts. Conversely, FCMC practices may enhance maternal and paternal sensitivity. McKay (1982) has succinctly described the essence of FCMC:

> The trend towards widespread availability of family-centered care is an important means of returning relevance and the human dimension to the practice of obstetrics—a medical specialty which has been faced with the almost overwhelming availability of technology, the massive application of which has often masked the human experience of giving birth. (p. 1)

CONSUMER PARTICIPATION

A vital element in the development of FCMC programs is consumer participation. Too often, health care professionals decide what consumers want or need without consulting them at all. When consumers do not have direct input into the planning of maternity services, they must exert indirect pressure in order to be heard. This pressure may come in letters or petitions to hospital administration, picketing of hospitals, or boycotting of services. The movement toward family-centered care started 20 years ago as a consumer movement via influential organizations. They are the American Society for Psychoprophylaxis in Obstetrics, Inc. (ASPO), the International Childbirth Education Association (ICEA), and La Leche League International. The activities of these and newer organizations that represent childbearing consumers are having a significant effect on the practice of maternity care, particularly in the United States.

An excellent example of consumer participation in planning care can be found at Sutter Community Hospitals in Sacramento, California. At this hospital, a family-centered care committee composed of nurses meets two times each month; consumers attend one meeting (the pro-

gram planning meeting) each month. The three consumers on this committee are randomly selected, contacted by letter, and interviewed. The consumers serve 18-month terms staggered at 6-month intervals so that all three are not new to the committee at the same time. In order to serve on this committee, consumers must (1) have given birth at Sutter Community Hospitals within the past 4 years, (2) be willing to attend meetings on a regular basis, and (3) be willing to participate actively in planning. The hospital reimburses each consumer committee member for transportation to and from the hospital, as well as for necessary child care. Consumer committee members have initiated an active car restraint program and developed a hospital information pamphlet to stimulate discussion between families and physicians.

At Worcester Hahnemann Hospital in Worcester, Massachusetts, a committee of five or six consumers is consulted before changes are made in the family-centered program. Whatever the method chosen for consumer input, open and honest communication between health care providers and childbearing families is essential.

STAFF PARTICIPATION

In order to provide FCMC, the staff must assume a position of support instead of control. The childbearing family becomes a partner in decision making, with the staff offering expertise rather than authority. Interviews with professionals who have assumed this new role have revealed their overwhelming satisfaction with it, although many of them admit that the transition to this role was not painless.

During their educational and socialization process, most health care professionals have been imbued with a provider culture (Spector, 1979) that emphasizes the illness perspective or medical model viewpoint of health care. This unique preparation can create values and beliefs that do not sanction any methods of health care other than those that are "scientifically proved." As a result, the beliefs and value systems of providers often differ from those of consumers. Such incongruence can lead to conflict between a family's choices for childbirth and the health care professional's recommendations.

It is imperative for health care providers to understand why families want alternatives to traditional hospital birth. This understanding begins with their evaluation of their own values and beliefs about childbearing.

CHOICE OF BIRTH ALTERNATIVES

Why do women choose birthing rooms? A survey by Maloni (1980) showed that the elimination of the need to move from the labor room to the delivery room was the aspect of the birthing room experience that women most frequently liked. Tranquility was also an important feature. Other reasons given included the opportunity to share the birth experience with their husbands, immediate and unrestricted infant contact, the emotional climate of the birthing room, the lack of usual restrictions imposed by hospital procedures, the priority given to the patient's preferences over hospital procedures, and the supportive nursing care. The homelike atmosphere, while appreciated, was not nearly as important as these other features.

When Cohen (1982) compared women who chose to give birth in hospitals with those who chose to give birth in free-standing alternative birth centers, he found that women who chose a birth center planned to emphasize autonomy and independence rather than intimacy in their child rearing. Also, the people closest to them were much more supportive and involved in the birth than those close to women who chose hospital births. Women who gave birth at the Childbearing Childrearing Center at the University of Minnesota in Minneapolis (Rising & Lindell, 1982) reported that the three major reasons they chose the center were to have control over their childbirth experience, to have family-centered care, and to avoid routine procedures. Kieffer (1980) compared the attitudes of 109 women before and after they experienced birth in a birthing room. The four highest ranking reasons for choice of the birthing room were (1) philosophy, (2) no separation of mother and baby, (3) personal involvement in the birth, and (4) freedom to

make choices regarding labor and birth. These studies indicate that attitudes and choices in the childbirth experience are related to the degree of control that the families expected to exert over the birth event.

Philosophy

A philosophy for an institution, department, unit, or program is a "statement of the system of beliefs which direct the individuals in a particular group in the achievement of their purpose" (Moore, 1971, p. 11). Such a statement should explain why things are done as they are. In other words, a philosophy is a "belief" statement, covering those things about which the group is collectively concerned.

Beliefs are cognitive perceptual responses that can describe, evaluate, and advocate action with respect to an object or situation. Beliefs can be conscious or unconscious, and they can be inferred from what a person says or does. Some things that contribute to beliefs are (1) cultural background, (2) observations, (3) feedback from others, (4) socialization, (5) education, and, of course, (6) the media (Zimbardo, Ebbesen, & Maslach, 1979). Values are enduring beliefs that certain ways of behaving or certain life styles are preferable to others (Rokeach, 1970). An individual's value system is a learned organization of rules on which that person bases choices of overt actions or behavior.

Many of the staff's beliefs and values must be examined when a philosophy of FCMC is being developed. What do they believe about current trends in childbirth practices? How do they feel about alternative birth practices as opposed to traditional maternity care practices? What do they believe about the needs of childbearing families to share their experience? Are they willing to accept the term *family* to include significant or supporting others? What do they believe about the role of educational programs in the department? Should the people responsible for developing the programs be the same individuals who provide the direct care? Other areas in which the staff beliefs and values should be explored are the pregnant patient's rights and responsibilities, the advantages of establishing parent-infant bonding immediately after birth, and the benefits of FCMC to the staff and to the hospital.

All staff members must deal continually with their feelings about the program. Staff meetings to discuss feelings are vital. When a new FCMC program is being implemented, the leader for these meetings may use an attitudinal survey to begin discussion. Questionnaires can also be used to determine the ongoing needs of staff members who encounter difficulty in adjusting to the new concept after an FCMC program has been in operation for a while.

All new nursing staff members hired into an FCMC program must be interviewed as to their attitudinal feelings toward the program. It is imperative that they accept the program philosophy as their own.

A philosophy for an FCMC program should be a thoughtful expression of group values, such as this statement of philosophy from the Family Hospital in Milwaukee, Wisconsin:

As the people of Family Hospital, we stand for the *inherent worth* of all individuals, be they employees, physicians, patients, families, visitors or the community at large.

As employees of Family Hospital, we support, respect and have compassion for each other. We are all valued people, each with *unique* and *important talents* and *strengths* to contribute. Each of us has needs as well, and when those needs are met, we are better able to meet the needs of our patients.

We depend upon and nurture one another, supporting with encouragement, educating with grace and communicating with understanding.

We believe each patient must be viewed as an individual, a family member, and a member of the larger community.

We recognize that each patient is the master of his own life. Since this self-mastery may be threatened by illness and hospitalization, we are committed to helping each patient regain or maintain control of his own environment and life style.

Each patient has the right to expect that we will:

- Treat him with dignity and respect.
- Be gentle with due regard for his physical and emotional suffering.
- Render highly competent medical, nursing and supportive health care.
- Encourage his participation in planning his care and daily activities.
- Give him information and education in order to best deal with stress and changes in his life resulting from his hospitalization or physical condition.
- Enable him to remain in close contact with loved ones whenever desired and possible.

The family is a group of people who value and love each other and whom the patient declares are close to him and involved with him on a daily basis. Although there are legal constraints on us regarding the rights of relatives by blood or marriage, we recognize that a patient's family may well consist of others.[1]

Another example of a philosophy that clarifies the values of the group is that of the Community Hospital of Roanoke Valley in Roanoke, Virginia:

We at Community Hospital of Roanoke Valley, believe that the family is the basis of society. During these times when the future of the family is in question, we feel it is our responsi-

[1]Reprinted with permission of Family Hospital, Milwaukee, Wisconsin.

bility to support and promote this family unit.

Each family member should be recognized and is entitled to consideration in childbearing and childrearing situations that are unique and important functions of the family. Childbearing is an experience that is appropriate and beneficial for the mother, father, and/or significant others to share. Siblings should not be excluded from this important life event; their place in the family should be emphasized and all members of the family will benefit from their presence during the crucial days following birth.

We believe that childbirth is one of the most important life events. All persons involved should be supportive of the parent's expectations, within the realm of safety, to assure that the birth experience is a positive one.

Based on our central belief that the birth experience has a significant impact on the future growth and development of the family, CHRV chooses to promote the Family-Centered Concept of Maternity Care.[2]

The following basic beliefs make up the philosophy that guides mother-infant nursing care at the Queen's Medical Center in Honolulu, Hawaii:

1. WE BELIEVE childbearing is not an illness, but rather a time of emotional, social and physical change and stress.
2. WE BELIEVE in promoting family love and positive attachments/relationships by encouraging contact throughout the experience to the extent desired by the family.
3. WE BELIEVE families must be offered opportunities to gain knowledge in the following areas:
   a. Emotional and physiological changes in the mother during the postpartum period.
   b. Sexuality during the postpartum period and family planning.
   c. Growth, development, basic care and needs of the infant through one year.
   d. Breast and/or bottle feeding.
4. WE BELIEVE by implementing mother-baby couple care, the nursing staff will come to see the family as a whole unit, each member affecting the other.
5. WE BELIEVE in a multi-disciplinary approach to maternal-infant care.
6. WE BELIEVE a daily formalized infant and maternal biopsychosocial assessment is a part of the nursing care of patients.[3]

In summary, staff members at each institution must prepare their own philosophy, because it must reflect what they believe. A thoughtfully prepared philosophy can be the statement from which the unit, program, or facility takes its direction.

Goals

After the philosophy has been developed, goals can be set. Goals are broad and general statements about ways to make the philosophy functional. They are part of the broad plan for an FCMC program. In the past, goal setting and planning were done only by top management, while the function of the employees was to carry out the plans and help reach the objectives. It is now believed, however, that wider participation in goal setting results in greater utilization of an organization's resources, both human and technical, and in significantly better plans. In addition, plans to which many people at all levels of

[2]By Susan Crooks, RN; Donna Sams, RN; and Juanita Wade, RN. Reprinted with permission of Community Hospital of Roanoke Valley, Roanoke, Virginia.

[3]Reprinted with permission of Queen's Medical Center, Honolulu, Hawaii.

an organization have contributed are more likely to be realistic and attainable; they also have built-in support.

Each goal for an FCMC program should be given a priority. The top-priority goal may be to provide an environment that will best meet individual and family needs. Since goals are usually broad statements of long-range purpose, some of them may be unattainable; these may be expressed as "wish" statements for future planning. Other examples of goals are

- to facilitate the bonding process between parents and infant
- to increase the parents' feelings of self-worth
- to provide a choice of birth environments
- to provide an environment in which the family unit is minimally disrupted
- to promote family growth and education
- to meet the childbearing needs of all families
- to assist the expectant family to identify, determine, and meet their own health goals
- to assist the expectant family to understand and cope with the impact of pregnancy and parenthood
- to assist individuals and family to prepare for healthy and wanted pregnancies through family planning education
- to place special emphasis through education on adequate nutrition during all phases of the life cycle
- to prepare the expectant family to achieve a satisfying labor and delivery experience
- to teach and promote appropriate parenting skills

Objectives

Unlike goals, objectives are specific, measurable, and observable. Objectives are behavioral expectations that can be expressed in definite, tangible, quantitative terms. Every objective should (1) be written, (2) be clear, (3) outline the method by which it is to be achieved, (4) indicate the reason that it was developed, (5) set the time

by which it is to be achieved, and (6) include a method of evaluation (Skarupa, 1971).

In order to be useful, an objective must be stated in terms of the results to be achieved, instead of the method to be used. For example, the objective "Patients will be taught about breastfeeding" focuses on the activities of the nurse rather than on the resulting benefits to the patient. In contrast, a measurable objective would be stated as "By the second day postpartum, each new mother will demonstrate on her own breasts the correct method of hand expression of breast milk." With this objective, the focus is on results.

As is true in the development of philosophy and goals, the development of objectives calls for thoughtful examination of the reasons for them. Objectives that are written in terms of results to be achieved and behaviors to be observed can be useful tools for the evaluation of nursing care.

The comprehensive FCMC program at Sutter Community Hospitals in Sacramento, California, has an excellent statement of philosophy, goals, and objectives:

We believe in the inherent dignity and worth of each human being as an individual and as a member of a family unit. The principle guiding the delivery of our maternity health care program is to provide an environment that will support the family as a unit. Our philosophic goal is to meet each person, and family, at their own level of intellectual and social being, then provide the environment (educational, physical and attitudinal) that will best meet individual and family needs.

To ensure a comprehensive approach for delivery of this care, we set forth the following goals and objectives where appropriate:

I. Goal: Family Health Care Education

With specific focus on the individual who is in the child-bearing years of his/her life cycle, our approach to health care education must meet general as well as individual needs. Under the knowledgeable guidance of professional personnel, the ultimate goal of family education is to increase the person's sense of security in himself/herself prenatally, during the intrapartum period, during the postpartum stay, and upon return to the home setting.

Objective 1: Prenatal Education Programs

To provide (group/individual) experiences that will prepare the expectant parent(s) for his/her role during pregnancy, labor, delivery and parenthood. The preparation should include but not be limited to:

1. The process of pregnancy.
    a. Physiology, and normal events of pregnancy.
    b. Diet.
    c. Hygiene, clothing.
    d. Body mechanics during pregnancy.
    e. Breathing/relaxation methods for use during childbirth.
2. Events of labor and delivery.
3. Participation of family members in the events of pregnancy and childbirth.
4. Introduction to infant care needs and related topics.
5. Social-psychological support (group/individual) that will promote readiness and acceptance of the parenting role.

As a result of attending any or all:

1. Early pregnancy classes
2. Fitzhugh childbirth preparation classes
3. Lamaze childbirth preparation classes

4. Bradley childbirth preparation classes
5. Maternity tour
6. Homestyle birth program orientation
7. Individual discussion

the expectant parent(s) will be able to approach childbirth with increased ease and confidence by:

1. Utilizing tools to make labor and childbirth a more pleasant experience.
2. Utilizing support techniques that involve the father (or chosen support person) in a meaningful role during pregnancy and childbirth.
3. Approaching parenthood with more realistic expectations and increased confidence in beginning infant care skills.

Objective 2: Intrapartum Education

To provide the parturient with knowledgeable guidance that will support learned or innate techniques of coping during the process of labor and delivery including but not limited to:

1. High risk pregnancy testing combined with counseling and education to deal with anxiety regarding a real/potential threat to the mother and/or unborn infant.
2. Physical support during labor combined with guidance and use of techniques learned in prenatal education experiences, or provision of techniques that will be helpful in the control of labor discomfort.
3. A recovery experience fostering early parent-infant attachment.

Objective 3: Postpartum Education Programs

1. To provide (group/individual) experiences where parent(s) can acquaint themselves with their child, learn basic principles of infant care, and/or details of care specific to their child as a result of participating in demonstrations and/or discussions on:

   a. Bathing.
   b. Bottle feeding.
   c. Breastfeeding.
   d. Infant care.

2. To provide (group/individual) experiences where the parent(s) can acquaint themselves with the tasks and needs of a postpartum mother as a result of participating in individual/group discussions/demonstrations on maternal self care.

II. Goal: Physical Facilities

With specific focus on the individual who is in the childbearing years of his/her life cycle, our utilization of physical facilities while subscribing to the codes and recommendations of licensing agencies will be flexible to meet the needs of the consumer of maternity health care. We will provide an environment in which the family unit is minimally disrupted. The environment should maximize the healthy and smooth transition into parenthood with safeguards for infection control.

Objective 1: Family-Centered Care Program

While adhering to infection control policies, following the standards of nursing practice put forth by the department of nursing service, and adhering to the rules/regulations that govern the hospital as a licensed health care agency, involvement of family members during hospitalization will be achieved in the following manner:

1. The father, or designated substitute, may accompany and support the mother during the labor period.
2. With appropriate preparation the father, or designated substitute, may accompany the mother to the delivery room to participate in the delivery experience.
3. The father, or designated substitute, may visit with the infant in the recovery room.
4. Throughout hospitalization, the mother's desire for infant contact time will be set by her limits, desires or needs.
5. The father, or designated substitute, will be allowed liberal visitation privileges with the mother and infant to participate in educational activities pertinent to their needs.
6. Sibling visitation will be permitted in the mother's room at designated times.

Objective 2: Homestyle Birth Program

In addition to the above tenets of Family-Centered Care, the Homestyle Birth Program provides an alternative birthing experience for prepared families.

1. Low risk prepared expectant mothers may elect to participate with chosen support people in a more homelike birthing environment in which

labor, birth, recovery and initial infant assessment will take place. Minimal intervention and yet medical safeguards will be provided.
2. Minimal interruption or separation of mother (parents) and newborn will occur during hospitalization given an uncomplicated, healthy outcome.
3. Early discharge may be elected by the family after which home followup will be provided by a trained professional RN.

III. Goal: Professional Performance

With specific focus on the individual who is in the childbearing years of his/her life cycle, the nursing staff will act as the coordinator for the planning and implementation of nursing care activities that will promote family growth and education with appropriate utilization of physical facilities.

Objective 1: Clinical Nursing Activity

A clinically skilled nursing staff will work with the parent(s) to:

1. Assess the parent(s) readiness, physically and emotionally, to take on the beginning aspects of parenthood.
2. Identify what support measures will be necessary to assist parent(s) in developing this readiness.
3. Implement a nursing plan of care based on both general and specific needs of the individual patient (family).

4. Document nursing care activities.
5. Evaluate nursing care activities.

Objective 2: Family-Centered Care Committee

A committee composed of nursing representatives from all perinatal units, as well as maternity service social worker(s), perinatal educator(s), lay consumers and administrative personnel as appropriate, will meet at least once monthly to:

1. Plan and implement facets of the Family-Centered Care Program.
2. Make policy recommendations regarding unit(s) management in relation to family-centered maternity nursing philosophy.
3. Provide a mechanism for communication and problem solving.[4]

RESISTANCE TO CHANGE

Most hospitals are bureaucratic organizations characterized by a well-defined chain of command and a system of rules and procedures to control work activities. Labor is divided according to specialization. The reward structure is based on technical competence, and the leadership style, being autocratic, tends to foster impersonality in human relationships (Ashley, 1977).

In order to do well in a bureaucratic organization, employees must be loyal to the system and accept its rules and control. Historically, nursing and medical training has indoctrinated students with the value of the bureaucratic structure (Ash-

[4]Reprinted with permission of the Perinatal Center, Sutter Community Hospitals, Sacramento, California.

ley, 1977). Consequently, many of the staff in positions of authority in hospitals have a primary allegiance to the organization and resist consumer requests for change.

Within bureaucratic hospital settings, the staff is usually in complete control. Orders are issued, and families are expected to follow them submissively (Kalisch, 1975). It can be comfortable for providers to be the authorities on maternity care. "You cannot visit your mother because that is hospital policy " is much easier for the staff to say than to explain the scientific ration~¹ for such a policy.

STRATEGIES FOR CHANGE

Changing staff attitudes may be the biggest challenge in persuading hospitals to convert from traditional maternity care to FCMC. In planning for structured change, it is essential in the beginning to build a good, trusting relationship between the key person involved in making the change (the change agent) and the people involved in the change. The human needs of those involved must be taken into account, since change is more acceptable when it is understood and is not perceived as threatening. In building a relationship from which change can happen, the problems to solve must be identified (Havelock, 1973).

Excellent illustrations of this step in the change process were evident at all the sites visited. Some of the change agents interviewed began by building a trusting relationship with the hospital administration, medical staff, or nursing staff. Others established a collaborative approach between medical, nursing, and administrative personnel from the very beginning. In other words, each situation was a bit different. The change agent first analyzed the forces involved and then developed a trusting relationship with a sympathetic listener who could help. Ideally, that listener holds some decision-making power. Mullaly and Kervin (1978) "sold" the controversial idea of sibling visitation by gaining the support of a few physicians before they made a formal proposal. These nurses asked an enthusiastic physician to present the proposal

at a combined pediatric-obstetric staff meeting. He was able to counter the negative reactions from his colleagues. Unfortunately, a proposal made by nurses at that time probably would not have received the same attention as a proposal presented by a peer physician.

As the next step, groups wanting to implement change should gather information to substantiate the need for change. At this point, prospective patients and new parents can be interviewed. Candy (1979) reported on consumer requests for maternity services not provided by the Toledo Hospital in northwest Ohio, where consumers were threatening to patronize other hospitals for childbirth services. In addition to interviews, observations of current practice can be made and data collected from the relevant literature. With the rapid proliferation of books and articles on FCMC, it is not difficult to compile an array of documentation to support it.

By now, the people involved in the trusting relationship should be thoroughly familiar with the problem identified. Next, they need to deliberate, cite documentation from the research, generate a range of solution ideas, and refine and rethink approaches to the problem. Their goal is to choose the best situation in which to begin the change process. The importance of a written plan cannot be overemphasized (Easterwood, 1981).

Many change agents interviewed on site visits chose to begin in small ways. One started a series of prenatal classes, another established a "fathers are not visitors" policy, and another started on a postpartum unit with demonstrations of the proper way to bathe a baby. They all worked diligently to gain acceptance for their plans by including everyone involved in maternity care at their facilities. Since one of the most important aspects of FCMC is the attitude of the staff, development of a program must include all staff.

FCMC can be gradually introduced by in-service programs (Figure 1-1), conferences, and workshops. Admitting office and laboratory personnel, volunteers, clerical help, and those responsible for custodial services should also be included in education programs. Although much more difficult to control than some of the other

Figure 1-1 Content Areas for an In-Service Education Program

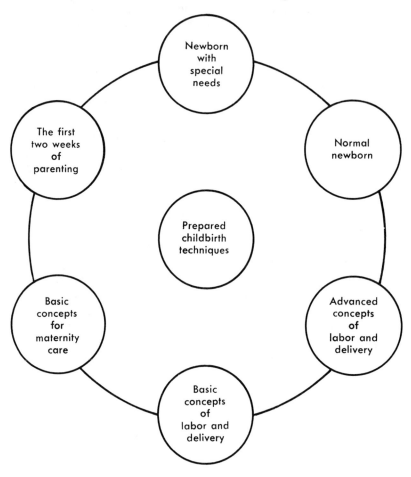

Source: Reprinted with permission from *Birthing Rooms* by P. Sumner and C. Phillips. St. Louis: C.V. Mosby, 1981.

planning variables, attitudes can be influenced by education of all those in contact with the childbearing family.

Bowden (1979) displayed articles strategically on bulletin boards, in lounges, and at nursing stations. Candy (1979) shared with physicians and nurses the content of the hospital-based prenatal classes. Films and videotapes demonstrating family-centered practices can be shown on the units. Staff members can be encouraged to attend conferences given by childbirth education groups, such as ICEA. The nursing director at Woman's Hospital in Texas has, herself, driven groups of staff nurses to ICEA conferences in the hospital van.

Simple successes will pave the way for more complicated change. In a description of change at Chicago Lying-In Hospital, Paukert (1979) noted that acceptance came as it was gradually demonstrated to the staff that FCMC works. As acceptance is gained, the change is stabilized. In order to be long-term, however, change must generate self-renewal. Periodic review and revision are necessary to keep relevant the changes made. Also, continuing reward and satisfaction for the staff are very important. As they experience the joyous births and exuberant "thank yous" of families, even the most traditionally oriented staff members will be converted to a philosophy of FCMC.

REFERENCES

Ashley, J. *Hospitals, paternalism, and the role of the nurse.* New York: Teachers College Press, 1977.

Bishop, J. (Ed.). *Family-centered maternity care: How to achieve it.* Spokane: The Cybele Society, 1980.

Bowden, M.S. How we did it: Family-centered care in a large community hospital. *Journal of the Association for Care of Children in Hospitals,* 1979, *8*(1), 14-17.

Candy, M. Birth of a comprehensive family-centered maternity program. *Journal of Obstetric, Gynecologic, and Neonatal Nursing,* 1979, *8*(2), 80-84.

Cohen, R.L. A comparative study of women choosing two different birth alternatives. *Birth,* 1982, *9*(1), 13-19.

de Chateau, P. Effects of hospital practices on synchrony in the development of the infant-parent relationship. *Seminars in Perinatology,* 1979, *3,* 45-60.

Easterwood, B. The process of change, a case study. *Journal of Obstetric, Gynecologic, and Neonatal Nursing,* 1981, *10*(5), 362-364.

Greenberg, M., & Morris, N. Engrossment: The newborn's impact upon the father. *American Journal of Orthopsychiatry,* 1974, *44,* 520-531.

Hales, D.J., Logaff, B., Sosa, R., & Kennell, J.H. The findings of limits of the maternal sensitive period. *Developmental Medicine of Child Neurology,* 1977, *4,* 454-461.

Havelock, R.G. *The change agent's guide to innovation in education.* Englewood Cliffs, NJ: Educational Technology Publications, 1973.

Interprofessional Task Force on Health Care of Women and Children. *Joint position statement of the development of family-centered maternity/newborn care in hospitals.* Chicago: Interprofessional Task Force on Health Care of Women and Children, 1978.

Jordan, D.A. Evaluation of a family-centered maternity care hospital program. *Journal of Obstetric, Gynecologic, and Neonatal Nursing,* 1973, *2*(1), 13-35; *2*(2), 15-27; *2*(3), 15-23.

Joy, L., Davidson, S., Williams, T.M.B., & Painter, S. Parent education in the perinatal period: A critical review of the literature. In P. Taylor (Ed.), *Parent-Infant relationships.* New York: Grune & Stratton, 1980.

Kalisch, B.J. Of half gods and mortals: Aesculapian authority. *Nursing Outlook,* 1975, *23*(1), 22-28.

Kieffer, M.J. The birthing room concept at Phoenix Memorial Hospital, Part II: Consumer satisfaction during one year. *Journal of Obstetric, Gynecologic, and Neonatal Nursing,* May/June 1980, *9,* 151-159.

Klaus, M., & Kennell, J. *Maternal infant bonding.* St. Louis: C.V. Mosby, 1976.

Klaus, M., & Kennell, J. *Parent-infant bonding.* St. Louis: C.V. Mosby, 1981.

Maloni, J. The birthing room: Some insights into parents' experiences. *American Journal of Nursing,* 1980, *5,* 314-319.

McKay, S. *Humanizing maternity services through family-centered care.* Minneapolis: International Childbirth Education Association, 1982.

Moore, M.A. Philosophy, purpose, and objectives: Why do we have them? *Journal of Nursing Administration,* 1971, *1*(3), 9-14.

Mullaly, L.M., & Kervin, M.C. Changing the status quo. *The American Journal of Maternal Child Nursing,* 1978, *3*(2), 75-80, 124.

O'Connor, S., Vietze, P., Sherrod, K., Sandler, H., & Altemeier, W. Reduced incidence of parenting inadequacy following rooming-in. *Pediatrics,* 1980, *66*(2), 176-182.

Paukert, S.E. One hospital's experience with implementing family-centered maternity care. *Journal of Obstetric, Gynecologic, and Neonatal Nursing,* 1979, *8*(6), 351-358.

Rising, S.S., & Lindell, S.G. The childbearing childrearing center: A nursing model. *Nursing Clinics of North America,* 1982, *17*(1), 11-21.

Rokeach, M. *Beliefs, attitudes and values: A theory of organization and change.* San Francisco: Jossey-Bass, 1970.

Skarupa, J.A. Management by objectives: A systematic way to manage change. *Journal of Nursing Administration,* 1971, *1*(2), 52-56.

Sonstegard, L.J., & Egan, E. Family-centered nursing makes a difference. *The American Journal of Maternal Child Nursing,* 1976, *1*(4), 249-254.

Spector, R. *Cultural diversity in health and illness.* New York: Appleton-Century-Crofts, 1979.

Sumner, P., & Phillips, C. *Birthing rooms: Concept and reality.* St. Louis: C.V. Mosby, 1981.

Williams, T.M. Continuities and discontinuities related to the development of maternal attachment. In T.M. Williams (Ed.), *The development of maternal attachment: A longitudinal study.* Symposium presented at the meeting of the Society for Research in Child Development, San Francisco, March 1979.

Zimbardo, P.G., Ebbesen, E., & Maslach, C. *Influencing attitudes and changing behavior* (2nd ed.). Reading, MA: Addison-Wesley, 1979.

Chapter 2

Family-Centered Antepartum Care

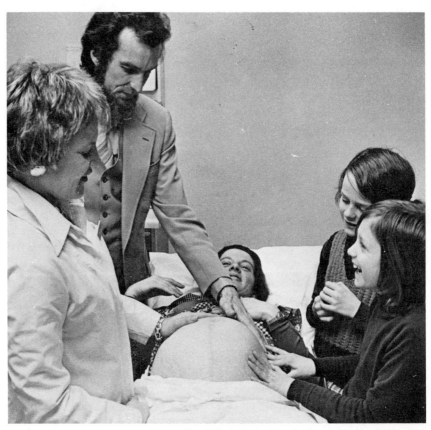

(photo © Alison E. Wachstein, from *Pregnant Moments*, Morgan & Morgan, 1979)

2

Although only the woman is physically pregnant, family members are also experiencing the shifts and changes in feelings, relationships, and life style that are associated with pregnancy. To care for the woman without including the people who live with her and love her is to ignore her most important support system and to provide fragmented care. On the other hand, the fact that family members may be physically participating in activities surrounding pregnancy does not in itself mean that family-centered care is being provided.

STRESS IN PREGNANCY

Much research interest has recently been focused on stress and its effects on pregnancy outcome. Most of the physiological research in this area has been done with animals, however, and it must be remembered that it is often not scientifically sound to extrapolate results of animal studies to humans. In animals unaccustomed to human contact, there appears to be a correlation between increased maternal catecholamine levels and decreased fetal heart rate and blood pressure, fetal hypoxia and acidosis, and electrocardiographic changes (Morishima, Pedersen, & Finster, 1978; Rosenfeld, Barton, & Meschla, 1976). These effects apparently occur because the uterine blood flow is decreased when the pregnant animals are subjected to stressful

stimuli, such as bright, flashing light; sudden loud noise or movement; and/or pain-inflicting devices.

Human studies on the effects of prolonged prenatal anxiety have indicated a correlation between high levels of maternal anxiety and outcomes such as prematurity or obstetric complications (Crandon, 1979; Newton, Webster, Binu, Maskrey, & Phillips, 1979; Standley, Soule, & Copans, 1979). Lederman (1978) found a correlation between women's anxiety levels and their labor progress, suggesting that high maternal anxiety levels result in poorer uterine contractility and, therefore, a slower labor progress. Scientists have been unable to demonstrate a correlation between human maternal stress or pain and fetal hypoxia, however.

Women who have a greater than normal amount of anxiety or who live in nonsupportive family situations should be identified early in pregnancy so that appropriate intervention plans can be developed and pregnancy outcome improved as a consequence. The stress that pregnancy exerts on each family member is caused in large part by developmental tasks and adaptational demands that can be puzzling and anxiety-producing. If the family is highly functional and able to be mutually supportive, psychological adjustment is smoother as pregnancy unfolds. Early identification of families who are experiencing difficulty with the process of adaptation permits early intervention and assistance in developing more functional patterns. As observed by Allen and Mantz (1981), there is more change in families if they are referred prior to 36 weeks' gestation. Allen and Mantz hypothesize that earlier contact allows the nurse to establish a supportive relationship with the mother and to define mutual goals prior to the infant's birth and the resulting stress of adapting to a changed family structure.

Expectant fathers, in particular, have been ignored in the health care system, which has focused almost exclusively on the mother—from assessment of pregnancy and its effects to the development of mother-infant bonding. As men are increasingly involved in the parenting of their children, the adaptational demands on an expectant father bear as much scrutiny as do those on the mother. For example, the normal process of the expectant father's experience may include physiological reactions, such as nausea, vomiting, and various aches and pains, as part of the adaptational process.

Including the father's adaptational changes in the assessment process, taking time to elicit and understand some of his fears and stresses and their changes as pregnancy advances (for example, from ambivalence and apprehension in early pregnancy to more positive feelings in later pregnancy), and planning for his inclusion in the care process and prenatal bonding are all part of family-centered maternity care. One simple way to begin is to include on the pregnancy record, which will later be forwarded to the birth facility, the father's responses to pregnancy, his description of the experience, and his stated concerns. Biller and Meredith (1975) believe that one of the best ways to improve family functioning is to concentrate on assisting and educating the father. Because his role is less biologically linked and less structured, the opportunity for changes from outside sources (for example, health care providers) may be greater.

Within the antepartum care facility, steps can be taken to identify and care for families that exhibit disproportional but perhaps not obvious amounts of life change, stress, marital or family discord, or other evidence of dysfunctional psychological patterns. Allen and Mantz (1981)

pointed out that the psychological needs of the many "normal" women who do not have a medical or obvious emotional-social problem are often ignored during the course of pregnancy unless acute problems surface. These women may be physically healthy but have social or emotional problems that are overlooked, either because the staff does not recognize them or because the women are not aware of or do not share their need. There are also pregnant women who are normal but who would benefit from preventive intervention because their background places them potentially at risk for problems caused by unresolved developmental conflicts, inability to trust others, poor communication skills, inadequate role models, or limited skills in using support systems.

Allen and Mantz (1981) described a program in which women originally designated "normal" were identified as potentially at risk and in need of further assistance. In this program, the community health nurse visited clients in the physician's office whenever possible. Because of this unique program structure, many women who would normally be underserved, such as those from rural areas, those with transportation difficulties, or those with extended family problems that ruled out home visits, could be seen. Referrals to other community helping agencies increased as a result of this approach. Data gathered by the community health agency after the program was initiated indicated that referrals from private practice to the community health agency tripled and that more than three-quarters of the referrals were for problems identified in women from the "normal" group. Postpartum referrals from the hospital also increased.

The criteria used in this program to identify women at risk appear useful and significant in identifying problems in both parents. The risk criteria were as follows:

1. Significant ambivalent or negative feelings toward pregnancy after 20 weeks gestation:
   a) No questions are asked about pregnancy, labor and delivery, or infant care. Plans for managing these are vague.

b) Patient is uninterested in or refuses to listen to fetal heart rate, to feel fetal outline or to discuss fetal growth.

c) Expectations for labor and delivery and postpartum adjustment are unrealistic, e.g., "just knock me out," or "everything will be great."

d) Past experiences with pregnancy or labor and delivery are perceived as negative.

e) Patient refuses to take classes or help with labor and delivery review, and has done little preparation on own.

f) Patient denies pregnancy, body changes, or awareness of fetal movement (when professional staff can document its presence).

g) Patient has persistent feelings of wanting to run away or "get it over with," especially prior to the last month of pregnancy, or to greater degree than the normal feeling of being tired of pregnancy at late gestation. These feelings are often accompanied by persistent physical complaints such as insomnia, nausea, vomiting, etc., which increase in intensity over the course of time. Frequently patient will not comply with normal comfort suggestions or important health care aspects, such as good nutrition, rest, exercise, etc.

h) Patient sees pregnancy and/or parenthood as interfering greatly with life style or self-image.

i) Patient indulges in activities that could be potentially harmful to self or fetus.

2. Insecure or negative feelings about her own mothering skills:

a) Experience caring for young children is limited.

b) Patient is youngest child in the family, i.e., may long have assumed baby role of the family and has difficulty accepting dependence of infant; often seen by extended family as incompetent and unable to make decisions; may have limited experience in nurturing or limit-setting with others.

c) There is no history of a positive parenting role model.

d) There is a history of abuse in the patient's family or with other children in the nuclear family.

e) Adolescent developmental needs are in conflict with parenting responsibilities.

f) Patient's adjustment experience with previous children was difficult.

g) Current parent-child interaction problems are perceived by parent or professional staff, e.g., the parent may not recognize older child's needs for preparation, planning.

h) Patient is willing to let others assume most of the responsibility for care of baby or is very critical of own abilities.

3. Inappropriate positive feelings about pregnancy or mothering:

a) Patient may enjoy pregnancy but makes no plans for the infant.

b) Patient anticipates infant as a friend (i.e., "someone who will love me/keep me company/listen to me") or otherwise demonstrates role reversal or unrealistic expectations of newborn.

c) There may be evidence of role reversal or unrealistic adult expectations of older children (e.g., children are seen as

always good or as acting too
mature).

4. Inadequate nuclear family support:
   a) There may be marital stress
      acknowledged or unacknowl-
      edged. Mother may say "he
      [father] never helps with the
      children," or she may want the
      father present during labor so
      she can "show him." There
      may be a history of wife abuse,
      alcoholism, or drug abuse.
   b) If patient is unwed: Is the father
      of the infant assuming an inter-
      ested supportive role? Has he
      abandoned the woman? What is
      his anticipated role with the
      infant?

5. Inadequate extended support system:
   a) Patient has no friends who
      could help out in an emergency.
   b) Extended family offers criti-
      cism, discounts patient's skill
      as a parent or is in conflict over
      other family matters.
   c) Extended family lives at some
      distance or is in poor health,
      thus, is not available to help.
   d) Grandparents take over parent-
      ing of the infant to exclusion of
      parents, in the extreme instance
      keeping parent in the role of the
      infant's sibling.

6. Current or historically significant
   psychiatric problems:
      Depression, suicidal ideation,
      schizophrenia, etc. This infor-
      mation must be elicited. If the
      client is obviously in dise-
      quilibrium, she may be identi-
      fied as at risk, but if in a func-
      tional state support may help to
      maintain equilibrium which
      would otherwise be lost.[1]

[1]Reprinted with permission from "Are Normal Patients at
Risk during Pregnancy?" by E. Allen and M. Mantz, *Journal of Obstetric, Gynecologic and Neonatal Nursing*, 1981,
10, 350-351.

FAMILY FUNCTIONING

Because the quality of family life and the
availability of family support during pregnancy
are important to a positive pregnancy outcome,
an assessment of family functioning should be an
integral part of antepartum care. If the family is
functionally competent, the baby is likely to be
adequately nurtured. If the family is dysfunctional, appropriate intervention can be instituted
early in pregnancy. In many instances, the family needs only minimal guidance to establish and
maintain healthy patterns of family functioning.

Unfortunately, assessment of family functioning is usually far down the list of "shoulds" in
antepartum care. Considered far more important
are blood pressure and urine screening, nutritional evaluation, and educational activities.
Antepartum care is strongly oriented toward
physiological events that lend themselves to scientific measurement. Although more elusive in
its measurability, family functioning warrants
close attention early in the course of antepartum
care. The signs of dysfunctional or less than
optimal family functioning are as important as
physiological variations that signal a trouble-
some course during pregnancy.

Smilkstein (1978) proposed a system of evaluating family functioning that he termed the
Family APGAR. This assessment tool is simple
to use and rapidly identifies families that would
benefit from intervention. The Family APGAR
provides a basic index of family functioning by
means of five parameters: *A*daptation, *P*artner-
ship, *G*rowth, *A*ffection, and *R*esolve. Table 2-1
includes a definition of each component, open-
ended questions that can be asked for further
information on the level of family functioning,
and an explanation of the functional area being
measured.

The information needed to determine the
Family APGAR can be obtained by means of a
simple questionnaire on which family members
are asked to evaluate areas of nuclear satisfaction, frequency of disagreement, communication, problem solving, and feelings of happiness
and closeness (Exhibit 2-1). It can be administered to family members during a 15-minute
time period. Using data obtained from the ques-

Table 2-1 Summary of Family APGAR Components

Component	Definition	Open-Ended Questions for Family Function Information	What Is Measured
Adaptation	The utilization of intra and extrafamilial resources for problem solving when family equilibrium is stressed during a crisis	How have family members aided each other in time of need? In what way have family members received help or assistance from friends and community agencies?	How resources are shared or the degree to which a member is satisfied with the assistance received when family resources are needed.
Partnership	The sharing of decision-making and nurturing responsibilities by family members	How do family members communicate with each other about such matters as vacation, finances, medical care, large purchases, and personal problems?	How decisions are shared, or the members' satisfaction with mutuality in family communication and problem solving.
Growth	The physical and emotional maturation and self-fulfillment that is achieved by family members through mutual support and guidance	How have family members changed during the past years? How has this change been accepted by family members? In what ways have family members aided each other in growing or developing independent life styles? How have family members reacted to your desires for change?	How nurturing is shared, or the members' satisfaction with the freedom available within the family to change roles and attain physical and emotional growth or maturation.
Affection	The caring or loving relationship that exists among family members	How have members of your family responded to emotional expressions such as affection, love, sorrow, or anger?	How emotional experiences are shared or the member's satisfaction with mutuality in family communication and problem solving.
Resolve	The commitment to devote time to other members of the family for physical and emotional nurturing. It also usually involves a decision to share wealth and space.	How do members of your family share time, space, and money?	How time, space, and money are shared or the member's satisfaction with the time commitment that has been made to the family by its members.

Source: Adapted and reprinted with permission from "The Family APGAR: A Proposal for a Family Function Test and Its Use by Physicians" by G. Smilkstein. *Journal of Family Practice,* 1978, *6,* 1232-1234.

tionnaire, the health care provider can ask open-ended questions, such as those in Table 2-1, to elicit further information about family functioning.

A family APGAR score of 7 to 10 indicates a highly functional family that has the resources to adapt to its changing life situation. Scores ranging from 4 to 6 suggest moderate dysfunction, while scores of 0 to 3 are indicative of severely dysfunctional families. When dysfunction is moderate or severe, supportive therapy or referral to a provider skilled in family therapy is appropriate. The concern is not only for present patterns of family functioning, but also for their effect on the unborn child; the increased risks of pregnancy, labor, and birth that are associated with dysfunctional family patterns; and the increased risks of parenting inadequacy and child abuse when family functioning is less than optimal.

Resources to provide sufficient help during the childbearing year may be lacking within the family unit. Such resources include adequate extra- and intrafamilial social interaction,

Exhibit 2-1 Family APGAR Questionnaire

The following questions have been designed to help us better understand you and your family. You should feel free to ask questions about any item in the questionnaire.

Comment space should be used if you wish to give additional information or if you wish to discusss the way the question applies to your family. Please try to answer all questions.

"Family" is the individual(s) with whom you usually live. If you live alone, consider family as those with whom you now have the strongest emotional ties.

For each question, check only one box

	Almost always	Some of the time	Hardly ever
I am satisfied that I can turn to my family for help when something is troubling me.	☐	☐	☐
Comments:			
I am satisfied with the way my family talks over things with me and shares problems with me.	☐	☐	☐
Comments:			
I am satisfied that my family accepts and supports my wishes to take on new activities or directions.	☐	☐	☐
Comments:			
I am satisifed with the way my family expresses affection, and responds to my emotions, such as anger, sorrow, or love.	☐	☐	☐
Comments:			
I am satisifed with the way my family and I share time together.	☐	☐	☐
Comments:			

Exhibit 2-1 continued

Who lives in your home?* List by relationship (eg, spouse, significant other,** child, or friend).			Please check below the column that best describes how you now get along with each member of the family listed.		
Relationship	Age	Sex	Well	Fairly	Poorly
_____	—	—	☐	☐	☐
_____	—	—	☐	☐	☐
_____	—	—	☐	☐	☐
_____	—	—	☐	☐	☐
_____	—	—	☐	☐	☐
_____	—	—	☐	☐	☐

If you don't live with your own family, please list below the individuals to whom you turn for help most frequently. List by relationship, (eg, family member, friend, associate at work, or neighbor).			Please check below the column that best describes how you now get along with each person listed.		
Relationship	Age	Sex	Well	Fairly	Poorly
_____	—	—	☐	☐	☐
_____	—	—	☐	☐	☐
_____	—	—	☐	☐	☐
_____	—	—	☐	☐	☐
_____	—	—	☐	☐	☐
_____	—	—	☐	☐	☐

*If you have established your own family, consider home to be the place where you live with your spouse, children, or significant other; otherwise, consider home as your place of origin, eg, the place where your parents or those who raised you live.
**"Significant other" is the partner you live with in a physically and emotionally nurturing relationship, but to whom you are not married.

Source: Adapted and reprinted with permission from ''The Family APGAR: A Proposal for a Family Function Test and Its Use by Physicians'' by G. Smilkstein. *Journal of Family Practice*, 1978, 6, 1231-1239.

religious and cultural support, economic stability that allows the family to meet the monetary demands of pregnancy, easily available medical care, and enough education to understand the changes and adjustment inherent in the childbearing year and to participate as resources in problem solving. Smilkstein (1978) used the acronym SCREEM to describe these resources: Social interaction, Cultural pride or satisfaction, Religion, Economic stability, Education of family members, and Medical care.

LIFE CHANGE

Although not an illness, pregnancy is a major life change that requires adaptation in many areas of family life. The Holmes-Rahe Schedule of Recent Events (SRE) lists life events that similarly require adaptive or coping behavior (Exhibit 2-2). Each item on the SRE has been assigned a numerical value according to the magnitude of the life adjustment it requires. When an individual experiences a sufficient number of life change events, as indicated by a score, that person's health status is more likely to change. For example, a score between 150 and 300 indicates a 50% possibility of a change in an individual's health status, whereas a score of 300 increases the likelihood of a health change to 90%.

The SRE can be used during pregnancy as an information-gathering tool and as a basis for discussion of the effects of pregnancy on life style. Expectant parents whose scores suggest that their adaptational energies are likely to be overtaxed by too many simultaneous changes may require assistance from health care providers or community sources of support. Families should be informed that a clustering of life changes may make the adjustment to pregnancy, childbirth, and the early weeks of parenting more difficult and that either avoiding unnecessary change or postponing it permits them to focus more adaptational energy on these adjustments. Thus, the use of the SRE in early pregnancy serves as a tool for anticipatory guidance for families.

Another simple form can be used beginning with the first prenatal visit to assess clients who

may be at risk (Exhibit 2-3). The interview questions can serve as a guide for family interviews.

CONCERNS OF PREGNANT WOMEN

Glazer (1980) studied the specific concerns and anxiety levels of pregnant women from both a clinic setting and a private group practice. Concerns were found to differ according to the trimester of pregnancy. During the first trimester, the most frequently mentioned concerns related to self, childbirth, and medical care; during the second trimester, the concerns more often focused on medical care, childbirth, and subsequent pregnancies. The greatest number of concerns were expressed during the third trimester, and they pertained to self, childbirth, and its effects on the baby, finances, family, and subsequent pregnancies. Over the entire course of pregnancy, the greatest number of expressed concerns involved the baby and childbirth.

Twenty-nine major concerns were identified by at least 50% of the pregnant women studied (Table 2-2). Glazer recommended that nurses use these concerns as a guide in prenatal interviews or in discussion groups with pregnant women, changing the focus of the interview or discussion to reflect the most common concerns of the various trimesters of pregnancy.

As anxieties, concerns, and family functioning problems are identified, plans can be made to provide follow-up for women who need assistance. This may take the form of

- education and support of family members as they experience role change
- referral to familial and community support systems (for example, early pregnancy classes, fathering groups, La Leche League, parenting groups, public health nurses, community mental health services)
- discussion groups for expectant parents
- ongoing assessment (for example, repeat of family functioning index on a monthly basis) to estimate progress and change
- support of the decision-making abilities of family members to increase their self-confidence and sense of involvement

Exhibit 2-2 The Social Readjustment Rating Scale

Life Event	Mean Value
1. Death of spouse	100
2. Divorce	73
3. Marital separation from mate	65
4. Detention in jail or other institution	63
5. Death of a close family member	63
6. Major personal injury or illness	53
7. Marriage	50
8. Being fired at work	47
9. Marital reconciliation with mate	45
10. Retirement from work	45
11. Major change in the health or behavior of a family member	44
12. Pregnancy	40
13. Sexual difficulties	39
14. Gaining a new family member (e.g., through birth, adoption, oldster moving in, etc.)	39
15. Major business readjustment (e.g., merger, reorganization, bankruptcy, etc.)	39
16. Major change in financial state (e.g., a lot worse off or a lot better off than usual)	38
17. Death of a close friend	37
18. Changing to a different line of work	36
19. Major change in the number of arguments with spouse (e.g., either a lot more or a lot less than usual regarding childrearing, personal habits, etc.)	35
20. Taking out a mortgage or loan for a major purchase (e.g., for a home, business, etc.)	31
21. Foreclosure on a mortgage or loan	30
22. Major change in responsibilities at work (e.g., promotion, demotion, lateral transfer)	29
23. Son or daughter leaving home (e.g., marriage, attending college, etc.)	29
24. Trouble with in-laws	29
25. Outstanding personal achievement	28
26. Wife beginning or ceasing work outside the home	26
27. Beginning or ceasing formal schooling	26
28. Major change in living conditions (e.g., building a new home, remodeling, deterioration of home or neighborhood)	25
29. Revision of personal habits (dress, manners, association, etc.)	24
30. Troubles with the boss	23
31. Major change in working hours or conditions	20
32. Change in residence	20
33. Changing to a new school	20
34. Major change in usual type and/or amount of recreation	19
35. Major change in church activities (e.g., a lot more or a lot less than usual)	19
36. Major change in social activities (e.g., clubs, dancing, movies, visiting, etc.)	18
37. Taking out a mortgage or loan for a lesser purchase (e.g., for a car, TV, freezer, etc.)	17
38. Major change in sleeping habits (a lot more or a lot less sleep, or change in part of day when asleep)	16
39. Major change in number of family get-togethers (e.g., a lot more or a lot less than usual)	15
40. Major change in eating habits (a lot more or a lot less food intake, or very different meal hours or surroundings)	15
41. Vacation	13
42. Christmas	12
43. Minor violations of the law (e.g., traffic tickets, jaywalking, disturbing the peace, etc.)	11

Source: Reprinted with permission from T.H. Holmes and R.H. Rahe: The Social Readjustment Rating Scale. *Journal of Psychosomatic Research* *11*:213-218, 1967.

Exhibit 2-3 Form To Assess Clients at Risk for Crisis

Mother's Name _____ **Age** _____ **Religion** _____
Father's Name _____ **Age** _____ **Religion** _____
Married: Yes_____ No_____ **Length of Time Married**_____ **Number of Children**_____
Pregnancy Planned: Yes___ No___ **Gravida**___ **Para**___ **Abortion:** Elective___ Spontaneous___ **Stillbirths**___

History of birth defects, prematurity, or illness in infants or family:_____
_____

Current Health Status: Mother_____
                       Father_____
                       Other Children_____
Are there any close friends, relatives, or organizations with whom they can talk or turn to for support? Yes__ No__
Name two:_____

INTERVIEW QUESTIONS

1. How does the woman feel about being pregnant?_____
_____

2. Has anything happened in the past or is there a current condition which is causing the client concern?_____
_____

3. What effect does the individual believe this pregnancy will have on her future lifestyle?_____
_____

4. What has been the expectant father's reaction to the pregnancy?_____
_____

5. What child rearing practices were used by the individual's parents when she was a child?_____
_____

   a. Which of these child rearing practices will the couple use with their child?_____
_____

   b. Which practices will they avoid?_____
_____

6. What does the couple do when faced with a serious problem?_____
_____
_____

7. Do they plan to attend childbirth education classes? Yes_____ No_____
   Why?_____
8. Does the expectant father plan to be with the woman during labor and delivery? Yes_____ No_____
9. Does the woman plan to have rooming-in? Yes_____ No_____
10. How much physical help do they anticipate:
    a. During pregnancy:_____
    b. After pregnancy:_____
    c. From whom:_____
11. To what extent will this pregnancy and the infant alter the couple's plans for:
    a. Career and employment:_____
    b. Education:_____
    c. Lifestyle:_____

ADDITIONAL COMMENTS_____
_____
_____
_____
_____
_____
_____
_____
_____

Exhibit 2-3 continued

NOTE
Increased risk for crisis should be considered if:
1. the mother experiences any pregnancy complications.
2. there is the probability of multiple birth.
3. mother and/or infant requires transfer to a high-risk center.
4. there is continued stress that has not been alleviated.
5. the client and/or family have no support systems.

Source: March of Dimes Birth Defects Foundation, 1981.

Table 2-2 Major Concerns Expressed by 100 Pregnant Women

Concern	Women (%)
Baby	
Whether your baby will be healthy and normal	94%
Whether your baby will be a boy or girl	70%
Self	
How you look	91%
Your own health	80%
Gaining too much weight	70%
Change in your way of living	69%
Being depressed	65%
Doing all the housework	60%
Being nervous	53%
Medical care	
Medication you might receive during childbirth	77%
What drugs are safe to take during pregnancy	70%
Being able to follow the diet your doctor ordered	62%
Whether the doctors will give you good care	58%
Whether the nurses will give you good care	58%
Whether the doctors are able to help you	57%
Childbirth	
Your baby's condition at birth	93%
Any unexpected things that might happen during childbirth	89%
Pain of childbirth	83%
Your condition during childbirth	81%
Whether your baby will be premature	70%
The cut the doctor makes when your baby is delivered	61%
Being torn when the baby is born	58%
Whether your baby will be overdue	56%
Whether you will have a miscarriage	54%
Whether something will happen to the baby because of something that might happen during delivery	69%
Finances	
Managing the added cost of having a child	66%
Being able to buy the things your partner and you will need and want	55%
Being able to buy the things your other children will need and want	52%
Subsequent pregnancies	
Type of birth control you will use after this baby is born	54%

Source: Reprinted with permission from "Anxiety Levels and Concerns among Pregnant Women" by G. Glazer. *Research in Nursing and Health*, 1980, *3*, 110.

FAMILY ATTACHMENT

As the questions concerning family functioning and psychological adaptation of family members are answered, it is logical to ask how well each family member is able to develop a relationship with the yet-to-be-born baby. Although research about the postbirth attachment process, particularly mother-infant attachment, has been extensive, less is known or understood about the formation of parent/child relationships during pregnancy—sometimes called prenatal bonding.

As a sensitive receiver of family messages, the fetus is thought to be influenced not only by the mother's responses, but also by the father's. For example, there is solid evidence that hearing the father's voice has a profound emotional effect on the fetus (Verny, 1981). Several studies have shown that newborn babies who heard their fathers' voices during pregnancy were able to pick out and respond to their fathers' voices even in the first 1 or 2 hours of life.

As knowledge of fetal responsiveness expands, practices in antepartum care will be oriented toward facilitating the family-infant attachment process during pregnancy. Especially from the 6th month of pregnancy (and perhaps earlier) when the fetus is capable of hearing, tasting, and primitive learning, care that takes into account these capabilities can be provided.

Encouraging family members to accompany the woman on antepartum visits is one way to involve everyone in the pregnancy and to enhance the formation of affectional bonds with the unborn family member. It may be necessary to schedule appointments on weekend days and evenings to provide times when family members can be present. Especially during the first antepartum visit, the father should be included as an integral part of the care process in the hope that he will show continuing interest. His active involvement will facilitate the establishment of bonds with his baby not only during pregnancy, but also after birth. Health care providers can help expectant parents to explore and articulate their needs and expectations and to construct with their partners a kind of picture of their future lives together as parents by sharing their hopes and fears and fantasizing about their future roles.

Children in the family can accompany their parents on these visits, assisting with care procedures, feeling fetal movements, listening to the fetal heartbeat, and learning about pregnancy and the birth process. Attractive visual displays of fetal development, picture books, and media programs designed for children can educate and involve them.

Family members can be encouraged by health care providers to participate in self-care activities. The Maternity Center Association in New York City holds the philosophy that families can adequately care for themselves if provided with principles and guidance, and that the best preparation for the responsibilities of child care is learning to take care of the fetus. The program of self-care at the Maternity Center Association includes teaching fathers or other support persons to take blood pressure, to palpate the abdomen, to measure fundal height, and to check fetal heart tones. Mothers test their own urine and record their weight, plotting it on graphs. Such activities can increase families' involvement in the pregnancy and their confidence in their ability to care for their child.

Innovative classes for expectant parents are being developed to address the complexities of the attachment process during pregnancy. Jones (1980) developed consciousness-raising groups for expectant fathers beginning in the 4th or 5th month of pregnancy. In the group meetings, the expectant fathers learn about pregnancy, the father's role, and what other men think about it. Jones noted that, prior to the late 1970s, fathering classes probably would not have been accepted; only recently, as the emotional importance of fatherhood is increasingly recognized, family structures are changing, cultural definitions of masculinity are shifting, and men are moving toward study of self, have men been seeing themselves in a different light. (See Chapter 6 for an outline of Jones' fathering classes.)

Schwartz (1980) established pregnancy support groups for men and women wanting to explore their feelings during the childbearing year and to make an emotional connection with their yet-to-be-born children. She observed about the groups:

> In a sense we were engaging in a ''prenatal bonding'' ritual; although we could not hold and touch the babies, we could speak to them, fantasize about them and prepare ourselves for the next stage by making the transition to familyhood on a gradual basis rather than in one sudden plunge after labor and delivery. (pp. 15-16)

She suggested that groups be geared toward first-time parents who are all starting at the same level of experience, that they begin as early in pregnancy as possible—the 3rd month being ideal because by this time the pregnancy is very real to the couple—and that groups be limited to 8 to 10 members. Schwartz used a spectrum of guided exercises, including fantasy, Gestalt awareness, meditation and focusing techniques, drawing and work with clay, journal writing, psychodrama, massage, and body awareness. At times, men and women were separated for a portion of a session, especially beneficial for men who seldom have the opportunity to express their conflicting emotions outside the bonds of the couple relationship.

ANTEPARTUM NURSING ASSESSMENT

The history and assessment form used in the antepartum care setting should be the focus for care planning during the childbearing year. Use of separate plans by each health care provider and facility fosters fragmentation of care and duplication of effort. Therefore, the plan should be shared and used by care providers throughout the childbearing year. Included in the plan should be the family's preferences.

Information is initially obtained from the family during an interview session. The form used to record the information gathered in the family interview should reflect an interest in family functioning and in the emotional adaptation of family members to the pregnancy. Several ante-

partum visits may be required before sufficient family and medical data have been gathered to develop a plan of care with the family. The resultant plan can be included in the prenatal record or developed separately on a Kardex form to be reviewed and updated during each prenatal visit.

Meserve (1982) believes that, if the client and professional work together to determine goals and acceptable courses of action, all persons will benefit from clearer communication. She developed a record form that facilitates client participation and provides information in an effective and easily comprehensible manner (Exhibit 2-4). The form is designed as a single sheet of paper folded into four pages with a pocket between the third and fourth pages that can hold original laboratory tests and correspondence. All information required to assess pregnancy status, determine needs, and plan care is readily available when the form is opened. If necessary, additional information can be included on plain lined paper that can be inserted in the folder. This information may include assessment scores for family functioning, adaptational responses to pregnancy, nutritional evaluation, detailed preference profile sheets, and assessment of risk factors. The record form is intended for use with normal women who use nurse-midwifery services; with some adaptation, however, it can be used in any setting.

If a more traditional medical record is used, it can include a nursing information record that summarizes the family's situation, its concerns, problems related to the pregnancy, and the family members' knowledge and attitudes concerning birth and infant care. The information form can travel from the antepartum care facility to the labor/birthing room, to the postpartum unit, to the public health nurse, and back to the antepartum facility.

ANTEPARTUM FAMILY EDUCATION

Although much prenatal education may take place in hospital- or community-based classes, the primary responsibility for effective antepar-

Exhibit 2-4 Antepartum Record Form

pt #_____

name				birth date
address	city	state	zip	phone
occupation	place of employment			bus. phone

father of the child		birth date
occupation	place of employment	bus. phone

past occupations

height	weight	blood pressure	blood type/Rh
tobacco	alcohol		drugs

health/significant history

insurance company/responsible party

address

Check if record sent

☐   hospital
_____

☐   family health care provider
_____

☐   infants care provider
_____

Problems/Recommendations

Summaries of Care Provided

Pregnancy
Labor/Delivery
Postpartum
Involutional check
Infant

Exhibit 2-4 continued

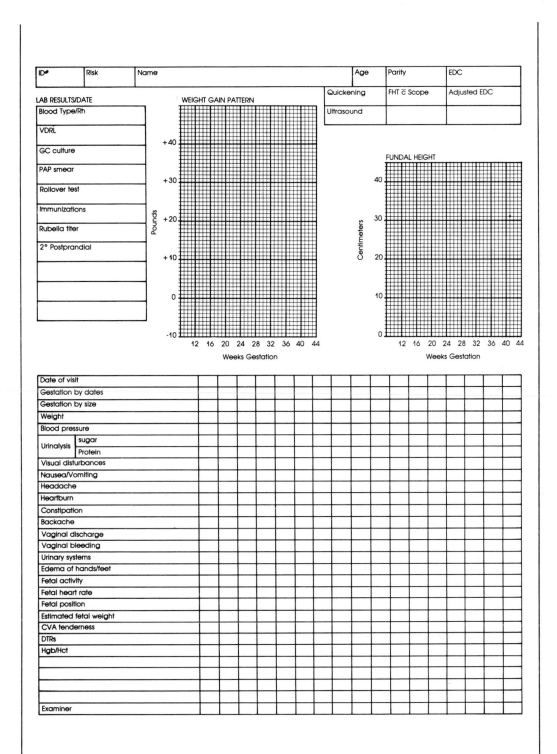

Exhibit 2-4 continued

TEACH/COUNSEL	OK	date	init.
Early pregnancy class			
Fetal/growth devel.			
Progress of pregnancy			
Clinic routines			
WIC referral			
Alcohol, drugs, tobac.			
Sexuality			
Danger signs			
Discomfort/relief			
Emotional changes			
Nutrition			
Mid pregnancy classes			
Nutrition/fluids			
Progress of pregnancy			
Activity/exercise			
Sexuality			
Relaxation measures			
Discomfort/relief			
Breastfeeding classes			
3rd trimester classes			
Progress of pregnancy			
Nutrition/fluids			
Danger signs			
Signs of labor			
Physiology of labor			
Exercise/rest			
Sexuality			
Breast preparation			
Hospit. adm. proced.			
Sibling preparation			
Family planning			

CLIENT PREFERENCES

Place   Hospital   Birth Room

        Home   Birth Center

        address: _____

Medication/anesthesia

        none/minimal   PCB

        Pudendal   local

Delivery: Bed   Table

        Position:

        LeBoyer   Other:

Postpartum: Room in   Early Discharge

        Other:

Labor coach _____

Siblings present: _____

date	PROBLEMS/NEEDS	OK	init.	ALERT LIST		
				MEDICATION	start	DC'd

Nutrition Assessment   at risk   yes   no

height	nonpregnant weight	ideal weight	Hx. preg. Wt. gain

24 hour diet recall
3 day diet history
Protein intake   Calcium intake
Folic acid   Vitamin C.
Iron
Ethnic
Craving   dislike/allergy
Referral
Supplements (Fe, vit)
Diet instructions

NOTES

_____

_____

_____

_____

_____

_____

_____

_____

_____

_____

_____

_____

_____

_____

_____

_____

_____

_____

_____

_____

Exhibit 2-4 continued

FAMILY HISTORY (Circle if someone has had one of these and explain below)

1. Diabetes	4. Tuberculosis	6. Varicose veins	8. High blood pressure	10. Multiple births
2. Cancer	5. Heart disease	7. Birth defects	9. Kidney disease	11. Cesarean births
3. Other:				

Number & explain:

PAST HISTORY (Circle those which you have or have had and explain below)

1. Allergies	7. Kidney/urinary disease	13. Rheumatic Fever	19. Tuberculosis
2. Asthma	8. Neuro/nervous problems	14. Heart disease	20. Alcoholism
3. Drug sensitivity	9. Serious injury/illness	15. Thyroid disorder	21. Smoking
4. Anemia	10. Reaction to anesthesia	16. Bleeding disorder	22. Abnormal blood pressure
5. Drug addiction	11. Painful intercourse	17. Drug addiction	23. Varicose veins
6. Convulsions	12. Problems with intercourse	18. German measles	24. Chicken pox
			25. Other

Number & explain

Operations & dates

Education	Occupations

OBSTETRICAL HISTORY   (record all pregnancies) (circle those which you have had)

1 Rh Babies   2 RhoGam   3 Toxemia   4 Miscarrage   5 Abortion   6 Ectopic pregnancy   7 Hydatiform mole

Year	Sex	Weight	Gestation	Length of labor	Type delivery	Place	Complications	Present health

GYNECOLOGICAL HISTORY (Circle those which you have had and explain)

1 Vaginal infection   2 Veneral disease   3 Sexual abuse   4 Pelvic/gyn surgery

Number & explain

Menarche	cycle/regularity	days/duration	amt. of flow	pain/treatment	gyn disorders

types/dates of contraception/reason for stopping

HISTORY OF THIS PREGNANCY (Circle those which you have experienced with THIS pregnancy)

1. Nausea	4. Cramping	7. Alcohol	10. Constipation	13. Injury/illness	16. Hallucinogens
2. Vomiting	5. Swelling	8. Caffeine	11. Breast changes	14. German measles	17. Addicting drugs
3. Bleeding	6. Headache	9. Smoking	12. Dizziness	15. Mood changes	18. Vaginal discharge
					19. X-rays

List medications taken (include vitamins & aspirin)

Planned pregnancy	yes	no	pleased to be pregnant	yes	no	reaction of baby's father

INITIAL PHYSICAL				INVOLUTIONAL PHYSICAL		
1	General			1	General	
2	Skin			2	Skin	
3	HEENT			3	HEENT	
4	Neck			4	Neck	
5	Breasts/nipples			5	Breasts/nipples	
6	Chest/back/CVA			6	Chest/back/CVA	
7	Heart/lungs			7	Heart/lungs	
8	Abdomen			8	Abdomen	
9	Extremities			9	Extremities	
10	Neuro			10	Neuro	
11	Pelvic:External			11	Pelvic:External	
12	Perineum/BUS			12	Perineum/BUS	
13	Vagina			13	Vagina	
14	Cervix			14	Cervix	
15	Uterus			15	Uterus	
16	Adnexa			16	Adnexa	
17	Rectal			17	Rectal	Pap Smear

Pelvimetry: DC	Spines	IS	Infant feeding
RTPA	Pubic arch	Coccyx	Interaction with infant
Sacral curve	Sidewalls	BI	Contraception/Instructions
Clinical impression			

Source: Reprinted by permission of the publisher from "A New Approach to Prenatal Care Records: Client Participation in Identifying Needs, Planning Care, and Recording Data," by Y. Meserve, *Journal of Nurse-Midwifery 27,* 18-19. Copyright 1982 by The American College of Nurse-Midwives.

Table 2-3 Prenatal Teaching Guide

1st-12th Weeks	12th-24th Weeks	24th-32nd Weeks
Woman more concerned with herself, physical changes with pregnancy, and her feelings about the pregnancy.	*Woman has usually resolved the issue of the pregnancy and becomes more aware of the fetus as a person.*	*Woman becomes more interested in baby's needs as a corollary to her own needs now and after birth.*
Changes that are normal for pregnancy Breast fullness Urinary frequency Nausea & vomiting Fatigue	Growth of fetus Movement FHT	Fetal growth & status Presentation & position Well-being—FHT
EDC—calculate & explain. Compare with uterine size	Personal hygiene Comfortable clothing Breast care & supportive bra Recreation, travel Vaginal discharge	Personal hygiene Comfortable clothing Body mechanics & posture Positions of comfort
Expectation for care Initial visit Subsequent visits	Employment or school plans	Physical & emotional changes
Clinic appointments	Method of feeding baby Breast or bottle Give literature re methods	Sexual needs/changes. Intercourse
Need for iron & vitamins	Avoidance or alleviation of Backache Constipation Hemorrhoids Leg ache, varicosities, edema, cramping Round ligament pain	Alleviation of Backache Braxton Hicks contractions Dyspnea Round ligament pain Leg ache or edema
Resources available Education Dental evaluation Medical service Social service Emergency room		Confirm infant feeding plans Prepare for breast or bottle feeding Nipple preparation Massage & expression of breast
Danger signs Drugs, self-medication Spotting, bleeding Cramping, pain	Nutritional guidance Weight gain Balanced diet Special nutritional needs	Preparation for baby Supplies Household assistance
		Danger signs Preeclampsia Headache, excessive swelling, blurred vision
		Tubal ligation (papers prepared ahead)

tum education lies with the ongoing informal teaching program in the care facility. A strong emphasis on education and counseling provides families with opportunities to learn about their bodies, the effects of life style choices, and self-care habits that can positively affect family health. Because of pregnancy, most families are at an especially teachable period in their lives; pregnant women, in particular, are often willing to forsake or modify their health habits so that their yet-to-be-born children will have a better start in life.

A blitz approach to antepartum education via one or several intensive educational sessions is probably a waste of both staff and family time. A survey by Chamberlain and Chave (1977) showed that the majority of clinic patients felt that group talks by physicians and midwives were not helpful. Rather, these patients found that asking questions in the prenatal clinic and one-to-one contact in the clinical situation were most rewarding. Yet, in the nursing literature, not infrequently a 2- or 3-hour session (or longer!) during an early antepartum visit is pro-

32nd-36th Weeks	36th Week to Term
Woman anticipates approaching labor and caring for baby after birth.	*Woman should feel "ready" for labor and for the assumption of care-taking responsibilities for baby, even though she may feel anxious about both of these as well.*
Fetal growth & status	Review signs of labor (or teach)

Personal hygiene
  Positions of comfort
  Rest & activity
  Vaginal discharge
	Review or continue instruction re relaxation &
	  breathing techniques
	
	Finalize home preparations
	Anticipation of hospitalization

Alleviation of discomfort
  Backache
  Round ligament pain
  Constipation or hemorrhoids
  Leg ache or edema
  Dyspnea
	Admission (ER & labor admitting room)
	  Examination, IV, shave, possible enema
	  Care in labor
	  Medication & anesthesia available
	  Postpartum care
	  Supplies needed: bra, personal items, money
	  May have 2 visitors

Recognition of "false labor"—Braxton Hicks
  contractions
How to cope & "practice" with these
	Tour of maternity unit
	
	Confirm plans to get to hospital; care of other children.
	  When to go and where

Nature of "true labor"signs. Difference between "bloody show" & bleeding	Consider family planning needs

What happens during labor
  Labor contractions & progress
  What she will experience
	Emergency arrangements
	  Precipitate delivery
	  Premature rupture of BOW e' or s' contractions
	  Care away from home

Relaxation techniques	Vaginal bleeding

Breathing techniques
  Abdominal
  Accelerated pattern
  Panting & pushing	

Involvement of husband or significant other	

Provision for needs of other children
  Anticipation of baby
  Care for children at home while mother is in hospital	

Source: Reprinted with permission from "Priorities in Prenatal Education" by J. Roberts. *Journal of Obstetric, Gynecologic, and Neonatal Nursing,* 1976, 5, 18-19.

posed for educational purposes. Although information may be conveyed by this approach, family members who are bombarded with medical and health care information probably retain only a minimal proportion of the content.

The current trend is to fashion antepartum self-care and educational activities around family needs rather than around a predetermined schedule of content. The emphasis is on information sharing and family participation in determining educational needs. Roberts (1976) observed that classes should not replace answer-ing questions at office visits, providing anticipatory guidance, or informing patients about pregnancy progress, childbirth, or institutional policies. Roberts recommended that information be organized according to the gestational period in which it can most appropriately be used by the family. Roberts categorized components of antepartum care that can be shared during various parts of pregnancy (Table 2-3).

Other approaches to self-care education could include (1) an unstructured group discussion format in which the word *class* is avoided, there is no formal teaching plan, and cues are taken directly from participants; and (2) discussion groups focusing on personal care in pregnancy for women less than 28 weeks pregnant, labor and delivery for women 30 to 38 weeks pregnant, and infant care for women who have completed the labor and delivery session. As health care providers become more comfortable with the idea that families should decide what information they need and want to learn, creative educational programs can be offered both in clinics and in private practices. Most health care providers find it easier to teach families with educational and social backgrounds similar to theirs (usually middle class). Those involved in outreach teaching may find group discussion situations initially frustrating and personally threatening, because they do not know how to relate clinical content to patients' concerns, or how to express it in patients' terms.

According to Pahlka (1982), the classes that were most successful and reached the largest numbers of women were those held in the clinic waiting room at the same time as prenatal appointments. She described the minimal teaching aids needed and emphasized use of oneself while cautioning against using norms for the curriculum of classes given to the private sector. Pahlka encouraged an approach whereby discussion is based on clients' experiences and questions are treated seriously.

In discussion groups, it is essential to convey to participants an attitude of positive regard and respect for what women say they want—whether or not it fits with the nurse's notion of what women *should* want. For health care providers involved in outreach teaching, the International Childbirth Education Association (ICEA) publishes an excellent guide, *Outreach Teaching* (McCormick, 1979), that comprehensively addresses the challenges, methods, format, and diversity of outreach education.

INFORMED DECISION MAKING

A basic tenet of family-centered antepartum care is the commitment to include family members in the decision-making process, helping them to participate in their care and encouraging them to choose from available options. The aim is not to place the burden of responsibility on the family, but to encourage, with professional guidance, family participation in decision making. Although some families will prefer to let others make choices for them, a family-centered approach includes providing families with enough information to participate in decision making and to give their informed consent to the course of action chosen.

Informed consent is an issue that is of increasing concern to health care providers, because courts have mandated that providers must obtain patients' informed consent for treatment. The following elements currently set the standards for informed consent:

1. The nature and purpose of the proposed procedure will be adequately identified and explained in lay language.
2. Risk, inconveniences, hazards, and problems in recuperation will be disclosed so that all information material to the decision of a reasonable person will be communicated.
3. Alternative forms of treatment will be discussed.
4. The identity of who will perform the procedure is revealed.
5. The patient will have all his/her questions answered.
6. Then, and only then, can consent "free from duress" be given. (Rockwell & Pepitone-Rockwell, 1979, p. 1342)

Some assert that informed consent and participation in decision making safeguards individual rights in the medical context; others say that this is a myth and that patients do not understand, cannot understand, and do not want to be told. The question of understanding is central to the issue of informed consent. Even when the risks and benefits of various medical procedures have been discussed, the level of understanding has not been found to be very high when patient recall has been tested. Although efforts have been made to increase patients' understanding by using videotape, pamphlets, structured discussion, and informal discussion, it is not known whether any of these media significantly improves understanding. It has been found, however, that clients who are given the opportunity to discuss the content of written forms understand information better than those who have only read the forms. Timing is also important. A reasonable interval between obtaining informed consent and the performance of a procedure may be necessary to enhance understanding.

During the antepartum period, there is usually ample time for the decision-making process to be instituted, for materials to be provided, for discussions to be held, and for questions to be answered. A first step in this direction is to provide all client families with a copy of the Pregnant Patient's Bill of Rights and the Pregnant Patient's Responsibilities (Exhibit 2-5) and to discuss its contents. At the same time, the way in which the antepartum care facility obtains consent can be explained. (For example, information may be provided first in written form by audiotape, or by videotape; recall may be tested by a simple paper and pencil test or by discussion; further discussion may follow to ensure understanding; only then is consent obtained. Although informed consent procedures can be tedious and time-consuming, they can also be viewed as educational opportunities—a way for people to understand more about their bodies and the effects of proposed medical intervention. As informed consumers, they will be better able to cooperate with the medical regimen, increasing the odds of a healthy pregnancy outcome.

PREFERENCE PROFILES AND BIRTH PLANS

In order to ensure that family preferences for the intrapartum and postpartum periods are understood in advance, health care providers at many antepartum and intrapartum care facilities discuss them with the family, put them in writing, and make them available to the birth facility staff so that all in contact with the family understand their preferences. Because preference profiles, also called birth plans, encourage parent involvement in the decisions surrounding their baby's birth and early care, they should be viewed as a positive and practical tool for communication between health care providers and family members. Birth plans or preference profiles may be written in several ways. Some facilities use a checklist or form (Exhibit 2-6); in others, couples may write a narrative explaining their preferences.

When couples draw up their own birth plan without consulting health care providers and present it for the first time on admission during labor, the result can be anger and hostility. Such negative feelings are less likely to arise if the antepartum care personnel initiate the development of the birth plan and make sure the family's preferences are communicated to birth facility staff prior to labor. To help families become aware of their choices and options, lists of alternatives can be provided.

COMPONENTS OF FAMILY-CENTERED ANTEPARTUM CARE

The following components of family-centered antepartum care are designed to emphasize family participation during pregnancy:

1. philosophy of care with clearly defined goals and objectives

   - Philosophy is developed and understood by all care providers.
   - Philosophy is available in writing for each client family and is discussed with family members.

2. team approach

   - Team includes the woman and her family, health care providers, and the community.

Exhibit 2-5 The Pregnant Patient's Bill of Rights and the Pregnant Patient's Responsibilities

THE PREGNANT PATIENT'S BILL OF RIGHTS

THE PREGNANT PATIENT'S RESPONSIBILITIES

The International Childbirth Education Association (ICEA) is an interdisciplinary, volunteer organization representing groups and individuals who share a genuine interest in the goals of family-centered maternity care and education for the childbearing year.

ICEA constantly seeks to expand awareness of the rights and responsibilities of pregnant women and expectant parents. Most pregnant women are not aware of their rights or of the obstetrician's legal obligation to obtain their informed consent to treatment. The American College of Obstetricians and Gynecologists has made a commendable effort to clearly set forth the pregnant patient's right of informed consent in the following excerpts from pages 66 and 67 of its *Standards for Obstetric-Gynecologic Services.*

"It is important to note the distinction between 'consent' and 'informed consent'. Many physicians, because they do not realize there is a difference, believe they are free from liability if the patient consents to treatment. This is not true. The physician may still be liable if the patient's consent was not informed. In addition, the usual consent obtained by a hospital does not in any way release the physician from his legal duty of obtaining an informed consent from his patient.

"Most courts consider that the patient is 'informed' if the following information is given:

- The processes contemplated by the physician as treatment, including whether the treatment is new or unusual.

- The risks and hazards of the treatment.

- The chances for recovery after treatment.

- The necessity of the treatment.

- The feasibility of alternative methods of treatment."

"One point on which courts do agree is that explanations must be given in such a way that the patient understands them. A physician cannot claim as a defense that he explained the procedure to the patient when he knew the patient did not understand. The physician has a duty to act with due care under the circumstances; this means he must be sure the patient understands what she is told."

"It should be emphasized that the following reasons are not sufficient to justify failure to inform:

1. That the patient may prefer not to be told the unpleasant possibilities regarding the treatment.

2. That full disclosure might suggest infinite dangers to a patient with an active imagination, thereby causing her to refuse treatment.

3. That the patient, on learning the risks involved, might rationally decline treatment. The right to decline is the specific fundamental right protected by the informed consent doctrine."

On the following pages ICEA sets forth the **Pregnant Patient's Bill of Rights**
along with the **Pregnant Patient's Responsibilities.**

Exhibit 2-5 continued

THE PREGNANT PATIENT'S BILL OF RIGHTS

American parents are becoming increasingly aware that well-intentioned health professionals do not always have scientific data to support common American obstetrical practices and that many of these practices are carried out primarily because they are part of medical and hospital tradition. In the last forty years many artificial practices have been introduced which have changed childbirth from a physiological event to a very complicated medical procedure in which all kinds of drugs are used and procedures carried out, sometimes unnecessarily, and many of them potentially damaging for the baby and even for the mother. A growing body of research makes it alarmingly clear that every aspect of traditional American hospital care during labor and delivery must now be questioned as to its possible effect on the future well-being of both the obstetric patient and her unborn child.

One in every 35 children born in the United States today will eventually be diagnosed as retarded; in 75% of these cases there is no familial or genetic predisposing factor. One in every 10 to 17 children has been found to have some form of brain dysfunction or learning disability requiring special treatment. Such statistics are not confined to the lower socioeconomic group but cut across all segments of American society.

New concerns are being raised by childbearing women because no one knows what degree of oxygen depletion, head compression, or traction by forceps the unborn or newborn infant can tolerate before that child sustains permanent brain damage or dysfunction. The recent findings regarding the cancer-related drug diethylstilbestrol have alerted the public to the fact that neither the approval of a drug by the U.S. Food and Drug Administration nor the fact that a drug is prescribed by a physician serves as a guarantee that a drug or medication is safe for the mother or her unborn child. In fact, the American Academy of Pediatrics' Committee on Drugs has recently stated that there is no drug, whether prescription or over-the-counter remedy, which has been proven safe for the unborn child.

The Pregnant Patient has the right to participate in decisions involving her well-being and that of her unborn child, unless there is a clearcut medical emergency that prevents her participation. In addition to the rights set forth in the American Hospital Association's "Patient's Bill of Rights," (which has also been adopted by the New York City Department of Health) the Pregnant Patient, because she represents TWO patients rather than one, should be recognized as having the additional rights listed below.

1. *The Pregnant Patient has the right,* prior to the administration of any drug or procedure, to be informed by the health professional caring for her of any potential direct or indirect effects, risks or hazards to herself or her unborn or newborn infant which may result from the use of a drug or procedure prescribed for or administered to her during pregnancy, labor, birth or lactation.

2. *The Pregnant Patient has the right,* prior to the proposed therapy, to be informed, not only of the benefits, risks and hazards of the proposed therapy but also of known alternative therapy, such as available childbirth education classes which could help to prepare the Pregnant Patient physically and mentally to cope with the discomfort or stress of pregnancy and the experience of childbirth, thereby reducing or eliminating her need for drugs and obstetric intervention. She should be offered such information early in her pregnancy in order that she may make a reasoned decision.

3. *The Pregnant Patient has the right,* prior to the administration of any drug, to be informed by the health professional who is prescribing or administering the drug to her that any drug which she receives during pregnancy, labor and birth, no matter how or when the drug is taken or administered, may adversely affect her unborn baby, directly or indirectly, and that there is no drug or chemical which has been proven safe for the unborn child.

4. *The Pregnant Patient has the right* if Cesarean birth is anticipated, to be informed prior to the administration of any drug, and preferably prior to her hospitalization, that minimizing her and, in turn, her baby's intake of nonessential pre-operative medicine will benefit her baby.

Exhibit 2-5 continued

5. *The Pregnant Patient has the right,* prior to the administration of a drug or procedure, to be informed of the areas of uncertainty if there is NO properly controlled follow-up research which has established the safety of the drug or procedure with regard to its direct and/or indirect effects on the physiological, mental and neurological development of the child exposed, via the mother, to the drug or procedure during pregnancy, labor, birth or lactation — (this would apply to virtually all drugs and the vast majority of obstetric procedures).

6. *The Pregnant Patient has the right,* prior to the administration of any drug, to be informed of the brand name and generic name of the drug in order that she may advise the health professional of any past adverse reaction to the drug.

7. *The Pregnant Patient has the right* to determine for herself, without pressure from her attendant, whether she will accept the risks inherent in the proposed therapy or refuse a drug or procedure.

8. *The Pregnant Patient has the right* to know the name and qualifications of the individual administering a medication or procedure to her during labor or birth.

9. *The Pregnant Patient has the right* to be informed, prior to the administration of any procedure, whether that procedure is being administered to her for her or her baby's benefit (medically indicated) or as an elective procedure (for convenience, teaching purposes or research).

10. *The Pregnant Patient has the right* to be accompanied during the stress of labor and birth by someone she cares for, and to whom she looks for emotional comfort and encouragement.

11. *The Pregnant Patient has the right* after appropriate medical consultation to choose a position for labor and for birth which is least stressful to her baby and to herself.

12. *The Obstetric Patient has the right* to have her baby cared for at her bedside if her baby is normal, and to feed her baby according to her baby's needs rather than according to the hospital regimen.

13. *The Obstetric Patient has the right* to be informed in writing of the name of the person who actually delivered her baby and the professional qualifications of that person. This information should also be on the birth certificate.

14. *The Obstetric Patient has the right* to be informed if there is any known or indicated aspect of her or her baby's care or condition which may cause her or her baby later difficulty or problems.

15. *The Obstetric Patient has the right* to have her and her baby's hospital medical records complete, accurate and legible and to have their records, including Nurses' Notes, retained by the hospital until the child reaches at least the age of majority, or, alternatively, to have the records offered to her before they are destroyed.

16. *The Obstetric Patient,* both during and after her hospital stay, has the right to have access to her complete hospital medical records, including Nurses' Notes, and to receive a copy upon payment of a reasonable fee and without incurring the expense of retaining an attorney.

It is the obstetric patient and her baby, not the health professional, who must sustain any trauma or injury resulting from the use of a drug or obstetric procedure. The observation of the rights listed above will not only permit the obstetric patient to participate in the decisions involving her and her baby's health care, but will help to protect the health professional and the hospital against litigation arising from resentment or misunderstanding on the part of the mother.

Exhibit 2-5 continued

THE PREGNANT PATIENT'S RESPONSIBILITIES

In addition to understanding her rights the Pregnant Patient should also understand that she too has certain responsibilities. The Pregnant Patient's responsibilities include the following:

1. **The Pregnant Patient** is responsible for learning about the physical and psychological process of labor, birth and postpartum recovery. The better informed expectant parents are the better they will be able to participate in decisions concerning the planning of their care.

2. **The Pregnant Patient** is responsible for learning what comprises good prenatal and intranatal care and for making an effort to obtain the best care possible.

3. Expectant parents are responsible for knowing about those hospital policies and regulations which will affect their birth and postpartum experience.

4. **The Pregnant Patient** is responsible for arranging for a companion or support person (husband, mother, sister, friend, etc.) who will share in her plans for birth and who will accompany her during her labor and birth experience.

5. **The Pregnant Patient** is responsible for making her preferences known clearly to the health professionals involved in her case in a courteous and cooperative manner and for making mutually agreed-upon arrangements regarding maternity care alternatives with her physician and hospital in advance of labor.

6. Expectant parents are responsible for listening to their chosen physician or midwife with an open mind, just as they expect him or her to listen openly to them.

7. Once they have agreed to a course of health care, expectant parents are responsible, to the best of their ability, for seeing that the program is carried out in consultation with others with whom they have made the agreement.

8. **The Pregnant Patient** is responsible for obtaining information in advance regarding the approximate cost of her obstetric and hospital care.

9. **The Pregnant Patient** who intends to change her physician or hospital is responsible for notifying all concerned, well in advance of the birth if possible, and for informing both of her reasons for changing.

10. In all their interactions with medical and nursing personnel, the expectant parents should behave towards those caring for them with the same respect and consideration they themselves would like.

11. During the mother's hospital stay the mother is responsible for learning about her and her baby's continuing care after discharge from the hospital.

12. After birth, the parents should put into writing constructive comments and feelings of satisfaction and/or dissatisfaction with the care (nursing, medical and personal) they received. Good service to families in the future will be facilitated by those parents who take the time and responsibility to write letters expressing their feelings about the maternity care they received.

All the previous statements assume a normal birth and postpartum experience. Expectant parents should realize that, if complications develop in their cases, there will be an increased need to trust the expertise of the physician and hospital staff they have chosen. However, if problems occur, the childbearing woman still retains her responsibility for making informed decisions about her care or treatment and that of her baby. If she is incapable of assuming that responsibility because of her physical condition, her previously authorized companion or support person should assume responsibility for making informed decisions on her behalf.

Source: Prepared by Doris Haire, Chair, ICEA Committee on Health Law and Regulation, published by International Childbirth Education Association, Inc., Minneapolis, Minnesota.

Exhibit 2-6 Family Birthing Center Preference Sheet

The purpose of this sheet is to have all the necessary information on record to help you have the best childbirth experience possible. Please fill out and return the following information.

NAME:_____ PHONE:_____

ADDRESS:_____

　　　　　　street　　　　　　　　　　city　　　　　　　　　　zip　　　　　　major cross streets

DUE DATE:_____ OBSTETRICIAN_____ PEDIATRICIAN_____

OTHER CHILDREN (Names & Ages)_____

SUPPORT PERSON (during delivery)_____

OTHERS YOU WISH PRESENT_____

SIBLING PARTICIPATION (extent of)_____

DO YOU WANT A CIRCUMCISION FOR A MALE INFANT?_____ PICTURES?_____

Method of infant feeding planned_____

What experience/education have you had with this method?_____

What experience/education have you had with infant care? (Bathing, diapering, etc?)

_____

What information do you want about child care? ____Nutrition   ____Feeding   ____Bath

____Immunizations   ____Infant car seats   ____Home safety, poison control   ____Crying

____Toddlers   ____Sibling rivalry   ____Discipline   ____Other_____

What other information would you like to have? ____Breast self exam   ____Diet   ____Episiotomy

____Exercise   ____Sexuality   ____Depression   ____Family planning   ____Mothering

____Fathering   ____Annual pap test   ____ Recovery after birth

Do you have any specific concerns about your labor/birth/postpartum recovery?_____

_____

How can the nurses best support you?_____

Special requests for your birth experience:

Source: Reprinted with permission of Family Birthing Center, Southfield, Michigan.

- According to the setting, the team may include obstetricians, pediatricians, family physicians, certified nurse-midwives, nurse-practitioners, nutritionists, social workers, childbirth educators, and community or outreach workers.
- Cooperative interrelationships are developed between hospitals, birth centers, health care providers, and the community in an organized system of care.

3. assessment of family functioning by one or a combination of assessment tools to identify the need for intervention

4. family attachment

- Family members accompany the pregnant woman during prenatal visits.
- Appointments can be made on evenings or weekends.
- Family members assist with care procedures.
- Attractive visual displays of fetal development, picture books, and media programs are designed and provided for children.
- Fathering discussion groups are established.
- Parent support groups are formed.

5. antepartum education

   - Information is shared, and the family helps to determine learning needs.
   - A prenatal teaching guide is used for anticipatory guidance.
   - Unstructured group discussions are held.

6. informed decision making

   - Risks and benefits are explained and family understanding is assisted via discussion.
   - Adequate time is allowed between explanations and the performance of a procedure to ensure family understanding.
   - The Pregnant Patient's Bill of Rights and the Pregnant Patient's Responsibilities are made available and discussed with each family.
   - Birth plans and preference profiles are developed during pregnancy.
   - Options for childbirth are listed for the family with supplemental information provided.

7. initial contact with the antepartum care facility

   - The person answering the telephone and scheduling appointments has a warm telephone manner and communicates interest and concern.
   - From the first, it is emphasized that staff members are available to answer questions at any time, not just during appointments.
   - A hot-line number is available for family use, or the names of primary care providers and their telephone numbers are provided.
   - Appointments are scheduled as soon as possible after the initial contact.
   - The importance of self-care measures is communicated immediately, and follow-up information is sent by mail.

8. orientation procedures (especially appropriate if the interval between the initial telephone contact and the first antepartum visit is more than 1 or 2 weeks)

   - Small groups of families are invited to the antepartum care facility according to a flexible schedule (evening, weekend, and daytime scheduling).
   - Orientation is aimed at helping families become comfortable with the facility's operation, to understand basic components of self-care and medical care, and to appreciate the facility's philosophy about families.
   - Components of the orientation session may include introduction of staff and the system of care (a slide-tape program can be used for this purpose), physical layout of the facility, presentation of media materials (e.g., posters, tapes, literature, slide-tape programs), and an explanation of consent procedures.
   - Staff, trained volunteers, paraprofessionals, or a birth counselor (with a background in nursing, the social sciences, or health education) can be given the responsibilities for orientation, such as interviewing families and assessing their function, planning supportive services and intervention, and helping families choose the type of birth experience they desire.

9. first medical visit

   - The first visit is scheduled so that the father, other family members, or friends can accompany the woman.
   - A primary care nurse who is assigned to the family for the duration of pregnancy coordinates the plan of care.
   - The woman meets her medical care provider while still dressed.
   - Care providers are introduced, and the scheduling of family appointments is explained.

- Supervision in self-care procedures is provided.
- Families participate in record keeping. If a family's first language is not English, arrangements are made to provide information in the family's language. Records are "open" with space for family members to add notes.

10. supportive environment

- Walls are warmly painted.
- Posters that provide information on topics such as nutrition, avoidance of teratogenic substances, environmental hazards, safety, and the family's emotional well-being are rotated regularly.
- A play area is provided for children.
- Lighting is natural.
- A lending library, as well as free pamphlets written at educational levels appropriate for the clientele and in the language spoken by the families served, is available.
- Special adjustments are made for the handicapped.
- A kitchen area with nourishing snacks is available, and families who use it

assume the responsibility of caring for the kitchen area.

- Information about community prenatal care services, intrapartum services, and educational programs is prominently displayed.
- The area has plants and comfortable chairs.
- Audiotapes, closed circuit TV, or other media materials are available.

11. ongoing antepartum visits

- Each woman has an initial meeting with the primary care provider prior to her medical visit.
- Educational programs are appropriate to the clientele.
- Anticipatory guidance includes opportunities to express concerns and to ask questions.
- Supervision in self-care procedures is continued.
- Referrals are made to community- and hospital-based educational programs.
- Family functioning is periodically reassessed for the development of family problems, pregnancy concerns, and emotional/psychological changes.

REFERENCES

Allen, E., & Mantz, M. Are normal patients at risk during pregnancy? *Journal of Obstetric, Gynecologic, and Neonatal Nursing*, 1981, *10*, 348-353.

Biller, H., & Meredith, D. *Father power*. New York: Anchor Books, 1975.

Chamberlain, C., & Chave, S. Antenatal education. *Community Health*, 1977, *11*, 11-16.

Crandon, A.J. Maternal anxiety and obstetric complications. *Journal of Psychosomatic Research*, 1979, *23*, 109-111.

Glazer, G. Anxiety levels and concerns among pregnant women. *Research in Nursing and Health*, 1980, *3*, 107-113.

Jones, T. . . . *also of men born!* Portland, Ore.: Terry Jones, 1980.

Lederman, R., Lederman, E., Work, B., & McCann, D. The relationship of maternal anxiety, plasma catecholamines, and plasma cortisol to progress in labor. *American Journal of Obstetrics and Gynecology*, 1978, *132*, 495-500.

McCormick, B. (Ed.). *Outreach teaching*. Minneapolis: International Childbirth Education Association, 1979.

Meserve, Y. A new approach to prenatal care records: Client participation in identifying needs, planning care, and recording data. *Journal of Nurse-Midwifery*, 1982, *27*, 17-20.

Morishima, H.O., Pedersen, H., & Finster, M. The influence of maternal psychological stress on the fetus. *American Journal of Obstetrics and Gynecology*, 1978, *131*, 286-290.

Newton, R.W., Webster, P., Binu, P., Maskrey, N., & Phillips, A. Psychosocial stress in pregnancy and its relation to the onset of premature labor. *British Medical Journal*, 1979, *2* (6187), 411-413.

Pahlka, B. Childbirth preparation: An important service for all. II. A clinical perspective. *Journal of Nurse-Midwifery*, 1982, *27*(4), 34-36.

Roberts, J. Priorities in prenatal education. *Journal of Obstetric, Gynecologic, and Neonatal Nursing,* 1976, *5,* 17-20.

Rockwell, D., & Pepitone-Rockwell, F. The emotional impact of surgery and the value of informed consent. *Medical Clinics of North America,* 1979, *63,* 1341-1351.

Rosenfeld, C.R., Barton, M.D., & Meschla, G. Effects of epinephrine on distribution of blood flow in the pregnant ewe. *American Journal of Obstetrics and Gynecology,* 1976, *124,* 156.

Schwartz, L. *The world of the unborn.* New York: Marek, 1980.

Smilkstein, G. The family APGAR: A proposal for a family function test and its use by physicians. *Journal of Family Practice,* 1978, *6,* 1231-1239.

Standley, K., Soule, B., & Copans, S. Dimensions of prenatal anxiety and their influence on pregnancy outcome. *American Journal of Obstetrics and Gynecology,* 1979, *135,* 22-26.

Verny, T. *The secret life of the unborn.* New York: Summit, 1981.

Chapter 3

Family-Centered Intrapartum Care

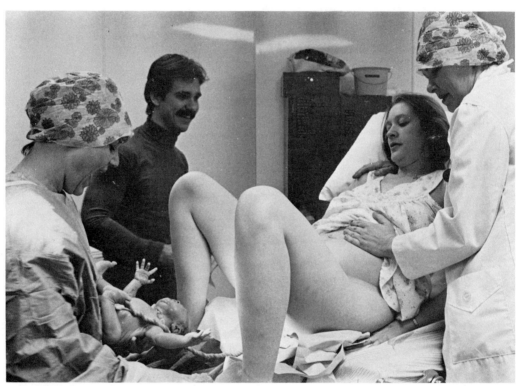

(photo © Alison E. Wachstein, from *Pregnant Moments*, Morgan & Morgan, 1979)

3

Family-centered care during labor and birth can offer many options to the childbearing family. Although specific features will vary, a family-centered birth is just as feasible when medical intervention is required because the pregnancy is at risk as it is when the pregnancy is normal. Segregation of families so that some are eligible for family-centered intrapartum care while others are not is discriminatory and masks the goal of a family-centered program—that is, to provide for the needs of all family members, regardless of the specifics of the birth experience.

The most basic component of any family-centered intrapartum program is that the father or support person participate to the extent that he (or she) and the mother desire. Other family members, too, may be included if that is the wish of the couple. Another central component of family-centered intrapartum care is attention to the attachment process both during labor and after birth. Although the importance of providing an atmosphere in which the attachment process can develop has been widely accepted, attention to bonding is likely to be greater in a birthing room or alternative birth center than in the more traditional setting of a delivery room. There is *no* reason, however, that the encouragement of attachment between family members cannot be fostered, regardless of the setting for birth.

INTRAPARTUM AREAS

Several types of physical facilities should be available to families during the childbirth experience (Interprofessional Task Force, 1978; International Childbirth Education Association, 1978).

Family Waiting Area and Early Labor Lounge

The lounge provides space for family visitation, preparation of snacks, telephone contact with other family members and friends, intercom contact with the labor and birth area, pleasant decor with windows, a nonhospital atmosphere that includes TV, radio, games, reading materials, and other diversionary activities. There should be ample space for walking or lounging; ideally, adjacent grounds are available so family members may go outside.

Diagnostic/Admitting Room

Women in early labor can be examined to assess cervical dilation or emergency conditions without being admitted to the birth facility. There is usually minimal or no charge for this care and for the time spent in the lounge area waiting until labor status has been determined.

51

Labor/Birthing Rooms

Comfortably furnished, with windows and a private bath or shower, the labor room may also be used for birth if the woman wishes and her birth attendant agrees. Although many birth facilities are organized so that a woman either labors in a labor room and is transferred to the delivery room for the birth or she uses a birthing room or alternative birth center, all labor rooms can be set up to double as childbearing rooms. A number of hospitals are moving toward this concept (Fenwick & Dearing, 1981; Notelovitz, 1978). For example, Fairview Hospital in Minneapolis, Minnesota, has nine labor/birthing rooms. Equipment in each room includes fetal monitors built into each bedside cabinet and a labor/birthing bed. A birthing chair is available in a separate room for those who wish to use it.

Hennepin County Medical Center in Minneapolis has a nurse-midwifery unit that has birthing rooms for each family; medical care and specialized equipment are immediately available, and special equipment is nearby to be transported into the room if complications arise. There is no central nursery, since parents and baby are never separated after birth. Dismissal is usually within 24 hours. At the University of Utah Medical Center in Salt Lake City, birthing rooms are used for most laboring women, including those whose babies are at risk. A high-risk birthing room adjoins the nursery, and there is a window between the two rooms so that the baby can be passed to the nursery for care immediately after birth.

As hospital maternity departments are renovated, many are changing to the birthing room concept for all families. This eliminates the need to "risk out" (deem ineligible) women whose status changes during labor, often as high as 30% or more of those originally assessed to be "normal." The cluster system concept of care described by Fenwick and Dearing (1981) encompasses the management of risk conditions, including cesarean delivery, in the birthing room. In this set-up, the childbearing room is equipped with a bathroom, closet, maternity bed, infant crib, bedside table, comfortable lounge chair, and routine items (e.g., suction apparatus, oxygen, and electrical outlets). Specialized delivery equipment is shared among childbearing rooms and is stored in a central area to be moved into the childbearing rooms when it is needed.

Hospitals with insufficient space to add birthing rooms can convert each labor room into a comfortable birthing environment. A hospital atmosphere can be avoided by including amenities such as wallpaper or walls painted in noninstitutional colors, tape cassette or musical equipment, a mirror, subdued lighting, a rocking chair, and whenever possible, a natural source of light.

Delivery Rooms

Much of the hospital austerity of delivery rooms can be removed by simple measures. Inclusion of the support person is foremost. A mirror allows the couple to watch their baby's birth. A backrest on the delivery table increases the woman's comfort and helps her work more physiologically with labor. Some delivery rooms are equipped with a birthing chair as an alternative to a delivery table. At Hampton General Hospital in Hampton, Virginia, a stereo plays music selected by the parents, and the delivery room lights can be adjusted according to the parents' preferences.

Recovery Rooms

In the immediate postbirth period, family members can be together in the delivery room, birthing room, or recovery area. Regardless of the setting, a family-centered approach means that the new baby can be "admitted to the nursery" at the mother's bedside. Instead of the baby being taken to the nursery, the nursery goes to the baby; routine procedures can be either postponed or done while the baby is held in the mother's or father's arms. Weighing may be deferred, or a scale may be brought to the mother's bedside.

Nurseries are being used less and less, and babies are being kept with their parents as much as possible. At Rose Medical Center in Denver, Colorado, babies are taken to the recovery room in an incubator and stay there with their mothers and other family members. The Cybele Cluster System does not include a central nursery for well babies. In this system, babies are taken to a small glassed-in baby room adjacent to the nurses' station if either mothers or babies require special care.

THE TRADITIONAL LABOR AND DELIVERY ROOM

As family systems have changed in their composition, flexibility in visitation and support person policies has become necessary. Life styles such as single parenthood and communal living have made archaic the traditional rule that only the father may be present to support his wife during labor and birth. Old policies die hard, however. It is still common for hospital policies to include the following statements: "Persons other than husbands must be approved by the physician and must have attended childbirth classes," or "Only one support person is allowed to be with the laboring woman, and this person is designated as the only support person throughout hospitalization." One woman who wanted her live-in companion (the father of her baby) to be with her during labor and birth was denied this privilege by the hospital because they had not married. She went to court to protest this regulation and won the right to have the father with her at birth.

The rationale for such restrictive policies may be related to concerns about infection, although there is no evidence that the presence of visitors who are healthy and free of symptoms increases the risk of infection. In alternative birth centers where family members, relatives, and friends may be present, there has been no reported increase in infection rates. In the birth facilities the authors visited, the infection rates were *never* reported to have increased as a result of the liberalization of visitation policies. Prudence demands, however, that any visitors with acute infectious illness, particularly upper respiratory tract infection, purulent or draining skin infections, or infectious diarrhea, be excluded from the labor and birthing rooms. It is also necessary

to wash hands, wear clean clothes, and use sterile procedures, as appropriate. If the basic precautions are taken, the question of who should visit then becomes an issue of control, with the power to make decisions about visitors vested in either the parents or the staff.

If birth is family-centered and managed according to the parents' wishes, the parents should decide who is to be with them. Room size may restrict the number of visitors who can be accommodated at one time. The number and appropriateness of chosen visitors should be discussed during pregnancy. For example, some women may find the presence of their mothers increases their tension, whereas others may find this deeply comforting. At Family Hospital in Milwaukee, there is one designated support person; if the presence of a second person (for example, a special labor coach or photographer) is desired, this is cleared in advance with the birth attendant. Other persons visit for brief intervals during labor if the mother desires and her condition warrants. The following is a sample policy for father or support person participation during labor and birth:

> *Purpose:* To provide physical support to minimize discomfort, encourage relaxation, and help make the childbirth experience a satisfying one.
> *Policy:* Every woman in labor will have a support person in attendance. Other visitors will be welcomed according to the wishes of the woman and as her condition permits.
> *Procedure:*
>
> 1. During labor and birth, the husband or support person designated by the woman remains with her. It is strongly recommended that this person attend preparation for childbirth classes.
> 2. If the woman wishes to have a second person present during labor and birth, this should be discussed with the birth attendant during pregnancy and

recorded on her preference sheet.

3. Because of the limited space available, it is requested that other visitors be kept to a minimum. Grandparents, children, or other persons may visit briefly if the woman desires. The woman may visit friends and relatives in the labor lounge if she wishes unless she is under the influence of medications or there are medical complications which preclude her doing so.

4. During birth, the father and designated support person are asked to ensure that they are free of infection, to wash their hands, to don proper scrub attire (cap, mask, scrub clothes, and shoe covers), and to stay with the woman at the head of the delivery table.

5. Family members may be together in the recovery room.

6. A release of responsibility form is to be signed for family participation in labor (Exhibit 3-1).

In addition to flexible visitation policies that do not separate the woman from her support person at any time during labor and provide access to friends and relatives of her choice, other amenities increase the woman's comfort during labor. Personal touches that improve the quality of the childbirth experience may include meals or snacks provided for the support person. Pictures can be taken during labor and birth. Sometimes, Polaroid pictures are provided by the birth facility. Most important is attention to what the woman and her family desire. In most cases, their requests can be met with minimum effort. The resulting positive feelings have long-term effects on their perception of the care they have received.

Bonding can be encouraged by giving the baby to the parents immediately after birth and placing the baby on the mother's abdomen during initial care procedures (e.g., suctioning, cutting the cord). The father may be invited to cut the cord after it has been clamped by the physician or midwife. The temperature of the delivery room can be increased to prevent excessive cooling of the infant, and the baby can be dried and placed skin-to-skin on the mother's chest, with a warm cover over them. A stockinette cap on the baby's head retards heat loss, as does a warming light placed over mother and baby or a change of covering periodically.

The baby can be cared for in the mother's or father's arms. Identification tags can be placed, Apgar score determined, and vitamin K administered while one parent holds the baby. As an alternative, an infant-warming unit can be placed next to the mother and procedures completed while she watches. Ophthalmic eye ointment or drops can be delayed for at least 1 hour (or longer, depending on state law) to allow unimpeded eye contact between parents and baby. Breastfeeding on the delivery table is an

---

Exhibit 3-1 Release of Responsibility during Labor and Birth

I, _____ , assume all responsibility for myself during the time I spend with _____ when she is in labor and giving birth. I hereby release _____ Hospital from all responsibility from incidents as a result thereof.

Date: _____   Signature: _____

Time: _____ am / pm   Relationship: _____

Witness: _____

option that can be exercised according to the mother's wishes. She may prefer to wait and nurse her baby in the recovery room.

The following is a sample policy and procedure for family-centered care in the traditional delivery room:

Policy: Parents will be encouraged to be with their baby as much as possible after birth so that early and optimal parent-infant contact will provide an atmosphere in which attachment can be fostered, while at the same time ensuring safe care for mother and baby.

Procedure:

1. If the baby's condition is stable, he or she is put on the mother's abdomen to be dried and suctioned. After the cord is clamped, the father may, if he wishes, cut the cord.

2. The baby is wrapped in a warmed sheet and blanket, and a stockinette hat is put on the baby's head. The baby is given to the mother to hold. As an alternative, the baby may be put skin-to-skin on the mother's chest and both covered with a warmed sheet and blanket. The warmed blanket and wrapper are changed after 5 minutes, and the baby's axillary temperature is taken to assess stabilization of body temperature.

3. Care procedures (Apgar scoring, suctioning, identification) are done while the baby is held in the mother's or father's arms. If they prefer, an infant warmer is placed next to the mother so that the parents may watch while procedures are completed. The administration of eye ointment or drops, injection of vitamin K, determination of hematocrit, and application of Dextrostix are delayed for at least 1 hour after birth.

4. Breastfeeding can begin as soon as the mother wishes.

5. The baby is continually assessed for color and respiratory status. Vital signs and other observations are recorded on the delivery room nurses' notes.

6. Mother and baby are taken to the recovery room together, accompanied by the father and/or support person. The baby is weighed at the mother's bedside, using a portable scale, and is observed frequently for color and respiratory response. Temperature is checked at 15-minute intervals. Vitamin K, Hematostix, and Dextrostix procedures are performed at the mother's bedside. Ophthalmic eye ointment or drops are administered between 1 and 2 hours after birth—after parent-infant contact has been initiated and the baby is no longer in an alert state.

7. The baby stays with the mother, transferring with her to her postpartum room. If the mother wishes, the baby may be taken to the nursery; or, preferably, rooming-in may begin.

8. If neonatal complications make it necessary to care for the baby in the nursery, the father or support person may accompany the nurse. After washing and gowning, he or she may enter the nursery. As soon as possible, the mother can be taken by wheelchair or walk to the nursery where she may see and touch her baby.

LEBOYER BIRTH

The Leboyer approach to gentle birth emphasizes the importance of easing the baby's transition into the world by eliminating environmental factors that may be upsetting to the infant (Salter, 1978). It is based on the concept that babies are human beings who are capable of feelings and may have remembrances of the birth that can be a lifelong influence. The baby therefore is eased out of the birth canal with an emphasis on quietness and calm, subdued lighting, and gentle handling.

Controversy has surrounded the use of the Leboyer method, particularly because of its emphasis on subdued lighting. There had been concern that the status of the newborn could not be assessed adequately and that the infant's temperature would not be maintained at the appropriate level under these conditions. However, as birth attendants have used the Leboyer method, it has become clear that, with flexibility during the postbirth period, it is possible to provide the amenities of the Leboyer approach without compromising safety.

The following is a sample policy and procedure for Leboyer gentle birth:

Policy: The Leboyer method of nonviolent childbirth is available and encouraged.

Purpose: To provide the opportunity for early and optimal parent-infant attachment in order to meet the emotional needs of both mother and infant. At the same time, good recovery care for the mother and transitional observation of the infant are emphasized.

Procedure:

1. Thorough hand-washing by the father or support person is requested.
2. The father or support person is present in the delivery room.
3. The air conditioner is turned off before birth, and the room temperature is maintained at 22.2 to 23.3 degrees C (72 to 74 degrees F).
4. During birth, the overhead lights are dimmed, and noise is kept to a minimum.
5. When the cord stops pulsing, the physician or midwife clamps the cord; if desired, the father or support person may cut the cord.
6. After suctioning, the baby is placed on the mother's abdomen. She massages, cuddles, dries her baby, and wraps the baby in a warm blanket.
7. The father or support person places the baby in the bath. The tub is filled with warm sterile water. A wooden-backed thermometer is floated in the water, and the water temperature is maintained at 37.8 to 40 degrees C (100 to 104 degrees F). The tub can be placed on a table under a radiant warmer or in a Kreiselman incubator. (A substitute for a tub is a plastic nursery cot.)
8. When the baby is removed from the bath, he or she is dried and wrapped in warm blankets. A stockinette cap is placed on the baby's head. The baby is given to the mother to hold and nurse, if she desires.

BIRTHING ROOMS

Also called labor/delivery rooms or single unit delivery systems (SUDS), birthing rooms are rapidly becoming common throughout the United States—not only as a reaction to the disadvantages of delivery room births, but also as a result of consumer demand for more humanized childbirth. In its purest form, birthing room births are available to all women regardless of risk status; all labor rooms can also be birthing rooms.

Moving from a labor room to a delivery room may interfere with labor or may disrupt its progress. When a woman gives birth in a birthing room, however, she is able to concentrate on delivering her baby and does not need to expend energy moving to a stretcher and then moving again to the delivery table. Her vital signs may be taken continuously, and, if necessary, the fetus may be electronically monitored until the moment of birth. The father is able to provide continuous support and does not have to be redirected to the new location. If rapid delivery is required, the woman's legs may be placed in the leg supports and the baby delivered without the delay caused by transport to a delivery room. Other advantages of a birthing room include

- The nursing staff no longer has to decide when to move the mother to the delivery room.
- There is no second room to be set up, so the nurses have ample time to prepare for an in situ delivery.
- It may be possible to reduce costs, since fewer rooms are used, less laundry and equipment are involved, and utilization of hospital space is better.

The concepts underlying hospital birthing rooms are that the birth experience should be humanized, intervention minimized, and continuity of care provided. These facilities do not employ rigid screening criteria. Instead, they offer a two-tiered model of care, low-risk and high-risk, and emphasize individualizing the birth experience. Local anesthesia, forceps, fetal monitoring, and so on are used when deemed necessary by the physician, nurse, or mother to facilitate a safe but still joyous birth.

The birthing room concept in the United States originated in 1969 at Manchester Memorial Hospital in Manchester, Connecticut where Dr. Philip Sumner pioneered the idea that "prepared" low-risk couples could experience birth in a combined labor/delivery room. The experimentation period proved highly successful, and the birthing rooms at Manchester Memorial were made available to any family, regardless of preparation during pregnancy. The basic philosophy of the birthing room concept was that childbirth should be oriented toward a humanistic experience that can influence positive parenting rather

than toward pathology (Carlson & Sumner, 1976; Sumner & Phillips, 1981).

SUDS, an option introduced in the Republic of South Africa in 1970, is similar to Sumner's model (Notelovitz, 1978). The purpose of SUDS is to provide privacy, comfort, and safety during labor and childbirth for women with normal pregnancy risk. Births are attended by either physicians or midwives. Expanding on this concept is the cluster system (Figure 3-1) proposed by Fenwick and Dearing (1981), which meets all the needs of childbearing women except for those that require tertiary care facilities. Women labor, give birth, and spend their postpartum hospitalization in the same room. Cesarean deliveries can be performed, and other complications, such as infant distress, can be managed in these rooms. Specialized equipment can be brought to the woman in her room from a central location rather than moving the woman to an operating room.

When criteria were initially developed to determine the women who would be allowed to use birthing rooms, they were necessarily stringent so that the safety of birthing room births could be evaluated. Over a decade of utilizing birthing rooms in the United States has proved that birth can be a humanized, safe experience in this setting (Barton, Rovner, Puls, & Read, 1980; Grad, 1979; Kieffer, 1980; Klass & Capps, 1980; Sumner & Phillips, 1981).

Variations in the birthing room concept are found in many hospitals today. Some of these rooms offer compromises between traditional delivery rooms and alternative birth centers. Others continue to impose the old restrictive criteria for use. By continuing to subscribe to such rigid criteria, these hospitals often lose the intent of family-centered care in a pathological orientation to birth, precisely what birthing rooms are supposed to avoid. Family Hospital in Milwaukee, Wisconsin has simplified its policy for utilization of birthing rooms with the statement: "Any pregnancy greater than 34 weeks' gestation free of medical and obstetrical complications will be eligible to use the birthing room." The tone of the policy is positive and encouraging, unencumbered by numerous risk criteria.

Figure 3-1 Cluster System Floor Plan Proposed for Northern Dutchess Hospital, Rhynebeck, New York

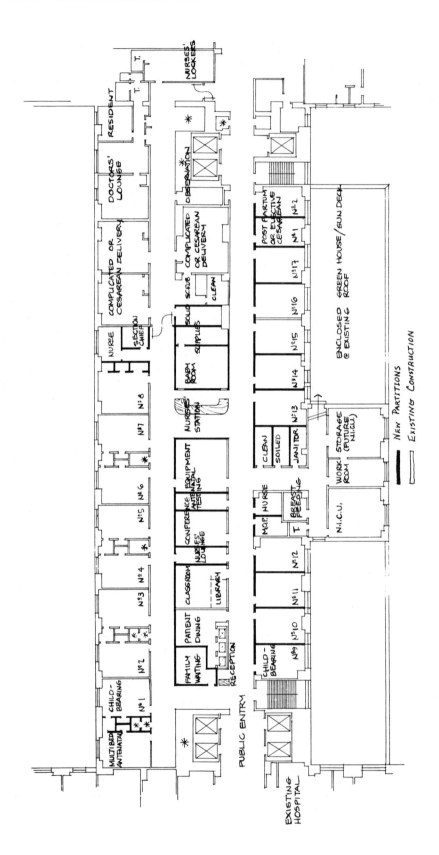

Source: Reprinted with permission of the Cybele Cluster Unit at St. Mary's Hospital, Minneapolis, Minnesota. Designed by the Cybele Society to meet individual needs of patient population and medical-nursing staff.

The following is a sample birthing room policy that delineates major criteria for use without being overly restrictive:

> *Statement of Philosophy.* The concept of a birthing room is based on the premise that many childbearing families are searching for physical, psychological, and social alternatives to the more structured or traditional institutional birthing process. We hold the belief that, for most women, pregnancy is a healthy state and the birth process a normal one. Women who continue in this healthy state and normal process can safely give birth in the birthing room, since modern perinatal techniques and technology are immediately available. We believe that, if the woman and her newborn are healthy, if the woman has received instruction on the care and observation of her newborn, and if appropriate pediatric follow-up is available, the newborn can be discharged safely between 6 and 24 hours after birth.
>
> *Admission Criteria.* Families must request the birthing room during pregnancy. A full-term vaginal birth should be anticipated. At least three prenatal visits to a physician or midwife are required. Couples are requested to attend preparation for childbirth classes and to attend the hospital's birthing room orientation program.
>
> *Transfer to Regular Delivery Room Services.* In the following circumstances, the woman may labor in the birthing room but will be transferred to the main delivery room for birth or for postbirth care:
>
> 1. administration of inhalant anesthesia required
> 2. breech delivery
> 3. unusual fetal presentations that do not correct themselves during labor

> 4. cesarean births
> 5. manual removal of the placenta
> 6. multiple births
>
> *Support Persons and Family Members.* The woman chooses one or two support persons to be with her during labor and birth. Children may visit their mother during labor and be present for birth if they are accompanied by a responsible adult. Families are urged to prepare their children thoroughly if they wish them to participate. Ill children should not visit.
>
> *Other Visitors.* Visitors who are not members of the immediate family or support persons may be present for brief periods of time if this is the woman's wish. Visitors may be asked to leave at the discretion of the staff. All visitors should be free of communicable disease and should not have been recently exposed to infection.
>
> *Consent Forms.* The following consent forms will be completed: birthing room permit, physician or midwife's agreement for use of the birthing room, agreement to infant care in the birthing room (Exhibit 3-2).

Birthing Room Facilities, Equipment, and Supplies

The birthing room must be designed and furnished to comply with the state department of public health codes, state fire marshal regulations, and hospital infection control policies. In order to comply with these regulations, the following provisions should be made:

1. Walls should have washable coverings.
2. A nonporous tile material should be used on the floor to facilitate frequent cleaning.
3. The birthing room should have a nonporous ceiling.
4. Furnishings should be covered with a nonporous material for easy cleaning.

Exhibit 3-2 Birthing Room Agreement

I have read and fully understand the criteria for eligibility to use the birthing room at _____ _____ Hospital. I understand that it is not a conventional delivery room and that I and the persons I choose to be with me have a large measure of responsibility in preparing for and participating in the labor and birth process. To this end I agree that:

1. I am aware of the possibility that medical problems may arise necessitating care for the high-risk mother and baby. This care may include transfer from the birthing room to the traditional labor and delivery area. I understand that in this eventuality I will be fully informed and will be a participant in the decision making about my care.
2. I will obtain the approval of my physician or midwife and the baby's physician for use of the birthing room.
3. I will attend childbirth preparation classes and the birthing room orientation class with my partner and/or the support persons who will be with me during labor and birth.
4. I will be accompanied during labor by at least one support person—either my partner, a relative, a monitrice,* or a friend.
5. I will review any plans for family participation and my preferences during childbirth with my physician or midwife. I will review those preferences having to do with the baby with the baby's physician.

Date: _____ Expectant Mother's Signature: _____
Due Date: _____ Witness: _____

Physician's/Midwife's Agreement for Use of the Birthing Room

_____ has discussed with me her plan to labor and give birth in the birthing room at _____ Hospital. I am in agreement with her plan, and I am willing to attend her delivery in the birthing room. I will forward her prenatal record in her 8th month which will be _____ .

Date: _____ Physician/Midwife: _____

Agreement to Infant Care in the Birthing Room

_____ has advised me that she plans to use the birthing room for the labor and birth of her baby. I am in agreement with her proposed plan. I am willing to care for her infant in the birthing room. I understand that normal discharge from the birthing room is between 6 and 24 hours after birth.

Date: _____ Physician: _____

_____

*A monitrice is a nurse who is skilled in the art of labor support and may be hired by the couple or by the hospital staff to stay throughout labor and the early postpartum period.

5. Cabinets and cupboards should be constructed of material impervious to water or solutions.
6. Window coverings should be made of washable material and designed for easy removal.

The birthing room should have the following fixed equipment:

1. scrub faucet with elbow controls
2. two oxygen outlets
3. one suction outlet
4. six electrical outlets (two emergency outlets)
5. overhead ceiling light fixture and procedure lamp (gooseneck or high intensity)
6. wall mount blood pressure apparatus

7. telephone
8. nurse call bell or intercom system
9. kick bucket and laundry hamper
10. rocker
11. bassinette
12. birthing room bed to facilitate quick transfer to delivery room with capabilities for lithotomy, Trendelenburg's, and sitting position
13. clock with second hand
14. patient gown, bed linen, extra wash cloths and bath blankets, towels, and absorbent pads
15. adjoining bathroom with toilet, sink, and bathtub (or shower)
16. mirror, either on a stand or portable so that it can be attached to the bottom of the bed for easy visualization during birth
17. curtains, bedspread (can be removed after family enters room), paintings or wall hangings, and inexpensive radio or tapedeck
18. log book for couples to record their comments during labor and/or after birth
19. overbed table

The following equipment should be available close to the room and brought into the birthing room as needed:

1. infant isolette with overhead warmer
2. electronic fetal monitor
3. spotlight
4. warm bath blankets
5. warm baby blankets
6. Leboyer tub
7. warmed sterile water in 500-ml or 1,000-ml containers

The following sterile supplies should be stored on a movable cart or in a cupboard in the birthing room:

1. instrument tray with two pair of scissors, one needle holder, one tissue forceps, two sponge forceps, two medicine glasses, two hemostats, cord clamp, bulb syringe, and cord blood tube
2. placenta basin
3. extra baby blankets and baby caps (knitted or stockinette)
4. double and single sterile gloves
5. sterile drape and towel pack
6. sterile gowns (two)
7. DeLee mucus traps
8. sutures
9. sterile $4'' \times 4''$ and $2'' \times 2''$ gauze pads
10. extra sterile bulb syringe, scissors, and cord clamps (individually wrapped)
11. scrub brushes
12. extra cord blood tubes

Also stored on a cart or in the cupboard should be miscellaneous supplies, such as

1. masks, caps
2. oxygen apparatus and tubing
3. adult suction equipment
4. prepping solutions
5. emergency drugs, syringes, needles, alcohol swabs
6. medications, such as ophthalmic eye ointment and/or drops, vitamin K, Methylergonovine Maleate (Methergine) 2 mg, synthetic oxytocin (Syntocinon) 5 and 10 units, and oxytocin citrate (Pitocin) 10 units
7. pudendal tray and anesthetic solutions
8. sphygmomanometer and stethoscope (adult and infant size)
9. identification cards and bracelets
10. amnihooks
11. Dopplers and gel
12. fetoscope
13. intravenous tray with solutions, tubings, and necessary equipment
14. Peripads, Chux, and postpartum necessities
15. baby scale
16. stool
17. bucket
18. electric warming pad
19. culture tubes and applicators for cervical cultures
20. Ambu bags and laryngoscopes (adult and infant)
21. nitrazine paper
22. flashlight

23. 2″ × 2″ lancet, hematocrit tubes, large capillary tubes
24. Dextrostix
25. Surgigel
26. thermometers

Birthing Room Protocols

A protocol should be developed to provide guidelines for admitting and caring for the family in the birthing room. The following is an example of such a protocol:

   I. Admission procedure
     1. The staff nurse ascertains whether the woman is in active labor by assessing the contractions, i.e., when started, how long in duration, character, frequency; membranes, i.e., intact or ruptured; due date; dilation by vaginal examination; presence of show. If labor has not yet established itself fully, the woman is encouraged to return home or to remain in a nearby setting outside the birth facility.
     2. If the woman is to be admitted, the attending physician or midwife and the admitting office are notified. The following forms are obtained from the woman: (a) birthing room agreement, (b) physician/midwife's agreement, (c) agreement to infant care in the birthing room, (d) birth plan indicating the preferences of the woman and her family.
     3. During admission procedures, the woman and her partner and/or support person are not separated.
  II. Labor management
     1. The woman wears her own gown and robe if she chooses.

2. Identification band is placed on her wrist.
3. Woman and support person wash hands.
4. Routine use of enemas are discouraged, but available at the request of the woman or her birth attendant. No perineal shaving is performed.
5. Adequate fluid intake is encouraged.
6. Intravenous fluids are not used unless a problem arises or the birth attendant requests them.
7. Frequent urination (at least every hour) is encouraged.
8. Ambulation is strongly encouraged during labor. If the woman remains in bed for a sustained period, she is asked to change positions (side-lying, semisitting, kneeling, all fours) at least every 30 minutes. If the membranes have ruptured, ambulation is acceptable if the fetal head is engaged.
9. Maternal and fetal vital signs are monitored every hour in early labor and every 15 to 30 minutes as dilation progresses.
10. The focus of care is on encouraging and supporting the natural forces of labor with a calm, assured, nonintervening approach.
11. The father and other support persons may be in attendance throughout labor to provide support, companionship, and help.
12. A labor/birthing bed is used for labor and birth with or without stirrups.
13. Minimal or no medication is used unless other measures

have not helped and the woman requests medication.

III. Imminent birth

1. The physician/midwife is notified.
2. The father and/or support persons are requested to wash their hands.
3. Items needed for the birth are brought to the birthing room, e.g., a spotlight and the infant resuscitation cart, if needed.
4. The birthing room is prepared as follows: open sterile packs on overbed table, open physician or midwife's gown (if used), place electric warming pad and blanket for baby in cradle, turn heat in room to 23.9 degrees C (75 degrees F).
5. Woman may or may not be draped, depending on whether the birth is conducted in a sterile field.

IV. Birth

1. Respect is given to the goals of gentle birth as part of the birthing room philosophy, i.e., respect for the newborn's sensitivity, vulnerability, and need for immediate contact.
2. The infant is suctioned, dried, and placed on the mother's chest skin-to-skin and covered with a warm blanket or heat lamp.
3. The infant is not forced or urged to nurse, but is placed in a position where the nipple can be reached.
4. If desired by the father, the baby is wrapped in a clean, warm, dry blanket, and the father holds the baby close to his body for warmth.
5. Use of Pitocin or Methergine is not routine and is left to the judgment of the attending physician or midwife and the wishes of the woman.
6. The baby is not placed in the birthing room crib except at the parents' request. Identification bands, Apgar scoring, and other procedures can be done while the baby is held in the mother's or father's arms.

V. Recovery period

1. Ideally, the infant spends the rest of the hospital stay with the parents.
2. Delivery equipment is taken out to be cleaned. Linens are changed and the parents made comfortable.
3. The recovery procedure to be followed for the mother includes checking vital signs, lochia, fundal height, and bladder distention.
4. The infant is monitored by the birthing room staff during this period, and the infant's status is documented. The baby is weighed and measured, temperature and footprints are taken, eye prophylaxis and vitamin K are administered at the bedside or in the nursery, according to the parents' choice.
5. Family members may be present in the birthing room as desired by the parents.
6. If the woman plans to be discharged by 6 hours after birth, the entire postpartum period is spent in the birthing room unless others are waiting to use the room. In this case, the woman remains in the birthing room as long as possible and then is transferred to a postpartum room. Maternal eligibility for early discharge shall be determined by joint

decision of the woman and her physician or midwife.

7. The following criteria are used for early maternal discharge:
   a. no intrapartum obstetric complications requiring closer postpartum observation (e.g., signs of infection or maternal exhaustion)
   b. blood loss less than 500 cc
   c. vital signs: temperature less than 37.8 degrees C (100 degrees F), pulse less than 100, blood pressure consistent with prenatal course
   d. fundus firm with no excessive bleeding
   e. ability to ambulate easily and care for infant
   f. ability to urinate adequately
   g. RhoGam therapy instituted, if indicated
   h. postpartum hemoglobin and hematocrit determined
   i. postpartum and infant care instructions given and understood
   j. pediatric follow-up plan developed

8. The following criteria are used for early infant discharge:
   a. physical findings within normal limits at examination by physician
   b. birth weight over 5 pounds and under 9.5 pounds
   c. vital signs stable: temperature 36.5 to 37.5 degrees C (97.8 to 99.6 degrees F), heart rate 110 to 160, respirations 30 to 60
   d. laboratory test results normal: Coombs negative, hematocrit 45 to 65, Dextrostix 45 or more
   e. good sucking reflex on breast or bottle demonstrated
   f. if infant has not urinated, special instructions obtained from the baby's physician
   g. meconium stool should be passed by 36 hours; if not, contact the baby's physician
   h. birth certificate filled out and signed by both parents
   i. no infant complications that require additional observation
   j. demonstrated ability of mother to handle and care for her infant

9. When mother and infant are discharged early, the family is contacted for follow-up either by a telephone call, a visiting nurse, or by an arrangement for the mother and infant to return to the office of the birth attendant for assessment.

Birthing Room Infection Control Procedures

Usually, the requirements for sterile procedures are more relaxed in a birthing room than in a delivery room. For example, although the medical and nursing staff wear scrub clothes and the physician or midwife wears sterile gloves during the birth, masks, hats, and shoe covers are not always used. Sterile drapes may not be used during the birth. Sterile procedure, of course, is followed. Thorough hand-washing by all those present for the birth is necessary.

Evaluation of Birthing Room Services

Completion of evaluation forms by families that have used the birthing room provides valuable feedback about how services can be improved. The form used at the Perinatal Center, Sutter Memorial Hospitals is shown in Exhibit 3-3.

ALTERNATIVE BIRTH CENTERS

Similar in many respects to birthing rooms, alternative birth centers may be variously known as family birth centers, homestyle birthing rooms, or 24-hour suites. They are often separately staffed from the rest of the obstetrics department, and they are usually set apart from the regular labor and delivery area. They may be located in the obstetrics department (for example, as part of the postpartum unit), but they are often geographically removed from the hospital obstetrics unit (for example, in an adjacent building or another part of the hospital). Organizationally, the alternative birth center is linked to the hospital and is a part of its services.

Alternative birth centers were developed largely in response to the home birth movement and to consumer pressure for more family-centered and humanized childbirth services. They have a strong appeal for couples who want to give birth in comfortable surroundings without medical intervention. Often, families who use birthing rooms cannot include as many family members and friends as they wish because of space limitations. Some couples choose the alternative birth center as a backup option in case their plans for a home birth do not materialize.

Staff members of alternative birth centers are frequently midwives and registered nurses. Their orientation toward birth is one of nonintervention, and the use of intravenous fluids, monitoring equipment, preps and enemas, or other "standard" procedures is uncommon. In contrast, it is not unusual for intravenous fluids, monitors, and even regional anesthetics, such as epidural blocks, to be used in birthing rooms.

Alternative birth centers have homelike accommodations, including a double- or larger-sized bed for the couple and a crib for the newborn. Emergency equipment and drugs are discreetly stored in cupboards, out of view, but easily accessible. The supplies and equipment needed for alternative birth centers are the same as those needed for birthing rooms. Private bathroom facilities are incorporated into each birth center. Also, there may be an early labor lounge or living room and small kitchen. Families are carefully screened; only low-risk and prepared women (couples) are eligible to use the alternative birth centers.

Ideally, the alternative birth center becomes the private space for one childbearing family throughout their birth experience. The family is admitted to the alternative birth center, labors there, gives birth there, and may remain there until discharge. If the family has to remain for more than 24 hours postpartum, the request for use of the alternative birth centers by other families may require transfer of the new family to a regular postpartum room.

While emphasizing normalcy, natural methods, self-help, and family participation, alternative birth centers are fully supported by the presence of an obstetric nurse or nurse-midwife and by the availability of obstetric and pediatric house staff at all times, with attending staff backup. If a situation that could threaten the safety of the mother or baby should arise at any time in labor, the mother is moved to the regular labor and delivery area. In such a situation the alternative birth center nurse and the father of the baby go with her.

Examples of Alternative Birth Centers

The Home-Like Birth Center at Booth Memorial Hospital in Cleveland, Ohio is located in a building separate from the hospital. It consists of four family suites, each with a living room, family room, a bedroom, and a bathroom. Families can share a kitchen and dining area, although most dine in their own suite. Midwives and registered nurses staff the birth center; women may choose either a midwife or a private physician as a birth attendant. If the need arises, laboring women can be transferred from the birth center to the hospital obstetrics department and, if circumstances permit, returned to the birth center. For example, if Pitocin is needed for

Exhibit 3-3 Sutter Memorial Hospital's Homestyle/Family-Centered Birth Program Evaluation

This questionnaire is to help us better meet the needs of families in our Homestyle Birthing Room Program. We would appreciate your comments. If you are being discharged early, the visiting RN will collect this form. If you remain in maternity for a few days, you may give it to the staff nurses. Thank you.

Name _____

Address _____ Phone _____

Name and relationship of support person _____

_____

My age is _____ This is baby _____ Baby was born on _____ /_____/ _____

Birth was attended by _____ , MD _____ RN

I gave birth in the Homestyle Birth Room _____ Delivery Room _____

If delivery, why? _____

My baby is a girl _____ boy _____ who weighed _____ lbs _____ oz. at birth and was _____ inches long.

I read the following books/pamphlets in preparation and thought:

Books/Pamphlets	Usefulness
_____	_____
_____	_____
_____	_____
_____	_____

I attended the following classes:

Class	Teacher	Evaluation
_____	_____	_____
_____	_____	_____

1. Did the Birthing Room orientation session adequately explain the program, labor, delivery, postpartum, discharge and followup? _____ Yes _____ No
    Comments:

2. Were your expectations of the birthing room met? If not, briefly explain.

    a. What was particularly helpful/not helpful during labor?
    b. Was there too much or too little intervention while you were in the birthing room?
    c. Were you given any conflicting information?
    d. Would you choose the same again?

3. Were your expectations of postpartum met? If not, briefly explain.

4. Were you given enough instructions from orientation and maternity nurses on infant care to feel comfortable in the care of your baby? _____ Yes _____ No
    Comments:

5. What was the experience of your support person(s) in the birthing room?

6. What suggestions do you have that would have made the program ''better''?
    Comments/Suggestions:

Source: Reprinted with permission of The Perinatal Center, Sutter Memorial Hospital, Sacramento, California.

labor augmentation, the woman temporarily must stay in the hospital obstetrical department. When the administration of Pitocin is discontinued, she may return to the birth center. Statistics gathered between 1977 and 1981* indicated a transfer rate ranging from 16 to 20 percent. The cesarean birth rate for women beginning labor in the birth center ranged from 3.6 to 6.7 percent.

At Booth's Home-Like Birth Center, the following statement of purpose and objectives guide the provision of care:

STATEMENT OF PURPOSE

Childbirth is a significant event in the course of life for all families in all cultures. Childbirth practices reflect the needs of family members and the way in which caring individuals and institutions function. As societies develop and change, the needs of families also change; and, so must the patterns of care giving.

A growing demand has been generated for health care which takes into account individual patient needs, increased patient rights and joint decision-making processes between the patient and health care providers. At the same time, there has been an increasing number of families which view childbirth as a very unique and personal event which should intimately involve family members and close friends. In the past, many families have had to choose between an intimate birthing experience in the home or hospitalization involving separations from family, friends and even the newborn child.

The Home-Like Birth Center at Booth Memorial Hospital is an option to families whose needs are no longer met by traditional modes of health care service.

The Home-Like program seeks to reconcile the safety of the hospital environment with personal care designed to meet the needs of patients desiring a warm and natural birth in the presence of selected family and friends. The program relies on a core of educational experience to prepare families for an increased decision-making role in their needs. Labor and delivery take place in a comfortable setting without obtrusive instrumentation. Safety and emotional support are assured by having nursing and house-staff available at all times who are in tune with the philosophy and individual needs of the family. Early discharge from the Center helps to reinforce the normal aspects of pregnancy and childbirth and allows the family to resume their life style with minimum intrusion and emotional upset. More of the family's energy is then free to welcome and care for the new infant. Home visits by professional staff will provide the family with support and information to insure the well being of the mother and infant until the family resumes the participation in the normal out-patient setting.

The service provided by the Home-Like program begins in pregnancy and continues through the postpartum course. It is designed primarily to meet the needs of low-risk patients who are anticipated to have a normal delivery without complications. Prenatal care to assure continued low-risk status is an integral part of the program. It is hoped that the Home-Like program will initiate unique services for prenatal patients which will provide a satisfying personal and safe experience—an experience which will contribute to the foundation for a close and intimate family life.

*Data provided by Sarah Danner, R.N., B.S.N., Head Nurse-Coordinator, Booth Home-Like Birth Center, Cleveland, Ohio.

OBJECTIVES

Major Objectives

1. To provide continuity of care to an identified group of patients and their newborns whose course is essentially normal.
   a. Maximal satisfaction is gained by both the patient and the nurse-midwife when continuity of care is provided to the patient over a period of time. Repetitive contacts with the same person or small group of persons promote: (a) the development of meaningful productive relationships, (b) higher quality of care through identification of one person who is responsible and accountable for the patient's care over time, and (c) economy of time by reducing the need for unnecessary communication.
   b. When a nurse-midwife assumes responsibility for the management of care, she is held accountable for her decisions and actions in relation to the patient's care.
   c. In order for the nurse-midwife to exercise judgment and skill and to promote optimal care, she requires the right of management of care without intervention about which she has not been informed.
2. To contribute to patient care in ongoing situations which require flexibility of team members to meet demands for care.
   a. Priority should be given to the development and maintenance of continuity of nursing and medical management of care for patients in the nurse-midwifery caseload. Involvement in other aspects of care, e.g., triage, caring for patients not assigned to the nurse-midwifery caseload, parents' education classes, in-service education, is legitimate utilization of the nurse-midwife, but should not jeopardize fulfillment of responsibility for the nurse-midwifery caseload.

Contributory Objectives

1. To develop and maintain working relationships with the various patient care, educational, and research units that affect or are affected by the nurse-midwife.
   a. The nurse-midwife functions more effectively within the health care system if she is involved in change processes and decision making relative to the development of policies and procedures.
   b. When nurse-midwifery functions overlap with functions performed by other health care personnel, division and/or sharing of responsibility should be mutually agreed upon.
   c. The quality and type of medical and nursing care provided by the nurse-midwife should be consistent with the care proposed by the Obstetric and Pediatric services.
   d. In an already highly organized health care system, the addition of the nurse-midwife should not impose undue confusion or expenditure of extra effort on the part of patients, nurse-midwives, nursing and medical colleagues, and other members of the health care team.
   e. By having the nurse-midwife exercise responsibility for the quality of nursing care for her patients through coordinated efforts with the nursing staff,

consistency and continuity of care may be promoted.

f. Since teaching and research should not jeopardize the patient's condition and satisfaction with care, the nurse-midwife must be informed of teaching and research activities in order to interpret the situation to the patient and to identify beneficial and/or deleterious effects such activities might have on patient care.

2. To provide means for nurse-midwifery staff orientation and development.

   a. The quality of the nurse-midwifery care depends upon adequate orientation and ongoing inservice educational opportunities.

   b. The nurse-midwifery caseload should be sufficient in size and diverse for the nurse-midwife to develop and maintain clinical competence in antepartal, intrapartal, postpartal (including family planning), and in the management of the normal newborn.

   c. The nurse-midwife should be responsible for the orientation and development of her own staff in relation to nurse-midwifery practice. Resource persons from other disciplines will be called upon to participate as appropriate.

3. To develop a system for the analysis and evaluation of the quality and quantity of patient care provided by the nurse-midwife.

   a. Improvement in patient care depends upon changes in practice based upon evaluation of service previously provided and the incorporation of innovative and current approaches to care.

   b. The objectives of the nurse-midwife should be allowed to change in response to future developments in the existing health care system.[1]

The Alternate Birthing Center at Hillcrest Medical Center in Tulsa, Oklahoma is housed on the main floor of Hillcrest Medical Center with quick access via elevator to the obstetrics unit. When couples enter the alternative birthing center, they come through a side door that bypasses the rest of the hospital, preserving the noninstitutional atmosphere that has been carefully created. Bright colors, carpets, and spacious hallways greet the eye. Roomy suites are designed to make the family feel at home; they include lounge and bedroom facilities, TV, bathrooms, and access to a kitchen complete with a microwave oven, stove, refrigerator, dishes, pots, and pans. Couples bring their own food to the center and prepare their meals, or, if they wish, they can order trays through the hospital food service. Minimum stay after birth is 6 hours. The philosophy and purpose of this center are as follows:

PHILOSOPHY

We recognize that pregnancy, the process of labor and birthing, are intense personal experiences and a time for adjustment for each individual. The birth produces a whole chain of events which have a profound and long-term effect on the individual, the family, and society.

It is our desire to recognize and provide those methods and practices of birthing which enhance and enrich this truly unique experience, and places birth in its true perspective in the flow of life experience. If, during this time of adjustments, adequate support systems are available, there is increased ability to cope with future life stresses; and a child growing to maturity in a family which is successful in coping

---

[1]Reprinted with permission of the Home-Like Birth Center, Booth Memorial Hospital, Cleveland, Ohio.

with the stresses of life has an increased opportunity for a well-adjusted and productive life. It is a human right to make informed choices regarding one's childbearing experiences. Active participation as a full partner with professionals in planning for a birth recognizes this right.

The Alternate Birthing Center is a beginning for a new approach to the childbearing-childbearing cycle [the beginning of pregnancy until one's own death or one's children's deaths] in which individualized humanistic health care fosters optimum levels of wellness at a reasonable cost for individuals and for the society.

PURPOSE OF ALTERNATE BIRTHING CENTER

The provision of comprehensive perinatal services requires that the needs of low-risk as well as high-risk women and their infants be addressed. Concomitant with increasing sophistication in technical resources for management of high-risk obstetrical situations has come recognition on the part of providers that normal childbirth needs are not being met by traditional obstetrical practices. This recognition has been heightened by the advocacy position assumed by professional leaders, by childbirth educators, and by greater consumer participation in health care. The increased costs of traditional care have contributed to many young couples choosing home delivery which offers the positive features of husband and family participation in a highly emotional human experience, with the result that home deliveries with their attendant hazards for mother and infant are growing in popularity.

The Alternate Birthing Center at Hillcrest Medical Center seeks to respond to the need to broaden the

spectrum of services for maternal and infant care, modifying traditional practices as needed to provide more natural, human experience within an atmosphere that is satisfying to young couples and consistent with safe and preventive perinatal care.

This will be accomplished by:

1. Provision of a room in which the mother may labor and deliver her infant, supported and assisted by the father and other support people in a home like environment that can be personalized to their satisfaction.
2. The care of mother and infant will be supervised by a licensed physician and by the presence of an obstetrical nurse throughout labor and delivery and by the availability of obstetrical, family practice, and pediatric staff at all times with attending staff backup.
3. Immediate rooming-in and early discharge will be additional important features of the Center's services including careful examination of mother and infant.[2]

Alternative Birth Center Policy

A typical policy for an alternative birth center is as follows:

1. The program is designed for healthy pregnant women who expect a normal labor, birth, and postpartum course.
2. The expectant mother should discuss with her physician or midwife her desire to give birth in the alternative birth center as early as possible in pregnancy.

---

[2] Reprinted with permission of Hillcrest Medical Center, Tulsa, Oklahoma.

3. When an agreement has been reached that the alternative birth center will be used, the woman and her partner and/or support person should register for the alternative birth center orientation classes. All persons who will be present during labor and birth are asked to attend the class series.
4. Attendance at childbirth preparation classes is important. If the expectant mother and her primary support person have attended classes during a previous pregnancy, a refresher class may be chosen.
5. A prenatal visit with the pediatrician or family physician of the parents' choice should be arranged so that plans can be made for the specific follow-up of the infant after birth and after discharge from the alternative birth center.
6. A specific plan for family participation during labor and birth should be developed during pregnancy in consultation with the birth attendant.
7. Consent forms that must be signed prior to admission to the alternative birth center are Patient's Consent Form, Physician/Midwife's Agreement, Verification of Infant Care, and Consent for Sibling Participation.

Admission and Transfer Criteria

The fundamental philosophical difference between the alternative birth center concept and a birthing room is that screening criteria are used to identify the birthing population eligible for the alternative birth center. There are very specific criteria for eligibility to give birth in an alternative birth center. In order to use the center, families must have no apparent medical problems, and a normal birth must be anticipated.

High-risk factors that exclude admission to the alternative birth center are

1. social factors

  - fewer than three prenatal visits
  - maternal age: primipara older than 35, multipara older than 40 (Relative contraindication—woman may use center after period of fetal monitoring.)

2. preexisting maternal disease

  - chronic hypertension
  - moderate or severe renal disease
  - heart disease, Classes II to IV
  - history of toxemia with seizures
  - diabetes
  - anemia: hemoglobin less than 9.5 gm/100 ml (Should a problem resolve, woman may be transferred to alternative birth center.)
  - tuberculosis
  - chronic or acute pulmonary problem
  - psychiatric disease requiring major tranquilizer

3. previous obstetric history

  - previous stillbirth of unknown etiology
  - previous cesarean section
  - Rh sensitivity
  - multiparity greater than five (Woman may use center with intravenous line in place during labor.)
  - previous infant with respiratory distress syndrome at same gestation

4. present pregnancy

  - toxemia
  - gestational age less than 37 or greater than 42 weeks
  - multiple birth
  - abnormal presentation (Primipara with a fetus with floating head will need evaluation by her obstetrician.)
  - third trimester bleeding or known placental previa

- membranes ruptured longer than 24 hours
- evidence of intrauterine growth retardation
- contracted pelvis on any plane
- pelvic disease, e.g., adnexal masses, uterine malformation, hydramnios, pelvic tumors, genital herpes
- treatment with reserpine, lithium, or magnesium
- induction: intravenous or buccal oxytocin (Pitocin)
- spinal or general anesthesia
- any other acute or chronic medical or psychiatric illness that, in the opinion of the medical staff, would increase risk to mother or infant

Transfer to the hospital labor and delivery rooms is required if one of the following high-risk factors develops after admission to the alternative birth center:

- hemoglobin: 9.5 gm/100 ml (Woman must have intravenous line in place during labor.)
- temperature 38 degrees C (100.4 degrees F)
- significant variation of maternal blood pressure from previously recorded values in office; fall or rise of maternal blood pressure of greater than 30/15 mm Hg
- significant vaginal bleeding
- development of any factor that requires continuous fetal heart rate monitoring
- any labor pattern or maternal or fetal complication that attending physician or nurse believes requires more sophisticated diagnosis or treatment than can be done in the alternative birth center

Should a problem resolve, the woman may be transferred back to the alternative birth center or give birth in the labor room.

Family and Support Person Participation

Just as well-defined criteria for admission of expectant mothers must be developed, guidelines for participation of other support persons and family members must be established. The following is a sample policy on family and support person participation:

1. The support persons who stay with the woman during labor, birth, and the postpartum period are there to assist her to labor and give birth. Her primary support persons are asked to attend childbirth preparation classes with her.
2. There are no specific limits on those the woman may choose to be with her during labor or how many people may be present. The expectant mother and her birth attendant need to come to an agreement during pregnancy about family and support person participation, however. Some women do best when accompanied by one or two emotionally supportive people, whereas others wish to include a larger group of friends and relatives.
3. All participants should be free of infection, wear clean clothes, and wash their hands when they arrive at the alternative birth center. Those who will have contact with the newborn baby must carefully scrub their hands before touching and holding the baby.
4. It is understood that the mother's safety and comfort are the first priority. Participants may be asked to leave if their presence seems distressing to the laboring mother and support persons assisting her or if the mother is transferred from the alternative birth center.
5. Participating children must have been prepared either through classes offered by the alternative birth center staff or by their parents.
6. Children under 12 years of age must be accompanied by an adult

who is not considered a primary support person for the expectant mother. This person will leave with the children if necessary—for example, if the mother is transferred, the children become upset, or a child is ill.

7. All participating children must be screened for signs of illness, including elevated temperature. Parents are asked to do this before they bring their children to the alternative birth center.

8. Children are to remain in the alternative birth center suite, or they are welcome to be with the family in the kitchen or lounge areas. They should not be in the halls, however. Parents should bring food and toys from home and sleeping bags if the children will spend the night.

9. If the children are to hold the newborn baby, they must wash their hands and put a gown on over their street clothes.

Nursing Care Protocols for the Alternative Birth Center

Just as written protocols are needed to ensure consistent high-quality care in the birthing room, so are they needed in the alternative birth center. The following is a sample protocol for intrapartum care in the center:

1. The emphasis is on encouraging and supporting the natural forces of labor with a calm, noninterventionist approach.

2. Adequate hydration is encouraged through the provision of honeyed teas, fruit juices, clear soups, water, and ice chips. The laboring woman can eat any available food.

3. Frequent urination is encouraged in order to keep the bladder empty, to encourage ambulation, and to monitor the woman's hydration.

4. The nurse or support person is in attendance throughout active labor in order to provide help and encouragement. Routines are discouraged and the nurse provides individualized care based on ongoing assessments.

5. A variety of positions during labor is encouraged, i.e., knee-chest, side lying, squatting, walking, or standing.

6. Vital signs and fetal heart tones (FHT) are taken and recorded as follows:
   a. temperature every 4 hours
   b. blood pressure, pulse, and respirations on admission, every hour during labor, and every 15 minutes for 2 hours postpartum
   c. FHT every 30 minutes in latent phase, every 15 minutes in active phase, and as frequently as indicated during second stage
   d. FHT every 5 minutes × 3 minutes when membranes rupture and then return to normal monitoring procedures
   e. Charting will be done as for all other laboring women

7. If the mother does not want an episiotomy and there is no obvious indication for one, the integrity of the perineum may be assisted by one or more of the following:
   a. hot soaks to perineum
   b. perineal massage with oil
   c. vaginal outlet stretching
   d. slow crowning of fetal head
   e. blowing during contractions and pushing between contractions
   f. the squatting position for birth

8. Respect for the goals of nonviolent birth will be shown; i.e., the infant's sensitivity, vulnerability, and need for immediate loving contact can be respected by
   a. placing the baby on the mother's abdomen, immediately after

birth, skin-to-skin, dried off, and covered with a warm, dry blanket

b. having a Leboyer bath available to be used if desired and if the infant is stable

c. delaying eye prophylaxis to allow for early eye contact between parents and infant

9. Keeping the family together for the childbearing experience is given priority at all times.

A written protocol is also needed for postpartum nursing care in the alternative birth center:

1. Consistent with our goals of facilitating early mother-infant bonding, separation of mother and infant is kept at a minimum.

a. The family unit may remain in the alternative birth center for 2 hours postpartum, after which they are transferred to a postpartum unit.

b. The option of staying in the alternative birth center unit until discharge depends on whether nurses are available for monitoring the baby and mother and on whether another family needs the unit.

2. Immediate rooming-in care of the infant includes the following:

a. Vital signs are determined every 1 hour for the first 4 hours and then every 8 hours. The labor/delivery nurse initiates a pediatric chart and takes vital signs for the first 2 hours.

b. Weighing and measuring is done at bedside in the alternative birth center if possible.

c. Newborn 2-hour examination is done at bedside or in presence of parents; it may be done by a certified nurse-midwife. The pediatric house staff physical examination is done as soon as possible.

d. Breastfeeding may be initiated as soon after birth as infant and mother are ready. Water by bottle is not prescribed routinely and is a joint decision of the mother and the baby's care provider.

e. Ophthalmic eye ointment is administered and vitamin K injected and recorded by person responsible for vital signs.

f. A specific care plan after 2 hours is worked out with nursery staff or postpartum nurse.

g. A hematocrit and Dextrostix is done by 4 hours of age.

h. Blood type and Rh determinations and Coombs test are done on cord blood prior to discharge if the mother is type O or Rh-negative.

3. Early postpartum care of the mother includes the following:

a. Vital signs are taken on mother (temperature and blood pressure).

b. Fundus is checked for firmness and signs of excess bleeding.

c. Urination is encouraged.

Alternative Birth Center Consent Forms

Several forms must be completed before a family may use an alternative birth center. Such forms include a family's consent form (Exhibit 3-4), a physician/midwife's consent form (Exhibit 3-5), a patient/physician or midwife's agreement (Exhibit 3-6), a physician's agreement to infant care (Exhibit 3-7), a consent for sibling participation (Exhibit 3-8), and a family-centered birth program family summary/preference sheet (Exhibit 3-9).

Early Discharge from Alternative Birth Center

When mother and baby are both healthy, early discharge from the alternative birth center is an

Exhibit 3-4 Sample Family's Consent Form

I hereby request and authorize, _____, aided by such associates,
                                                        (birth attendant)
assistants, and hospital personnel as may be directed by him/her, to assist me in the delivery of my baby at the Family
Birthing Center of _____ Hospital.
_____ and the staff of the Family Birthing Center have explained to
        (birth attendant)
me that delivery in the Birthing Center will differ from the usual in-patient hospital procedures. Delivery will be in a
separate building attached to the hospital, not in the hospital delivery room. Delivery will be without the use of spinal or
general anesthesia. Other medications will be used only if requested or needed.

The above named physician or midwife and members of the Birthing Center staff have informed me that there are risks
during childbirth even in a traditional labor and delivery room. I understand that separation of delivery and my birthing
experience from the hospital labor and delivery rooms may delay the treatment of these conditions.

I nevertheless consent to giving birth at the Birthing Center, without the usual hospital delivery room procedures,
except those required by the Birthing Center. I understand that during the birth, conditions may arise which, in the
judgment of the above named physician or midwife may necessitate medical or surgical treatment other than that
contemplated. In that event, on behalf of myself and my baby, I authorize the above named physician or midwife, his or
her associates, assistants, and hospital personnel, to administer any such surgical treatment, or administer any such
medication or anesthetics, which in his or her judgment may be necessary or advisable to meet such emergency, except:

_____

_____

If, during the contemplated procedure, it becomes necessary or advisable in the judgment of the above named
physician or midwife I authorize my admission and/or the admission of my baby to _____ Hospital.

I also understand that conditions may develop after birth which would necessitate, or make advisable, the transfer and
admission of the baby to the Neonatology Unit of _____ Hospital. In that event I consent to such transfer
and admission.

During the contemplated delivery procedure, in addition to the above named physician or midwife, and such assistants
and hospital personnel as he or she may require, I consent to the presence of:

_____

_____

I also authorize my husband/partner to assist the above named physician or midwife in the birth of my baby.

_____	_____
Father	Mother
_____	_____
Witness	Witness
Dated: _____	Dated: _____

Certification by Physician/Midwife:
  In my opinion the consent of the mother to be and the father is an informed consent.

                                          _____
                                                  Physician/Midwife

  To be re-signed at the time of admission to the Family Birthing Center.

_____	_____
Father	Mother
Date: _____	_____
	Witness

Source: Adapted and reprinted with permission of Family Birthing Center, Providence Hospital, Southfield, Michigan.

Exhibit 3-5 Sample Physician/Midwife's Consent to Use of Alternate Birthing Center

My patient, _____, has discussed with me her wish to labor and deliver her baby in the Alternate Birth Center at _____. Since she has had a normal pregnancy and her history indicates she is of low-risk, I am in agreement with this plan and am willing to attend her delivery in the Center. Her prenatal record will be forwarded to the Center by her 36th week.
Her EDC is _____.

_____   _____
            Date   (signed)

                                    Name and Address:

                                    _____
                                           (Please print name)

                                    _____

                                    _____

                                    Phone: _____

Source: Adapted and reprinted with permission of Hillcrest Medical Center, Tulsa, Oklahoma.

Exhibit 3-6 Sample Patient/Physician or Midwife's Agreement

(To accompany consent form, must be signed by delivering physician/midwife and patient and returned to alternative birth center)

I have discussed these items with _____
(patient) and an agreement has been made as follows:
1. Perineal shave
   Mini _____   None _____
2. Enema
   Yes _____   No _____
3. Analgesia during labor _____
4. Anesthesia during delivery
   Local _____   Pudendal _____   Other _____
5. Leboyer delivery
   Yes _____   No _____
6. Number of support people present:
   A. During labor _____
   B. During birth _____
   C. Children _____
7. Support person's involvement:
   Support person only: Yes _____ No _____
   If more than support, please explain _____
   _____
   _____
8. Other

_____   _____
Patient   Physician/Midwife

Source: Adapted and reprinted with permission of Hillcrest Medical Center, Tulsa, Oklahoma.

Exhibit 3-7 Sample Physician's Agreement to Infant Care in the Family Birth Center

_____ has advised me that she plans to participate in the Family Birth Center Program at _____ Hospital for her labor and the birth of her infant. I have reviewed the criteria for the infant's care and am in agreement with the proposed plan for early discharge provided the infant has a normal physical assessment. I understand that a registered nurse trained in newborn assessment will be making a home visit 24 to 48 hours post discharge, and any unusual findings will be reported to me.

_____   _____
Date   Physician's Signature

My plan for follow-up care of this infant includes:

Obstetrician's Name _____

Source: Adapted and reprinted with permission of Sutter Memorial Hospital, Sacramento, California.

Exhibit 3-8 Sample Consent for Sibling Participation in the Family Birth Center Program

I request the presence of my child(ren)

_____   _____
Name   Age

_____   _____
Name   Age

in the Family Birth Center during my present labor and birth. I understand that the consent of my physician/midwife must be obtained. I agree that an adult other than my primary support person will assume all responsibility for the child(ren) and will care for him/her if it becomes necessary for the child(ren) to leave the Family Birth Center. The name of the support person for my child(ren) is: _____. I understand that at present there are inadequate data concerning the short-term or long-term psychological impact to children witnessing their mother's labor and birth of a sibling.

I release the hospital from liability from any effects to my child(ren) from being present during the labor and delivery.

I have prepared my child(ren) for the birth in the following ways: _____

_____
_____
_____
_____

_____
Patient's Signature

_____
Father's Signature

_____
Date

_____   _____
Physician/Midwife's Signature   Date

Source: Adapted and reprinted with permission of Sutter Memorial Hospital, Sacramento, California.

Exhibit 3-9 Sample Family-Centered Birth Program Family Summary/Preference Sheet

Name _____

Address _____

Obstetrician _____ Pediatrician _____

INFORMATION ON MOTHER

Number of pregnancies _____ Number of children _____ Date baby due _____

Medication taken, other than vitamins _____

Childbirth education: Method _____ Instructor _____ Date completed _____

Support persons during birth: 1. _____

                        2. _____

                        3. _____

Other children to visit following birth: 1. _____

                                2. _____

Feeding plans: Breast _____ Bottle _____ Circumcision desired: Yes _____ No _____

Special requests for the birth: _____

_____

_____

Early discharge (12-24 hours after the birth) desired: Yes _____ No _____

Discharge address _____

              Contact telephone _____

DO NOT WRITE BELOW THIS LINE

1. Birth program orientation date: _____
2. Informed consent, patient: _____
3. Physician/midwife's agreement: _____
4. Patient/physician or midwife's agreement: _____
5. Physician's agreement to infant care: _____
6. Sibling participation agreement(s): _____
7. Prenatal history observations: _____

Source: Adapted and reprinted with permission of Sutter Memorial Hospital, Sacramento, California.

option. Preparation of the family for early discharge ideally begins during pregnancy and continues throughout the intrapartum and postpartum periods (Avery, Fournier, Jones, & Sipovic, 1982).

Early Discharge Criteria

The following protocol includes discharge criteria for both mother and baby:

1. Infant eligibility for early discharge—6 to 48 hours postpartum
   a. physical examination within normal limits at time of discharge—to be done by pediatric house staff or baby's physician.
   b. vital signs—temperature 36.5 to 37.5 degrees C (97.8 to 99.6 degrees F) at 2 hours, heart rate 100 to 160, respirations 40 to 60.
   c. laboratory values—hematocrit 48 to 65 at age 4 hours; Dextrostix greater than or equal to 45 at 4 hours; type/Rh, Coombs, no evidence of incompatibility.
   d. feeding—baby's demonstration of good sucking reflex on mother's breast or from a bottle.
   e. birth certificate—filled out and signed.
   f. voiding—if infant has not voided before discharge, parents

alerted to watch for it and notify nursery if baby has not voided within 24 hours.

   g. meconium—if infant has not passed meconium before discharge, parents should be alerted to watch for meconium by 48 hours or report back to nursery.

2. Maternal criteria for early discharge—6 to 48 hours postpartum
   a. No intrapartum obstetric complication requiring close postpartum observation (e.g., signs of infection, maternal exhaustion, etc.).
   b. less than 3 degrees laceration or episiotomy repaired.
   c. blood loss less than 500 cc.
   d. normal delivery or low forceps.
   e. analgesia/anesthesia—mothers who have received spinal, caudal, epidural, or general anesthesia not discharged before 24 hours.
   f. vital signs—temperature less than 100 degrees F, pulse less than 100, blood pressure consistent with prenatal course.
   g. fundus firm with no excessive bleeding.
   h. ability to ambulate easily and care for infant.
   i. ability to void adequately.
   j. RhoGam eligibility determined and plan for administration developed.
   k. postpartum instructions and booklet given and understood
   l. two-week postpartum appointment made.
   m. pediatric follow-up plan worked out.

3. Home situation criteria for early discharge
   a. access to telephone and immediate transportation should a problem arise.
   b. check in by telephone within 24 hours of discharge.

4. Follow-up of early discharge patients
   a. All patients leaving by 6 hours should check in by telephone a few hours after getting home and agree on time for a 24-hour visit by the alternative birth center staff.
   b. All 12-hour discharge patients should check in by telephone within 24 hours to schedule a home visit within 48 hours of discharge.[3]

Home Visit Protocols

Written protocols should be used during the postpartum home visits after early discharge. The following is a sample protocol for nursing care of the mother.

  A. Vital signs (TPR, BP)
   If temperature is above 100.4, consult physician
   Check for any irregular cardiac rhythms when counting pulse
   BP should be within woman's own normal limits
  B. Breasts—check for breast consistency; presence of colostrum or milk; condition of nipples and areolae; advise on breast care
   Be sure mother knows manual expression of breast milk
  C. Costovertebral Angle—check for tenderness bilaterally. If tender, check for signs and symptoms of urinary tract problems
  D. Legs: Check for areas of swelling or tenderness, especially calves
  E. Perineum
   1. Check episiotomy or laceration repair if any. Note separation of suture line, edema, redness, ecchymosis, pain, discharge
   2. Lochia—check character, amount, odor

[3]Adapted and reprinted with permission of Sutter Memorial Hospital, Sacramento, California.

Normally: rubra × 1-2 days
serosa × 2-7 days
alba after 7-10 days
Amount: If pad is saturated in 2 hours, bleeding is too heavy. Some small clots are normal, may be associated with cramping. Some breakthrough bright red bleeding is normal through the first few weeks postpartum if associated with increased activity or breastfeeding.

3. Fundus—check height, firmness, size
Day of delivery fundus at umbilicus; at 4-5 finger breadths below umbilicus and well into pelvis by 7 days. Size of grapefruit initially; gets progressively smaller

4. Voiding—how often, amounts, burning or difficulty

5. Bowel Movements—should have BM by 3rd pp day

F. Review nutrition and fluid intake patterns

G. Review signs of illness and postpartum complications, review how to obtain assistance

H. Review contraceptive methods if woman desires

I. Assess mother's psycho/social adjustment postpartum
Review patterns of sleeping and rest periods; use of medication; complaints of pain and/or fatigue, depression; adequacy of help at home; feelings about breastfeeding, siblings' adjustment, regaining her figure, postpartum sexuality.[4]

Findings should be noted on a form especially designed to record the postpartum status of the mother (Exhibit 3-10).

An established protocol should also be followed for the examination of the infant during the home visit:

I. First Visit—within 24 hours of discharge from Center
The nurse performs a complete physical assessment including the following:

A. Baby Assessment

1. Temperature: (Axillary; normal range 97-99); check extremities for touch temperature, color

2. Heart: (Apical pulse normally 110-160); listen for any abnormal sounds

3. Respirations: Watch chest for one minute for resp. rate; normally 30-60/minute. Note any signs of respiratory distress. Listen to lung sounds.

4. Skin: Check for jaundice; arrange to have bilirubin drawn if indicated.

5. Cord: Check for moistness, odor, redness, bleeding. Remove cord clamp if cord is dry.

6. Circumcision: Check for bleeding, edema

7. Feeding: Breast
Evaluate number of feeds/24 hrs, length of time nursing, quality of suck. Determine number and amounts of any supplementary feedings.

8. Feeding: Bottle
Check for correct preparation of formula. Determine number of feedings/24 hrs;—what, how much, when offered

9. Weight—Check weight on day 3, compare with birth weight

[4]Reprinted with permission of New Beginnings, Inc., Warwick, Rhode Island.

Exhibit 3-10 Sample Record for Mother's Postpartum Status at Home Visit

MOTHER'S RECORD

Name _____ G _____ P _____ Type and RH _____ .

Delivered by _____ Date _____ Time _____

L & D Complications _____

	Discharge Date _____	Home Visit Date _____
Temperature, Pulse, Respirations		
Blood Pressure		
Diet (3 meals, good appetite, anorexia)		
Fluids (amount, type)		
Breasts (soft, filling, firm)		
Examined for lumps (yes, no, taught)		
Skin — color (normal, red)		
Nipples (clean, cracked, blistered, bruised) —Sore (first minute of feeding, throughout feeding, between feedings)		
Measures recommended:		
CVA tenderness (neg. or pos.)		
Extremities —Homan's sign (neg. or pos.)		
—Edema (neg. or pos.)		
Fundus (firm, central, level)		
Perineum (epis., lac. or intact) —Treatment using (peri bottle, sitz, tucks, Epifoam)		
—Clean, healing, edematous, bruised		
Lochia (color, amount, odor)		
Voiding (completely, any dysuria)		
Bowel movements (# and soft or hard)		
Exercises (taught, doing which)		
Family planning (discussed, method)		
Home-physical set-up (stairs, bathroom, meals, problems) —Assistance (what type, who, how long)		
Appointment for 6 weeks check-up		
Signature:		2/82

Source: Reprinted with permission of the Home-Like Birth Center, Booth Memorial Hospital, Cleveland, Ohio.

10. General characteristics—note alertness, responsiveness, reported sleep patterns, any specific problems

B. Parent Education and Support
1. Discuss signs of illness in a newborn and where to call for appropriate help (private pediatrician, E.R., pediatric clinic). Signs of illness include changes in behavior or feeding patterns, elevated temperature, diarrhea, jaundice, respiratory distress

If signs of illness present at nurse's visit, she will call pediatrician or other physician to report findings.

II. Second Visit—Day 3
A. Repeat infant assessment as outlined above
B. Give bath demonstration if parents interested
C. Do heel stick for PKU
D. Give parents urine PKU slip and instructions[5]

Findings should be recorded on a special form (Exhibit 3-11).

Following the home visit, the family physician is notified of findings by telephone. The new mother is reminded to make a postpartum appointment with her physician, midwife, or clinic. Signs of illness in the mother or baby are reviewed, as are birth control methods.

Infection Control in Alternative Birth Centers

No studies have indicated that family-centered birth increases the incidence of infection. *A National Nosocomial Infections Study Report*

---

[5]Reprinted with permission of New Beginnings, Inc., Warwick, Rhode Island.

from the Hospital Infections Branch, Bacterial Disease Division of the Bureau of Epidemiology (U.S. Department of Health and Human Services, 1979) included the following:

1. The presence in the birth room of children of the family who are healthy and have been instructed in what to expect and how to behave should not increase the risk of infection. Persons with acute infectious illness, particularly upper respiratory tract infection, purulent or draining skin infection, or infectious diarrhea should be excluded from the room. No studies have evaluated the relative risk of infection to mother or infant if family members and others in the birth room wear a hospital scrub suit or clean gown over regular clothing compared with being allowed to wear street clothes. Similarly, although requiring persons attending the birth to wear a cap and mask will probably reduce further any small risk of infection, it is unknown whether these are necessary.

2. Although the infant must be kept warm and be observed for signs of distress, allowing the infant to remain with his mother immediately after delivery probably does not increase the risk of infection. Family members and hospital personnel must wash their hands thoroughly and don a clean gown before holding or caring for the infant.

3. Allowing the father or another adult family member selected by the mother to have extended visiting privileges to assist in the care of the infant and mother to the extent desired by the mother probably does not increase the risk of infection. The other children in the family may require reassurance from their mother and reasonable visiting of the entire family, if all members are healthy, probably does not increase the risk of infection to mother or infant.

As mentioned earlier, in no instance was there a report of increased infection in the birth facilities visited by the authors. Infection control procedures varied in their thoroughness, and good

Exhibit 3-11 Sample Record for Infant's Postpartum Status at Home Visit

INFANT'S RECORD

Name_____ Mother_____

Birthdate _____ Time _____ Apgars. _____ / _____
                                                    (1 minute)   (5 Minutes)

Delivered by _____ Pediatrician for discharge PE _____

Weight _____ Hct. _____ Type RH _____ Coombs. _____ Bili. _____ T. Pro. _____

Urine_____ Stool_____   Retic. _____

L & D Complications
....

| | Follow-up | Phone | Discharge | Home |
| Pediatrician _____ | No. _____ | Date _____ | Visit Date _____ |

Temperature		
Heart rate sounds (normal, murmur heard)		
Femoral pulses (palpated, not palpated)		
Respirations rate-sounds	/	/
Fontanels (bulging, level, depressed)	/	/
Eyes react to light (pupil and movement)		
Mucous membranes (moist, dry)		
Moro reflex (good, passive)		
Activity (active, lethargic)		
Skin (rashes, color) Extremities		
(rashes, color) face and trunk		
Blood drawn for Bilirubin (results)		
—Physician notified — Family notified		
—Repeat — date to be done — (results)		
Cord condition (drying, wet/red around naval)		
—triple dye applied (clamp removed)		
—cultured — physician notified		
Circumcision (healing, edematous, bleeding)		
Feeding type (breast, bottle)		
No. of times in 24 hrs./minutes each side	/	/
Sucking (good, weak)		
Wet diapers, No. per day, Stool-Color-Frequency		
Problems		
PKU (date done or to be done)		
Signature:		2/82

Source: Reprinted with permission of the Home-Like Birth Center, Booth Memorial Hospital, Cleveland, Ohio.

138266

statistical information was not often available, partly because there have been no identified problems with infection. There was often a reliance on word of mouth; for example, a pediatrician would inform the obstetric staff of an infection in a newborn, and follow-up would be initiated to determine the causes and to correct any identified problems.

The compiling of accurate statistics is important, and infection rates of families using the alternative birth center should be systematically monitored. At Hillcrest Medical Center in Tulsa, Oklahoma, infection control measures include an infection surveillance form attached to a self-addressed stamped envelope that is to be returned to the hospital's epidemiology department if an infection is identified (Exhibit 3-12).

The Alternative Birth Center at Illinois Masonic Hospital in Chicago, Illinois has the following protocol for infection control:

Handwashing

All participants of the Alternative Birthing Center must scrub their hands and arms with a sponge scrubber for 3 minutes upon entering the unit. Hands must be washed (following handwashing procedure) after examining each patient.

Dress Code and Gowning

All ABC personnel must wear a scrub gown. A lab coat or a yellow disposable gown must be worn over the scrub dress when leaving the OB area.

All professional persons in the Birthing Center rooms during delivery must wear scrub attire. Personnel attending the delivery must wear sterile gloves.

Exhibit 3-12 Infection Surveillance Form for Alternative Birth Center

	Address
Operation Performed	
Date of Operation	
Date of Onset of Infection	
Date Returned to Office with Infection	
Manifestations of Infection	
Site of Infection	
Cultured yes: no:	Return completed form to HMC Epidemiology Dept. if patient exhibits
Treatment Initiated	symptoms.

Source: Reprinted with permission of Hillcrest Medical Center, Tulsa, Oklahoma.

Illness

1. All personnel must have annual physicals.
2. Personnel with a possible viral or bacterial illness should not be allowed to work in the Birthing Center during the period they are clinically ill.
3. Personnel having been ill with a sore throat must have a throat culture before returning to work.
4. Husbands, visitors and siblings showing signs of illness must be screened by the Nurse Clinician.

General Care of ABC

1. Follow protocol for care of discharge unit, after each use.
2. All non-disposable sterile supplies and equipment are rotated and checked for their sterility and expiration dates.[6]

LABOR AND BIRTH STAFFING

In most birth facilities visited, labor and birth staffing was on a one-to-one basis (one nurse to one family) or a one-to-two basis (one nurse to two families). If at all possible, one nurse remained with the family throughout labor and birth. When the labor went beyond an 8-hour tour of duty, some hospitals paid the nurse overtime to remain on duty. Most nurses chose to work standard 8-hour shifts, however.

There are numerous methods for assessing and meeting staffing needs. Whatever method is utilized, the primary goal must be to provide the best possible care to patients while being as fair as possible to the nursing staff. The answers to the following questions can help achieve that goal:

1. What is the census?
2. What is the patient classification (acuity)?

- post cesareans
- antepartum care
- intravenous lines

3. Are there any special procedures that must be done?

- nonstress testing
- phototherapy lights
- circumcisions
- surgery (scrub person needed)
- intrauterine transfusions
- ultrasound, amniocentesis
- blood transfusions
- diabetic blood draws

4. Are there pending admissions to labor and birth?
5. Are there pending discharges?
6. Are there special needs?

- dying infants
- family support
- parent teaching

Monitrices

The monitrice concept, as implemented at Manchester Memorial Hospital, Connecticut, is one solution to staffing hospital maternity units (Sumner & Phillips, 1981). A monitrice is an experienced maternity nurse who is trained in the psychoprophylactic method of childbirth and supports the woman and her family on a one-to-one basis throughout labor and birth. If a group of monitrices is available, a hospital literally has an on-call staff of private duty nurses for labor and delivery.

The monitrice is part of a team that includes regular nursing and medical staff. Nursing staff may assume responsibility for admission and support until the monitrice arrives. Care in the first hours postpartum may be given by a monitrice or by nursing staff. In case of complications or situations that require surgical intervention, monitrice and staff also work

---

[6]Reprinted with permission of Illinois Masonic Hospital, Chicago, Illinois.

together as a team. Maternity nurses who choose to work only a few days a week or full-time can find the role of monitrice very rewarding.

Some institutions may find it more efficient to subdivide the role of the monitrice into two separate ones: (1) a labor attendant who is not a registered nurse, but is knowledgeable and experienced in prepared childbirth and is highly motivated to provide continuous one-to-one emotional support; and (2) an obstetric nurse who monitors the mother's and the fetus' vital signs, but is otherwise free to leave the room to perform other duties. Under this system, childbirth educators who are not nurses have an opportunity to share in the drama of the birth.

Nurses in private practice may organize a private monitrice program, receiving a fee for services from the families served (Hommel, 1969). The Monitrices of Maryland, for example, have organized a private duty obstetric nursing service. Each monitrice may have her own professional insurance, or the group may purchase insurance coverage.

On-Call Staffing

A similar solution to the unpredictable demand for hospital maternity services is on-call staffing. Kowalski (1973) described the use of two-nurse teams to carry a caseload of patients through the prenatal clinic, labor, delivery, and the postpartum period. When a clinic patient is admitted in labor, the nurse on call goes to the hospital to provide care throughout labor and birth. According to Kowalski, "Each nurse is scheduled to be in the obstetric clinic 16 hours per week and on call for labors every other 24 hours and every other weekend." To ensure continuity of care, each team nurse tries to see each patient at least twice for antepartum care. Scheduling is such that each team nurse works an average of 40 hours per week. Regular staffing is modified, but the need for one nurse to care for six or more women in labor is less frequent than before on-call staffing. Both patients and nurses report satisfaction with the on-call system (Kowalski, 1973). In a service such as this, the nurse is employed by the fee-for-service clinic that provides the maternity care.

Many hospitals with birthing rooms also use on-call staffing; they develop a call list of staff nurses who volunteer or nurses who wish to work only on call. These nurses provide one-to-one nursing care throughout labor and birth. They are considered hospital employees, are paid by the hospital, and are covered by the hospital's professional practice insurance.

The Shared Beginnings nursing care program in the San Francisco Bay area is a variation of on-call staffing (Freeman, 1979). This program involves a group of nurses who are on call only for the birth itself and the first 4 to 6 hours after birth to provide nursing care and facilitate parent-infant bonding. They also make follow-up telephone calls after hospital discharge and follow-up home visits to the family, if requested. Since they are essentially private duty nurses, families pay them directly.

On-call programs offer close nursing observation and personalized care during heavy census periods when regular staff members are working at or beyond their limits. Regular staff members may see the on-call nurses as outsiders, however, and as a threat. Group meetings attended by both staff and on-call nurses are essential to keep communication open.

NURSE-MIDWIFERY

In many areas of the United States, nurse-midwifery services are growing rapidly. There is an increasing awareness that nurse-midwives are valuable and often essential members of the maternity care team. For example, at Mount Zion Hospital in San Francisco, California, certified nurse-midwives have had hospital privileges since 1978. At San Francisco General Hospital, nurse-midwives have attended the deliveries of over 1,000 low- to high-risk women since 1975; outcome statistics have been comparable to those of the obstetric department in general (Mann, 1981). At Hennepin County Medical Center, a nurse-midwife service was initiated in 1973. By January of 1980, the service had had experience with over 2,400 births. Maternal and neonatal morbidity has been low, and the service has demonstrated that highly individualized care for normal childbearing women can be provided by nurse-midwives with good results (Rising & Lindell, 1982).

In spite of these excellent reports, nurse-midwives often have great trouble obtaining hospital privileges. In many communities, organized medical groups do not even recognize them. While the controversy over nurse-midwife utilization continues, their numbers increase.

FREE-STANDING BIRTH CENTERS

Out-of-hospital (free-standing) birth centers are proliferating in the United States. Although controversial, these new centers are part of a growing trend to develop less costly and more family-oriented forms of health care than those traditionally provided by hospitals. Free-standing birth centers offer another option to couples seeking more responsibility and control over their birth experiences.

Maternity Center Association

A model for out-of-hospital birth centers has been the Maternity Center Association's Childbearing Center, which opened in 1975 in New York City. The Childbearing Center was designed as a demonstration project to test whether safe, satisfying, and economical out-of-hospital care could be provided to those families who did not want hospital births (Lubic & Ernst, 1978). Located on the first two floors of a former townhouse, the Childbearing Center has two labor/birth rooms. "It is like a maxi-home and not a mini-hospital (nor is it home birth which in New York State is defined as birth in a personal residence)" (Faison, Pisani, Douglas, Cranch, & Lubic, 1979, p. 527).

A labor lounge and a garden are available for couples to use in early labor. Families are accommodated in the center for prenatal care, classes in preparation for childbirth and infant care, labor and birth, pediatric examination, and postpartum care. The environment is personalized and homelike, emphasizing family involvement and parent responsibility.

Nurse-midwives, backed by obstetricians, provide most of the physical care. The physicians see each family twice during the prenatal period and are always available for consultation. The mother and baby are discharged to home within 12 hours of birth; follow-up care at home is provided by public health nurses within 24 hours of discharge and again on the 3rd to 5th postpartum day. As in hospital birth centers, patients are carefully screened prenatally and only those who anticipate a complication-free pregnancy and delivery are accepted. In order for the family to participate in the in-depth education program, enrollment at the center is required no later than the 22nd week of pregnancy. With thorough record keeping to validate their experiences, the staff of the Childbearing Center has demonstrated that low-risk pregnancies and births can occur safely in an out-of-hospital center—and at a cost "substantially below" that of birth in a hospital (Lubic & Ernst, 1978).

A $256,000 grant was awarded to the Maternity Center Association in New York City by the Hartford Foundation. The tasks of the grant are (1) to develop a manual of birth center standards, (2) to create a cooperative resource and information network, and (3) to promote wider public understanding of the birth center concept. Coordinating these tasks is the Cooperative Birth Center Network. Information on setting up free-standing birth centers can be obtained by writing to this organization at Box 1, Route 1, Perkiomenville, PA 18074.

Economy

Most free-standing birth centers are staffed by certified nurse-midwives and physicians who have privileges at the local hospital. Ambulance service and emergency procedures are readily available. Fees vary with the services provided and the ability of the family to pay (reduced-fee sliding scale). Several insurance companies, as well as Medicaid, reimburse these clinics for their services. For childbirth at the Maternity Center Association in New York, Blue Cross/ Blue Shield of Greater New York and Medicaid reimburse depending on contract (Faison et al., 1979). Some insurance carriers reimburse the cost of out-of-hospital birth at a lower rate than that applied to the cost of a conventional hospital/physician birth, however. Also, in states where there are no state regulations for out-of-hospital birth centers, insurance carriers will *not* always reimburse costs in centers.

A birth center fee usually includes in one comprehensive charge all prenatal visits, all childbirth preparation classes, labor and birth care at the center, and postpartum office and home visits. This fee usually does *not* include laboratory testing, any hospitalization or hospital service (for example, x-ray, ultrasound, Rho-Gam, cesarean birth), or any separate physician's fees for services at the hospital. The cost of circumcision is not covered in the basic fee. The comprehensive fees of the free-standing birth centers surveyed by the authors were approximately one-half to two-thirds the total charges for normal childbirth in a hospital setting with a private physician providing care.

Services

The following list of responsibilities of the family and the birth attendants is shared with families who give birth at New Beginnings, Inc. in Warwick, Rhode Island:

Childbirth is one of life's peak experiences; it is a family experience that is shared emotionally, physically and spiritually as the whole family joins together in receiving and welcoming the newborn.

Childbearing is a healthy process. Staying healthy during childbearing is the responsibility of the mother. She is assisted by other members of her family and by health care providers. As your health care providers, we at New Beginnings want you to realize what the responsibility of staying healthy entails. We also want you to know our responsibilities in assisting you to remain healthy.

Responsibilities of the Family

1. Mother has good nutritional pattern and hematocrit not less than 35 by the last month of pregnancy.
2. Mother has received good and consistent prenatal care.
3. Financial commitment to New Beginnings is met as agreed.
4. Childbirth preparation has been completed prior to birth.
5. Family is prepared as well as possible to experience childbirth without narcotics or sedatives.
6. Family members show themselves to be supportive of one another.
7. Provisions are made for someone to be continuously at home the first three days following birth to manage the household so that mother may rest.
8. Mother has contacted a local breastfeeding group for assistance at home after birth (if new at breastfeeding).
9. Family is willing to transfer care to a physician and the hospital in emergency and/or on decision of New Beginnings' staff.
10. Pediatric follow-up is arranged for the newborn.
11. Accurate and complete information about medical history for the family is provided to the nurse-midwife.

Responsibilities of Birth Attendants

1. Is fully aware of current medical status of the mother
2. Provides for emergency hospital back-up
3. Develops good rapport with the family

4. Is sensitive to special needs or unusual circumstances of a family situation
5. Is professionally qualified and legally licensed to provide normal pregnancy care and to attend birth
6. Is prepared to deal with childbirth emergencies until transfer to hospital can be made
7. Keeps family informed of the progress of the pregnancy
8. Involves the family in all decision making concerning their care
9. Keeps abreast of new developments in medical sciences which deal with care of the childbearing family so that the most up-to-date knowledge is used as a basis of care[7]

Facilities

The out-of-hospital birth centers surveyed were located in diverse sites. One is in a renovated townhouse (i.e., Maternity Center Association, New York City); another, in a large apartment (i.e., Familyborn, New Jersey). Others are in renovated parts of medical office buildings (e.g., ABC, Alaska, and New Beginnings, Inc., Rhode Island). The Denver Birth Center is located in a wing of the obstetric unit of a hospital. Some are in houses (e.g., The Childbirth Center, P.A., New Jersey; Birthplace, Inc., Florida; Southwest Maternity Center, Inc., New Mexico; The Birthplace, Washington; The Birth Home, California; Birth Center-Women's Health Center, West Virginia; Birth Center, Oklahoma).

These birth centers are usually decorated in homelike fashion; they have family living rooms, kitchens, and baths. Often, they also have lending libraries and referral files for community resources relating to childbirth and early parenting. Although statistics on maternal and infant morbidity and mortality differ from center to center, they are consistently comparable with hospital statistics.

COMPONENTS OF FAMILY-CENTERED INTRAPARTUM CARE

The following are the components of family-centered intrapartum care:

1. family waiting area or early labor lounge where the woman may be with her family and close friends

   - Healthy snacks are available or can be prepared by family.
   - Telephones are available.
   - There is an intercom with access to labor and birth area.
   - There is access to outdoors for walking.
   - The decor is pleasant, and there are windows.
   - Activities such as games, TV, radio, and reading materials are provided.
   - Furnishings are comfortable.

2. diagnostic/admitting room with minimal or no charge for assessment of labor status or for evaluation of emergency medical problems
3. labor/birth rooms (birthing rooms)

   - Rooms are furnished with labor/birth bed, rocking chair, infant crib, comfortable chairs, tape cassette or other audiovisual equipment, and clock with second hand.
   - There is a private bath with toilet and tub or shower.
   - Lighting is subdued.
   - Portable mirror is provided.
   - Decor is homelike and includes painted walls or wallpaper, pictures, plants.
   - Labor/birth staff provide support and manage labor according to normal physiological principles with no unnecessary

---

[7]Reprinted with permission of New Beginnings, Inc., Warwick, Rhode Island.

interference; women are encouraged to ambulate, change positions, bathe during labor, drink fluids, and may eat as desired.

- Chosen companions are welcomed at all times, even when procedures are being performed and labor progress is abnormal.
- Visitation policy is flexible.
- Meals are available for support person.
- Specialized equipment is accessible.
- Adherence to low-risk criteria is less stringent.
- Components of standard current medical practice and technology may be utilized.
- Staffing limitations may require, but not mandate, that mother and newborn be moved to the recovery room following birth; mother, infant, and father may remain together in the recovery room before being transferred to the family-centered care unit.

4. delivery room

- Adjustable backrest is on delivery table, or a birthing chair is available.
- Walls are warmly painted
- Lighting can be dimmed at birth according to the parents' wishes.
- A stool is provided for support person.
- A mirror is provided.
- Music of the parents' choice is played.
- Leboyer birth is an option.
- Polaroid pictures may be taken at the time of birth.
- Provision is made for the attachment process to begin.
- If an incubator is used, it is placed by the mother's side.
- Skin-to-skin contact between mother and baby, father and baby is encouraged.
- Ophthalmic eye ointment or drops administration is delayed for at least 1 hour after birth.

- Breastfeeding may begin on the delivery table.
- The delivery room is warmed prior to birth.
- Apgar scoring, vitamin K injection, and other procedures are done while the baby is held by the parents, if this is their wish.
- There is a telephone for contacting family members and friends.
- Parents and baby are not separated unless medically indicated or desired by the parents.

5. recovery room

- Family members are not separated during the recovery period.
- Early skin-to-skin contact of mother and infant is encouraged; newborn body temperature is maintained by a warm blanket over both mother and infant; contact by the father or support person may be extended, if desired.
- Recovery for both mother and newborn lasts for 2 to 3 hours postpartum before transfer to the family-centered care unit.
- Infant remains with the family throughout the hospital stay, depending on the infant's satisfactory adjustment, parents' desires, room availability, and staffing allowances.
- If the family desires and expects early discharge, primary support person may elect to stay with the new mother in her postpartum private room; all others will observe family-centered care visiting hours.
- Family is helped to gain necessary competency and self-confidence in infant care skills and satisfactory initiation of feeding.
- Discharge home is possible at approximately 12 to 24 hours postpartum following pediatrician's and obstetrician's evaluation and laboratory rounds.

6. alternative birth centers

- Room is comfortably furnished with a full-size "family" bed with firm mattress, rocking chair, infant crib, comfortable chairs, a couch that doubles as a bed, small refrigerator, tape cassette or other audiovisual equipment, clock with second hand.

- A wedge is available for support while pushing during the expulsion stage.

- A bean bag chair is provided for elevation of the hips for birth and for provision of space for physician/midwife assistance at birth.

- A stool is provided for the physician or midwife to sit on during birth and/or episiotomy repair, if desired.

- There is a private bath with toilet and tub or shower.

- A small kitchen is available.

- Lighting is subdued.

- Risk screening criteria for admission to the alternative birth center and transfer to traditional labor and delivery rooms are explained to family.

- Decor is homelike and includes painted walls or wallpaper, pictures, plants.

- Fetal monitors or intravenous fluids are not used routinely in the alternative birth center.

- Decisions regarding change of status from low to high risk necessitating a fetal monitor, intravenous fluids, labor augmentation, or birth in a delivery room are fully shared with the family by the physician and/or midwife.

- All participants in the birth who will have contact with the newborn are required to scrub.

- Siblings must be accompanied by responsible adults, other than the primary support person, to supervise them and to remove them, if appropriate.

- The primary support person and expectant mother must attend an orientation session to ensure understanding of their roles and responsibilities.

- All participants are screened for absence of communicable diseases, cough, rhinitis, sore throat, skin lesions, or diarrhea.

REFERENCES

Avery, M., Fournier, L., Jones, P., & Sipovic, C. An early postpartum hospital discharge program: Implementation and evaluation. *Journal of Obstetric, Gynecologic, and Neonatal Nursing,* 1982, *11*, 233-235.

Barton, J.L., Rovner, S., Puls, K., & Read, P.A. Alternative birthing center: Experience in a teaching obstetric service. *American Journal of Obstetrics and Gynecology,* 1980, *137*, 377-384.

Carlson, B., & Sumner, P. At home delivery: A celebration. *Journal of Obstetric, Gynecologic, and Neonatal Nursing,* 1976, *5*, 21-27.

Faison, J.B., Pisani, B.J., Douglas, R.G., Cranch, G.S., & Lubic, R.W. The childbearing center: An alternative birth setting. *Obstetrics and Gynecology,* 1979, *54*(4), 527-532.

Fenwick, L., & Dearing, R. *The Cybele cluster: A single room maternity system for high- and low-risk families.* Spokane: Cybele Society, 1981.

Freeman, M.H. Giving family life a good start in the hospital. *American Journal of Maternal Child Nursing,* 1979, *4*(1), 51-54.

Grad, R.K. Breaking ground for a birthing room. *American Journal of Maternal Child Nursing,* 1979, *4*, 245-249.

Hommel, F. Nurses in private practice as monitrices. *American Journal of Nursing,* 1969, *69*, 1447-1450.

International Childbirth Education Association (ICEA). *ICEA Position Paper on Planning Comprehensive Maternal and Newborn Services for the Childbearing Year.* Minneapolis: International Childbirth Education Association, 1978.

Interprofessional Task Force on Health Care of Women and Children. *Joint Position Statement on the Development of Family-Centered Maternity/Newborn Care in Hospitals.* Chicago: The American College of Obstetricians and Gynecologists, 1978.

Kieffer, M.J. The birthing room concept at Phoenix Memorial Hospital, Part II: Consumer satisfaction during one year. *Journal of Obstetric, Gynecologic, and Neonatal Nursing,* 1980, *9*, 151-159.

Klass, K., & Capps, K. Nine years' experience with family-centered maternity care in a community hospital. *Birth and the Family Journal,* 1980, *7*(3), 175-180.

Kowalski, K.E. "On call" staffing. *American Journal of Nursing*, 1973, *73*, 1725-1727.

Lubic, R.W., & Ernst, E.K. The childbearing center: An alternative to conventional care. *Nursing Outlook*, 1978, *26*(12), 754-760.

Mann, R.J. San Francisco General Hospital nurse-midwifery practice: The first thousand births. *American Journal of Obstetrics and Gynecology*, 1981, *140*, 676-682.

Notelovitz, M. The single unit delivery system—A safe alternative to home deliveries. *American Journal of Obstetrics and Gynecology*, 1978, *132*, 887-894.

Rising, S.S., & Lindell, S.G. The childbearing childrearing center: A nursing model. *Nursing Clinics of North America*, 1982, *17*(1), 11-21.

Salter, A. Birth without violence: A medical controversy. *Nursing Research*, 1978, *27*, 84-88.

Sumner, P.E., & Phillips, C.R. *Birthing rooms: Concept and reality*. St. Louis: C.V. Mosby, 1981.

U.S. Department of Health and Human Services. Alternative birth centers: Assessment of the risks and recommendations for operation. *A National Nosocomial Infections Study Report*. Department of Health and Human Services, Bureau of Epidemiology, 1979.

Chapter 4

Family-Centered Care for Pregnancy, Labor, and Birth at Risk

(photo © Alison E. Wachstein)

4

THE HIGH-RISK FAMILY

High-risk mothers and infants have a higher incidence of morbidity and mortality than does the general population of mothers and infants. Pregnancy is classified as high risk in the presence of certain conditions that have been identified as dangerous to the health and life of the mother and/or the infant. These conditions include medical disorders, obstetric disorders, and social and demographic factors (Wilson & Schifrin, 1980).

Risk Scoring

One of the methods used to identify those pregnancies that have a significantly greater statistical risk of perinatal morbidity and mortality is risk scoring. Numerous scoring systems have been developed to quantify obstetric risk. Some are based on as many as 100 factors that identify low, high, or extreme risk pregnancies; others use only 5 or 10 factors (Biggs, 1982). One type of risk-scoring system is integrated into Hollister's maternal/newborn record system. The Health History Summary (Exhibit 4-1) allows for initial recognition of risk at the first antepartum visit. The Prenatal Flow Record (Exhibit 4-2) and Obstetric Admitting Record (Exhibit 4-3) provide a continuing risk guide, since risk factors may change as pregnancy progresses.

It has been noted that, in large urban areas, up to 10% to 11% of all babies born alive need specialized neonatal care (Ferrara & Harin, 1980). According to Babson, Pernoll, and Benda (1980):

> Of the more than 3.5 million pregnancies each year that reach 20 weeks of gestational age, approximately 40,000 fetuses die before delivery. Almost the same number of neonates succumb in the first month of life after birth. Another 40,000 have severe (but often correctable) congenital malformations. (p. 1)

When a pregnancy is labeled high risk, the medical care is focused on the pathophysiology of the crisis. The attitudes of the health care providers often change dramatically when a pregnancy is identified as at risk. Family-centered maternity care practices are frequently limited to the "normal" childbearing population. This is unfortunate, not only because high-risk families need family-centered care as much as those with normal pregnancies do, but also because the special psychological challenges in providing care to high-risk families makes family-centered care even more important. According to Garbarino (1980),

95

Exhibit 4-1 Hollister Health History Summary

Health History Summary   Date:

HOLLISTER
maternal/newborn
RECORD SYSTEM

PATIENT IDENTIFICATION

Patient's name _____

Age_____ Race_____ Religion_____ Marital status_____ Years married_____ Education_____ Occupation_____

Home address _____ Home tel. _____ Work tel. _____

Nearest relative _____ Relative's employer _____ Work tel. _____

Referring physician _____ Attending physician _____

Medical History	Patient	Family	Check and detail positive findings including date and place of treatment. Precede findings by reference number.
1. Congenital anomalies			
2. Genetic diseases			
3. Multiple births			
4. Diabetes mellitus			
5. Malignancies			
6. Hypertension			
7. Heart disease			
8. Rheumatic fever			
9. Pulmonary disease			
10. GI problems			
11. Renal disease			
12. Other urinary tract problems			
13. Genitourinary anomalies			
14. Abnormal uterine bleeding			
15. Infertility			
16. Venereal disease			
17. Phlebitis, varicosities			
18. Nervous/mental disorders			
19. Convulsive disorders			
20. Metabol./endocrine disorders			
21. Anemia/hemoglobinopathy			
22. Blood dyscrasias			
23. Drug addiction			
24. Smoking/alcohol			
25. Infectious diseases			
26. Operations/accidents			
27. Blood transfusions			
28. Other hospitalizations			
29. **No known disease**			

Sensitivities (detail positive findings)
30.☐ **None known**
31.☐ Antibiotics
32.☐ Analgesics
33.☐ Sedatives
34.☐ Anesthesia
35.☐ Other

Preexisting Risk Guide
Indicates pregnancy/outcome at risk
36.☐ Age < 15 or > 35
37.☐ < 8th grade education
38.☐ Cardiac disease (class I or II)
39.☐ Tuberculosis, active
40.☐ Chronic pulmonary disease
41.☐ Thrombophlebitis
42.☐ Endocrinopathy
43.☐ Epilepsy (on medication)
44.☐ Infertility (treated)
45.☐ 2 abortions (spontaneous/induced)
46.☐ ≥ 7 deliveries
47.☐ Previous preterm or SGA infants
48.☐ Infants ≥ 4,000 gms
49.☐ Isoimmunization (ABO, etc.)
50.☐ Hemorrhage during previous preg.
51.☐ Previous preeclampsia
52.☐ Surgically scarred uterus
53.☐ _____

Indicates pregnancy/outcome at **high** risk
54.☐ Age ≥ 40
55.☐ Diabetes mellitus
56.☐ Hypertension
57.☐ Cardiac disease (class III or IV)
58.☐ Chronic renal disease
59.☐ Congenital/chromosomal anomalies
60.☐ Hemoglobinopathies
61.☐ Isoimmunization (Rh)
62.☐ Drug addiction/alcoholism
63.☐ Habitual abortions
64.☐ Incompetent cervix
65.☐ Prior fetal or neonatal death
66.☐ Prior neurologically damaged infant
67.☐ _____

Initial Risk Assessment
68.☐ No risk factors noted
69.☐ At risk
70.☐ At **high** risk

Signature

Menstrual History	Onset age	Cycle q.	days	Length days	Amount	L M P	mo/day/yr	quality

Pregnancy History	Grav	Term	Pret	A bort	Live	E D C	mo/day/yr	

No.	Month/ year	Sex	Weight at birth	Wks. gest.	Hrs. in labor	Type of delivery	Details of delivery: Include anesthesia and maternal or newborn complications. Use Risk Guide numbers where applicable.
1							
2							
3							
4							
5							
6							
7							
8							

 Hollister™

Exhibit 4-2 Hollister Prenatal Flow Record

Prenatal Flow Record

HOLLISTER®
maternal/newborn
RECORD SYSTEM

PATIENT IDENTIFICATION

Patient's name _____

Risk Guide for Pregnancy and Outcome

Preliminary Risk Assessment (detail risk factors from the HHS below)

- ☐ (0) No risk factors noted _____
- ☐ (1) At risk _____
- ☐ (2) **High risk** _____

Continuing Risk Guide (enter dates first noted and revise RISK STATUS)

Mo/day	Potential risk factors	Mo/day	High risk factors
/	3. Preg. without familial support	/	18. Diabetes mellitus
/	4. Second pregnancy in 12 months	/	19. Hypertension
/	5. Smoking (≥ 1 pack per day)	/	20. Thrombophlebitis
/	6. Rh negative (nonsensitized)	/	21. Herpes (type 2)
/	7. Uterine/cervical malformation	/	22. Rh sensitization
/	8. Inadequate pelvis	/	23. Uterine bleeding
/	9. Venereal disease	/	24. Hydramnios
/	10. Anemia (Hct < 30%:Hgb < 10%)	/	25. Severe preeclampsia
/	11. Acute pyelonephritis	/	26. Fetal growth retardation
/	12. Failure to gain weight	/	27. Premature rupt. membranes
/	13. Multiple pregnancy (term)	/	28. Multiple pregnancy (preterm)
/	14. Abnormal presentation	/	29. Low/falling estriols
/	15. Postterm pregnancy	/	30. Significant social problems
/	16.	/	31. Alcohol and drug abuse
/	17.	/	32.

Initial Prenatal Screen

Mo day	Test	Result
/	Hct/Hgb	
/	Patient's Blood type and Rh	
/	Father's Blood type and Rh	
/	Antibody	
/	Serology	
/	Rubella titer	
/	Urinalysis micro	
/	Pap test	
/	G.C.	

Additional Lab Findings

Mo/day	Test	Result
/	Hct/Hgb	
/	Hct/Hgb	
/		
/	Blood sugar	
/	Bacteriuria	
/		
/		
/		
/		

G	T	P	A	L	L M P	mo/day/yr	E D C	mo/day/yr

- ☐ Initial prenatal instruction
- ☐ Attends prenatal classes
- ☐ Cesarean section
- ☐ For sterilization
- ☐ Breast ☐ Bottle Feeding
- ☐ Circumcision

Quickening date ___ mo/day/yr

Anesthesia _____

Baby's physician _____

See Add Prog Note

Flow Chart

Date	Weight this visit	Blood pressure	Protein	Sugar	Est. weeks gestation (dates/size)	Fundal height	Fetal heart rate	Edema	RISK STATUS (0,1,2)

Physician's signature _____

Hollister™

Exhibit 4-3 Hollister Obstetric Admitting Record

Obstetric Admitting Record

HOLLISTER
maternal/newborn
RECORD SYSTEM

Basic Admission Data

G	T	P	A	L	L M P	mo / day / yr	E D C	mo / day / yr	A G E

Date _____ mo / day / yr _____   Time _____ : _____ ☐ AM ☐ PM

☐ Direct admit   ☐ Transport ↓   ☐ Other ↓

☐ Ambulatory
☐ Wheelchair
☐ Cart/stretcher

Next of kin _____   Tel. no. _____

Reasons for admission

☐ Onset of labor
Observation/evaluation
  ☐ Fetal status
  ☐ Medical complication
  ☐ Obstetric complication
☐ Spontaneous abortion
Cesarean section
  ☐ Primary   ☐ Repeat
Induction of labor
  ☐ Elective   ☐ Indicated

☐ Other _____
Detail reasons:

Patient Care Data

Contractions on admission   ☐ None

Frequency _____ Duration _____ Quality _____

Began on _____ mo / day / yr _____ at _____ : _____ ☐ AM ☐ PM

Membranes on admission   ☐ Intact

☐ Ruptured: date _____ mo / day / yr _____ at _____ : _____ ☐ AM ☐ PM

Fluid was: ☐ Clear   ☐ Meconium   ☐ Foul smelling

Vaginal bleeding   ☐ None

☐ Normal show   ☐ Bleeding (describe) _____

Patient has:

☐ Recent URI
☐ Exposure to infection
☐ Been vomiting
☐ _____
☐ Dentures
☐ Contact lenses
☐ Glasses
☐ _____

Plans for anesthesia   ☐ None planned

☐ Specify type: _____

Last oral intake _____ mo / day / yr _____ at _____ : _____ ☐ AM ☐ PM   ☐ Fluids   ☐ Solids

Current Medications   ☐ None

Name/type of medication	Last taken	Brought in No	Yes
_____	_____	☐	☐
_____	_____	☐	☐
_____	_____	☐	☐
_____	_____	☐	☐

Patient plans: No   Yes

☐ Private   ☐ Semi-private   ☐ ☐ Rooming in
☐ Smoker   ☐ Non-smoker   ☐ ☐ Husband in delivery
☐ Breast   ☐ Bottle feeding   ☐ ☐ Circumcision for boy
☐ Other: _____

Procedures ☐ Prep   ☐ Enema (results) _____

☐ Other: _____

Physician's name _____

Notified by _____

Date _____ / _____ / _____   Time _____ : _____ ☐ AM ☐ PM

Significant Prenatal Data

Prenatal lab tests   ☐ None

Patient's blood type	Father's blood type	Antibody	Serology
Rh titer	Rubella titer		

Fetal assessment tests   ☐ None

Date				
Test				
Result				

Allergies/sensitivities   ☐ None

Latest risk assessment   ☐ No risk factors noted at present

☐ At risk
1. _____   4. _____
☐ High risk
2. _____   5. _____
3. _____   6. _____

Prenatal education

☐ No ☐ Yes Attended classes _____ times/received instruction
☐ No ☐ Yes Received prenatal care
☐ No ☐ Yes Records available on admission
→ Source of prenatal data: _____

Baby's physician _____   Tel no _____

Admission Physical Examination

Ht. (in.)	Wt. (lbs.)	B.P.	Temp.	Pulse	Resp.

System	WNL	Abn.	Findings
HEENT	☐	☐	
Breasts	☐	☐	
Heart and lungs	☐	☐	
Abdomen	☐	☐	
Extremities	☐	☐	
Reflexes	☐	☐	

Fetal evaluation

Fundal height _____
Estimated fetal weight _____
FHR _____
Station _____
Effacement _____
Dilatation _____

Estimated weeks gestation _____

Presentation   **Position**

☐ Vertex
☐ Face/brow
☐ Breech (type) _____
☐ Transverse lie
☐ Compound

Urine	Blood sent	:	☐ AM ☐ PM	Nurse _____
Alb.	Hct	Hgb		
Glu.				Attending _____

Hollister.

When significant disruptions in early parent-child attachment occur, they are associated with increased risk for child maltreatment. This is particularly true when the child is difficult to care for or the parent's normal care-giving ability is impaired. (p. 590)

A simple screening procedure that was developed by the At Risk Parent Child Program, Inc. in Tulsa, Oklahoma can be used by antepartum care providers, postpartum care providers, or pediatric care providers; it can alert professionals to the need for more formal assessment. For example, at Hillcrest Medical Center in Tulsa, Oklahoma, the Kardex on the postpartum unit and in the nursery contains criteria to signal to the staff any potential problems. If a parent or child is found to meet one or more of the criteria listed in Table 4-1, intervention is initiated (Ayoub & Jacewitz, in press).

Developmental Tasks of Pregnancy

Pregnancy itself is a crisis involving physiological and psychological stress for all families. All expectant parents must accomplish certain developmental tasks in order to adjust to the physical and emotional changes of preg-

---

Table 4-1 Clinical Criteria Used in Making Assessment of a Family's Risk Status

Biological Alerts

1. premature infants
2. infants with congenital defects
3. infants with poorly established feeding or sleeping patterns, commonly called "difficult infants"
4. infants with complicating medical problems including feeding and developmental difficulties
5. mothers with a physical illness, particularly when occurring in vulnerable periods including pregnancy, childbirth, and postpartum period
6. recent history of serious illness or death in siblings or significant others
7. physical characteristics of child which do not meet parents' expectations: sex, physical features, etc.

Psychological Alerts

1. parental history of unhappy, physically and/or emotionally deprived childhood
2. parental emotional/social isolation
3. history of past emotional difficulties—depression, withdrawal, hostility, suspicion, confusion
4. moderate to severe intellectual limitations
5. parental addiction to drugs or alcohol

Social Alerts

1. poor living conditions
2. financial difficulties
3. unemployment
4. mobility
5. lack of transportation
6. history of violent and/or illegal activities
7. medical conditions resulting from lack of medical or nutritional care

Interactional Alerts

1. marital difficulties—discord or lack of support
2. family difficulties—discord or lack of support
3. parental-infant attachment difficulties

Source: Reprinted with permission from *Child Abuse and Neglect: The International Journal,* by C. Ayoub and M. Jacewitz. Families at Risk for Poor Parenting: A Model for Service Delivery, Assessment, and Intervention, in press, Pergamon Press, Ltd.

nancy. The following describes these developmental tasks:

1. In the first trimester (incorporation), a woman must accept the pregnancy and incorporate it as a part of her.
2. In the second trimester (differentiation), she must recognize the fetus as an individual, thus differentiating it from herself.
3. In the third trimester (separation), in preparation for birth, a woman must be able to let the fetus go . . . separating it from herself.

Expectant fathers often have similar developmental tasks, having first to accept and then to separate from the fetus in order to parent (Colman & Colman, 1971).

High-risk pregnant women and their families have special tasks to accomplish in addition to the developmental tasks necessary for all expectant families. These are tasks related to illness and tasks related to the combination of pregnancy and illness. Persons who are ill must adapt to the sick role, accept an uncertain outcome, and adapt to chronic illness. Tasks of women who are both ill and pregnant include

1. adaptation to long-term hospitalization and family separation;
2. frequent visits to physician's office or clinic;
3. undergoing special tests and procedures;
4. integration of ''I'm sick'' with ''I'm pregnant;'' and
5. fear of potential surgery (Johnson, 1979).

Psychological Effects of High-Risk Pregnancy

Stresses that occur normally in pregnancy are amplified in the high-risk pregnancy. Jones identified the psychological effects of high-risk pregnancy as denial, blame and guilt, feelings of failure, and ambivalence (cited in Johnson, 1979). In addition, high-risk families may focus on the uncertain outcome of pregnancy and thus experience great anxiety and fear. Antepartum

hospitalization for the management of medical problems may create further anxiety for the high-risk pregnant woman and her family. As a consequence, high-risk expectant mothers often withdraw from their usual role and increase their dependent behavior.

As outlined in *Standards of Obstetric, Gynecologic, and Neonatal Nursing* (Nurses Association of the American College of Obstetricians and Gynecologists, 1981),

Every effort must be made to allay the patient's fears without instilling false hope.

In collaboration with the physician, the nurse should:

1. explain the existing condition and the expected results of treatment;
2. explain individualization of care, so it will be understood that no single pattern of treatment fits all patients;
3. encourage dialogue that will allow the patient and her family to express their feelings and to ask questions; and
4. encourage communication among the patient, her family, and the health care team.

Books, pamphlets, films, or group class sessions may be used to increase the patient's knowledge of pregnancy, antenatal care, and her specific illness, and may help reduce fears she may be experiencing. Since the fetus may already be compromised, the patient should understand the possibility of further adverse effects due to inadequate diet and poor nutrition, smoking, alcohol abuse, the use of other drugs, and/or emotional hazards. If the illness extends beyond the hospital stay, it is especially important that both the patient and her family be instructed in health care, and be referred to the appropriate community resource(s) for follow-up after discharge. (p. 18)

The stress of hospitalization and feelings of dependency can be reduced by giving the woman and her family opportunities to control their environment. For example, Prentice Women's Hospital in Chicago offers an antepartum hospitalization program in which mothers are encouraged to wear their street clothes instead of hospital gowns. They are issued passes to go home for visits whenever possible, and family members are included in planning care. Visits to the neonatal intensive care units and anticipatory counseling are important parts of the Prentice program.

Children in high-risk families may develop a variety of problems. They may have difficulty sleeping or coping with separation from their mother if she is hospitalized for an extended period of time. Parents, feeling anxious about their children at home, may become overprotective and overindulgent. If the mother returns from the hospital without the baby, the children at home may fear that they have harmed their sibling by their thoughts. If the parents are having difficulty coping with the high-risk baby, their overattentiveness to their sick baby may limit the time and energy available for the other children (Johnson, 1979).

FAMILY-CENTERED NEONATAL INTENSIVE CARE

In caring for the family of a high-risk baby, the goal should be to send a well baby home as a family member, not as a stranger. Parents of a high-risk baby may lose their child through death or relinquishment (adopting out the baby), or they may be presented with a premature or defective child, thus losing the perfect child of their dreams. In the immediate newborn period, the holding, touching, and eye-to-eye contact important in establishing parent-infant attachment often have to be delayed so that immediate life support measures can be initiated. Prolonged separation from the infant not only may threaten the attachment process, but also may increase the potential for future problems, such as failure to thrive and neglect (Klaus & Kennell, 1982).

Whenever a baby is in an intensive care unit, the other family members also need special nurs-

ing care. The parents, siblings, and grandparents should be encouraged to visit their baby in the nursery and to participate in the care. Since the parents are responsible for providing lifelong physical and emotional care, they and their infant must be treated as a unit from the very beginning.

Infection

In the past, the threat of infection has excluded parents and other family members from hospital nurseries. Studies indicate, however, that there is no increased risk or occurrence of infection when mothers are present in the nursery (Klaus & Kennell, 1982). It has also been found that family members in newborn nurseries wash more thoroughly and more often than do hospital staff (Klaus & Kennell, 1982).

The fact that family contact with newborns does not increase the risk of infection is supported by the American Academy of Pediatrics (AAP), which stated that "visiting and physical contact with sick infants does not increase the risk of infection when parents follow the same hand washing and gowning procedures as nursery personnel" (1977, p. 6). The AAP also recommends that siblings be allowed to visit sick infants in the neonatal intensive care area.

Parental Responses

Early contact and frequent visits by the parents can accelerate their acceptance of the infant-at-risk (Klaus & Kennell, 1982). Some parents may want to touch or hold the baby on the first visit to the nursery, while others may be reluctant to do so. Many parents find it difficult to absorb any information during this emotionally charged first visit.

When the baby is born prematurely, the family has not had sufficient time to complete the developmental tasks of the third trimester. Frequently, these parents blame themselves for the premature birth and question what they did "wrong." They may feel inadequate, depressed, and angry. Brazelton (1982) identified three defenses that parents often use in dealing with the stress of a premature birth: (1) denial in order to defend themselves against disintegration, or "going to pieces;" (2) projection in order to displace their own feelings of inadequacy onto the medical personnel; and (3) detachment. When the outcome for the baby is very uncertain, parents may protect and prepare themselves for the possible death of the baby by withdrawing from contact with the baby.

The nurse needs to recognize and accept a wide range of feelings from the family while remaining realistic and not giving false assurances. The family members should be encouraged to express feelings, concerns, and expectations as they begin to adapt to the new situation.

Because the flashing lights and buzzers on the monitors and all of the equipment attached to the baby can be very frightening, family members need to be prepared before they visit the intensive care nursery for the first time. Visual aids, such as photographs of babies in the intensive care nursery with photographs and descriptions of equipment, are very helpful in preparing the family for what they will see.

Family members can be helped to see their baby as a unique individual if they are encouraged to touch and interact with the infant. The nurse can point out the baby's specific responses. If siblings are unable to visit, having them send baby clothes and toys for their baby and taking photographs to share with them can facilitate the attachment process. The baby's first name should be used by all personnel who talk with the parents. The earlier the baby is given identity, the sooner the family thinks of their infant as a person. Grant (1978) outlined tasks and parental responses that signal unhealthy or healthy outcomes in families of high-risk infants (Figure 4-1).

As the baby improves, the family should be encouraged to take an active role in care. Hospital staff's explanations must be in terms that the parents can understand. A family-staff interaction guide can be used to record visits by family members and to designate by a coding system exactly which person visits (Exhibit 4-4). It is an objective tool, providing a continuous record of parent-infant and parent-staff interactions. Such a tool can facilitate communication among professionals in various disciplines and can provide data for discharge planning.

Personalizing Care

At Brookwood Medical Center in Birmingham, Alabama, Polaroid pictures of the baby are taken daily and placed in the baby's "Special Diary." Nurses make daily notations to the baby's family from the baby, for example, "I ate well today. 3 P.M.: I drank 1½ oz. of my mother's milk and burped three times."

To personalize care further, the infant's name and daily weight progress can be displayed in a prominent place. Infants can be dressed in doll clothes or clothes made by the family. Special attention can be given to monthly birthdays and holidays.

Parent Support Groups

There are monthly meetings of a parent support group composed of families currently requiring high-risk newborn care at Brookwood Medical Center. Also, parents who previously had babies in the neonatal intensive care unit make weekly visits to current neonatal intensive care unit parents. These nonprofessional people offer a form of help not usually given by the professional staff. Their role is completely nonmedical; they are there to give support and hope, and to listen. Working with the parent support group(s) are a maternal child health (MCH) liaison nurse, a chaplain, and the neonatal social worker.

Members of the group assist parents directly by visiting them in the unit nightly, writing letters with pictures enclosed, visiting mothers in the local hospitals, and holding weekly peer group meetings. Support groups also assist in public relations by providing educational services, producing visual materials, making speeches, and giving television interviews about infants in the neonatal intensive care units and their families. Support groups also assist in the growth and development of hospital staff through in-service presentations and monthly meetings.

Figure 4-1 Parental Response during Crisis Period

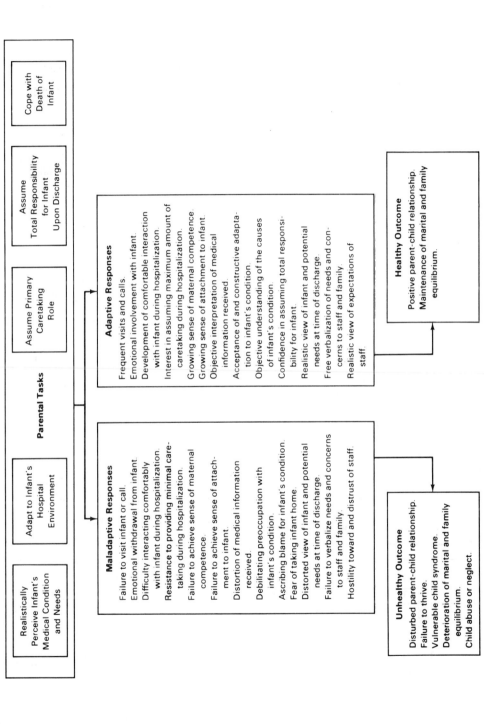

Source: Reprinted from "Psychosocial Needs of Families of High-Risk Infants," by P. Grant, *Family & Community Health*, 1978, *1*(3), 93, by permission of Aspen Systems Corporation, © 1978.

Exhibit 4-4 Family-Staff Interaction Guide

FAMILY–STAFF INTERACTION GUIDE

SPECIAL CARE NURSERY

MARTIN LUTHER KING, JR. GENERAL HOSPITAL
County of Los Angeles • Department of Health Services

DATE	CALLED	VIEWED	TOUCHED	HELD	BOTTLE FED	BREAST FED	DIAPERED	WRAPPED	BATHED		INIT.

RECORD ALL PARENT VISITS. USE CODES & INITIALS

Ⓜ – MOTHER Ⓕ – FATHER Ⓟ – PARENT

Ⓞ – OTHER (GIVE NAME) –

ADMISSION DATE	BIRTH WEIGHT

INFORMATION DISCUSSED	NURSE	M.D.	LIAISON NURSE	CHW MSW
VISITING & PHONING				
ENCOURAGED TO VISIT AFTER DISCHARGE				
SCRUBBING TECHNIQUE				
FACTORS PREDISPOSING TO PREMATURITY				
MEDICAL PROBLEMS				
EXPLANATION OF & NEED FOR				
INCUBATOR				
MONITOR				
IV EQUIPMENT				
OXYGEN EQUIPMENT				
RESPIRATOR				
BILI LITES				
DISCHARGE TEACHING				
BATH DEMONSTRATION				
CORD CARE				
CIRC CARE				
FORMULA PREPARATION				
SIBLING RIVALRY				
INFANT CARE, ROUTINE WHEN TO BATHE, FEED, ETC.				
ACTIVITIES OF THE MOTHER				
ENCOURAGED TO TREAT AS NORMAL INFANT				
DISCHARGED MEDICATION				
FOLLOW-UP APPOINTMENTS				
OTHER TEACHING				

PATIENT IDENTIFICATION

NAME

MLK NO.

MLK-763 (6-73)

Source: Reprinted with permission from *Pediatrics*, 1975, *55*(2), 288. Copyright American Academy of Pediatrics, 1975.

Nesting, Parenting, or Bonding Rooms

Hospitals today often provide parenting space, frequently at no cost, for high-risk families. For example, Brookwood Medical Center provides a "parenting" room, where parents of high-risk babies may stay with their child in the hospital.

> Since parents of high-risk babies have not had complete responsibility for the baby since he was born, they may want to learn to care directly for the child before leaving the hospital. To provide a sort of "halfway house" between the hospital and home, Brookwood offers a "parenting room." The parenting room is a private room in which the newborn, well enough to leave the NICU, rooms in for 24 or 48 hours with his mother and father (or somebody else directly involved in the child's care). There, the new parents care completely for the child, feeding, changing and tending him. The nursing staff is available to demonstrate any care techniques and answer any questions for the parents, so that they can feel secure in their ability to care for the child when they leave the hospital. (Brookwood Medical Center, *Nursery: Family Centered Maternity Care.*)

At Worcester Hahnemann Hospital in Worcester, Massachusetts, there is a "bonding room" next to the intermediate nursery. The room allows undisturbed times for family interaction and breastfeeding by mothers who have been discharged from the maternity unit but whose newborns must remain hospitalized. It is next to the nursery, and the door to the nursery has a window in it so that families can observe nursery care and be observed by nursery staff. Families using this room provide for their own personal needs. Use of this rooming-in arrangement helps parents learn care-giving skills, encourages breastfeeding, and facilitates family-infant interaction.

Discharge Planning and Follow-up

Continuity of care is particularly important for high-risk families. The admitting nurse becomes the primary nurse and cares for the infant while the infant's condition is critical and requires intensive care. This arrangement helps to provide stability in crisis situations, because there are fewer care-givers to whom parents must relate.

Careful record keeping is important to facilitate continuity of care between the hospital and community services. A discharge planning tool that shows optimal parental behaviors prior to discharge may be attached to the chart, clipboard, or Kardex utilized by nursing staff while the baby is in the nursery (Exhibit 4-5). Daily comments are made in pencil so that change can be recorded. When the baby is ready for discharge, all comments and suggestions are finalized in ink. Although this tool becomes a permanent part of the child's medical record, a copy is also sent to the person or agency that will follow the child and family. In addition, a maternal and newborn community nursing referral may be completed by the person initiating referral (Exhibit 4-6). A family assessment form may be completed by the community nursing agency and returned to the referral hospital (Exhibit 4-7).

Sample Protocol for Family-Centered Neonatal Intensive Care

Those providing family-centered neonatal intensive care should adhere to an established protocol. The following is an example of an appropriate protocol:

    I. The Neonatal Intensive Care Unit (NICU) provides extraordinary nursing and medical care on a concentrated and continuous basis for acutely ill infants who require intensive care, life support measures, and skilled observations.

    II. The care provided in the NICU recognizes the need for family

Exhibit 4-5 Discharge Planning Tool

Patient _____ Birthdate _____ Discharge date _____
Parents' names _____ Phone # _____
Primary nurse _____ Discharging nurse _____
Follow-up after discharge _____ Appointment date _____
PKU _____ Hct. _____ Head circ. _____ Ht. _____ Wt. _____ Eye exam. _____

Discharge Criteria	No	Yes	Comments
1. Parent knows phone numbers of SCN, Totline, and for source of follow-up			
2. Parent demonstrates bathing baby			
3. Parent demonstrates cord care			
4. Parent demonstrates care of circumcision			
5. Parent demonstrates diapering of baby			
6. Parent is able to take infant's rectal temperature, and accurately read thermometer			
7. Parent discusses action and side effects of prescribed medication			
8. Parent administers medication to baby and verbalizes medication schedule			
9. Parent satisfactorily completes any special treatment or procedure to be done upon discharge			
10. Parent has decided whether to breast or bottle feed			
11. Parent discusses frequency and amount of feeding			
12. Parent demonstrates feeding baby			
13. The mother who is breastfeeding discusses breast care, milk expression, diet, and identifies a source of support after discharge			
14. Parent discusses formula preparation/sterilization if bottle feeding			
15. Parent discusses conditions of home, and defines a plan for integrating the baby into the family			
16. Parent verbalizes expectations for infant's development, and plans for appropriate stimulation			
17. Parent discusses when baby may be taken out of the house			
18. Parent demonstrates appropriate bonding behaviors			
19. Parent verbalizes time and place for follow-up care (Name of clinic or pediatrician)			
20. Visiting Nurse has spoken with parent(s)			
21. Social work referral has been made (if indicated)			

SUMMARY AND FOLLOW-UP PLANS:

Source: Reprinted with permission of Lippincott/Harper & Row from ''A Discharge Planning Tool for Use with Families of High-Risk Infants,'' by J. Cagan and P. Meier, *Journal of Obstetric, Gynecologic, and Neonatal Nursing,* 1979, 8(3), 147.

Exhibit 4-6 Sample Maternal and Newborn Nursing Referral

BASIC FAMILY DATA
Mother's Name: _____
Address: _____
_____
Apt. No. _____ Floor _____
Telephone _____
Language spoken _____
Mother's Age _____
Marital Status: M___ S___ W___ D___ Sep___
Hospital Record No. _____
Insurance: Medicaid _____
      Blue Cross/Shield _____
      Other _____
Date of Admission _____

Date of referral _____
Referral hospital _____
Referred by: _____
Telephone: _____
Physician's Signature _____
Reason for referral _____

Visit to be made: _____ Prior to discharge of infant
             _____ After infant discharge

Policy Expiration Date _____
Policy No. _____

Date of Discharge _____

MOTHER'S MEDICAL HISTORY
Summary of Past History _____
_____

Obstetrical History: Gravida _____ Para _____ Ab _____ Stillborn _____ Multiple Births _____
   Complications: _____
_____

Present Pregnancy: EDC _____ Date of Delivery _____ Est. Gestational Age _____
   If At-Risk Pregnancy, please list indicators below:
     1. _____   3. _____
     2. _____   4. _____
Labor and delivery: Type of Delivery: 1. _____ Vaginal _____ Vertex _____ Episiotomy
                                _____ Breech _____ Forceps
                                _____ Natural
                  2. _____ C/S—Reason _____
   Type of Anesthesia: _____ Local _____ Spinal _____ Epidural _____ General
            _____ Other: _____
   Intrapartum Complications (Please indicate both maternal and neonatal): _____
_____
_____

Postpartum Complications: Active   Resolved
     1. _____ _____ _____
     2. _____ _____ _____
     3. _____ _____ _____
Follow-up Care: 6 week postpartum check-up to be done by _____
           Other agency referrals: _____
_____

Infant Status: _____ Discharge with mother _____ To remain in hospital _____ Transferred to another hospital

SPECIAL NEEDS AT TIME OF DISCHARGE (physical, social, emotional): _____
_____
_____
_____
_____

Exhibit 4-6 continued

INFANT DATA

Infant Name _____   Date of Birth _____

Hospital Record No. _____   Gestational Age _____

Place of Birth: _____ In hospital   Birth Weight _____

_____ At home   Discharge weight _____

_____ En Route   Sex _____ M _____ F

_____ Other hospital   Apgar Score(s) _____

If transferred, reason and age at time of transfer: _____
_____
_____

Newborn Care Provided in: _____ Normal Nursery   _____ Neonatal Intensive Care Unit

Summary of problems and treatments during hospitalization (Please include birth defects, medical problems, and summary of treatment, etc.)

Problems	Treatment
1. _____	1. _____
2. _____	2. _____
3. _____	3. _____
4. _____	4. _____

Discharge Plans: _____ Home   _____ Another hospital (name) _____

Date of discharge _____

Follow-up scheduled with _____ Private Physician _____

_____ Clinic _____

Feeding Status: _____ Bottle   Formula _____

_____ Breast

Special Instructions _____

SPECIAL NEEDS AT TIME OF DISCHARGE (please include physical, social, emotional & parental needs):
_____
_____
_____
_____
_____

Authorization

I hereby authorize the release of whatever information is necessary to assure continuity of care.

_____
Signature of Parent

Source: Reprinted with permission of Massachusetts Department of Public Health, Maternal Child Services. Provided by Karen Murphy, R.N., M.S., Clinical Specialist, NICU.

Exhibit 4-7 Family Assessment Form

Please return to Referral Hospital: Date of Home Visit _____

Mother's name _____   Person making visit _____

Address _____   Agency _____

Home or contact phone _____   Telephone No. _____

Did mother expect a community nursing visit?   Infant: _____ At home

      _____Yes _____No   _____ In hospital

1. Assessment of Home Environment: _____

      _____

      _____

2. Assessment of Socio-economic Status: _____

      _____

3. Please indicate current status of:

Infant	*Mother*
A. Diets: Formula _____	Eating pattern: _____
# of feedings _____	_____
B. Sleep patterns: _____	Postpartum course: _____
_____	_____
C. Elimination: _____	Elimination: _____
_____	Lochia: _____
D. Activities of daily living: _____	Activities of daily living: _____
_____	_____
E. Medications (include vits.) _____	Medications (include vits.) _____
_____	_____

4. Integration of infant into family (include mother, father, sibling interaction): _____

      _____

      _____

5. Is there anything about the infant's behavior which concerns the mother/father? _____

      _____

      _____

6. Describe the infant's activity at the time of your visit: _____

      _____

7. Physical assessment of infant: Pulse _____ Heart rate _____ Skin turgor _____

      Umbilical cord _____ Comments: _____

      _____

8. Has follow-up appointment been kept for infant care?

      _____ Yes   Where _____   When _____

      _____ No   When is appt. _____   Where _____

9. Overall assessment and summary of family _____

      _____

      _____

10. Follow-up plan: Special needs: _____

                         _____

              Visit plans: _____

                         _____

              Referrals: _____

                         _____

Source: Reprinted with permission of Massachusetts Department of Public Health, Maternal Child Services. Provided by Karen Murphy, R.N., M.S., Clinical Specialist, NICU.

support, the importance of opportunities for parent-infant bonding, and the effects of illness on parenting and family life.

III. State guidelines are adhered to, including the following:

A. The NICU is designed to include a nurses' station, medication room, physician work area, and supply areas immediately adjacent to the unit. There is provision for isolation of infants as necessary.

B. The activities of the NICU are directed by a multidisciplinary committee composed of pediatricians, obstetricians, nurses, and respiratory therapists.

C. Nursing care is provided by registered nurses who are responsible to the Head Nurse, who is in turn responsible to the Director of Nursing. The nursing staffing pattern, which is determined by acuity of illness, provides a range of 1:1 to 1:3 nurse-baby ratio.

D. Medical care is provided by the attending physician and/or consultant.

IV. Nursing Staff

A. Nursing personnel are selected to work in this unit according to the following criteria:

1. Nurses must be registered professional nurses who have had experience in infant care.

2. Nurses must demonstrate that they are capable of coping with stress and meeting the needs of patients with numerous and/or complex care problems.

B. Programs of orientation and preparation are provided for staff.

1. All registered nurse personnel attend a hospital orientation program and a special NICU orientation program.

2. All registered nurses are given additional instruction in the care of acutely ill infants, which includes management of electronic monitoring and respiratory care.

3. All registered nurses are provided education in teaching parents how to care for infants at home.

4. Support nurses, who generally work on other units, are trained to work with Level I and II babies, are given a special orientation to NICU, and work in NICU a minimum of 1 day per month.

5. Selected opportunities for continuing development in neonatal nursing are provided for experienced nursing staff through (a) staff development; (b) conferences, workshops, and seminars; (c) clinical experiences in selected Level III centers.

6. Selected nurses attend an advanced course in transport of the neonate after 1 to 2 years experience.

C. Staff members are responsible for their own continued development in the NICU. Opportunities are provided for them to attend continued educational programs outside the hospital, as well as in-service programs.

1. Staff are encouraged to participate in continuing educational programs, workshops, and seminars.
2. Problem solving and learning experiences are obtained through contact with clinical nurse specialists, nursing care conferences, and other resources (e.g., respiratory therapists and physicians).
3. Special learning modules on care of infants are used.
4. Current literature, reprints, and journals are reviewed.

D. Staff may play expanded roles.
1. Registered nurses and respiratory therapists are specially prepared to provide intensive care for high-risk neonates during transport.
2. Registered nurses who demonstrate clinical expertise are utilized to assist with orientation and development of staff, as well as with special projects.

Components of Family-Centered High-Risk Care/Neonatal Intensive Care

In order to provide family-centered care to high-risk families and family-centered neonatal intensive care, the staff should

- provide continuity in care-givers so that change in risk status as pregnancy progresses can be quickly identified
- acknowledge and accept the family's feelings and fears for less than optimum pregnancy outcome
- assist family to adjust their pregnancy expectations to reality by promoting anticipatory grief
- facilitate parents' sense of self-control and confidence in their parental role by including them in decision making

- help mother develop her mothering role when hospitalized prenatally:
  1. encourage ambulation instead of bed rest whenever possible
  2. give her control over daily activities, schedule, and own personal care
  3. assess her learning needs and teach about impending labor, birth, and neonatal intensive care
- encourage parents to verbalize feelings of guilt or personal failure or doubt about femininity, masculinity, mothering abilities, and fathering abilities
- provide opportunity for family to visit the neonatal intensive care unit and all premature and sick babies and meet with the high-risk nursery medical and nursing staff prior to birth of baby
- after birth, encourage discussion of labor and birth experience (an important psychological and developmental need)
- if newborn is well, help parents readjust from the risk state
- if infant is sent to another hospital:
  1. before leaving the referral hospital, bring the baby for parents to view and touch
  2. take photograph of baby with a Polaroid camera and leave photograph with parents
  3. if possible, have father accompany the infant in the transfer vehicle
  4. encourage frequent telephone calls to and from the neonatal intensive care unit
  5. transfer mother to the same hospital whenever possible
- encourage parents and siblings to visit and call in order to increase contact
- to promote bonding and prevent feelings of helplessness, have parents and siblings hold, fondle, and feed the infant as the infant's condition allows
- to promote continuity of care, assign one primary care nurse to each family when possible
- refer family to a community health nurse soon after infant's admission so that contin-

uous support is provided for the family through hospitalization and discharge

- be thorough, honest and appropriately optimistic in explaining baby's condition
- help family to understand diagnosis and developmental risks for the infant
- encourage nursing mothers to pump their breasts to provide breast milk for the infant
- begin positive infant stimulation programs, such as gently stroking, massaging, and/or singing to the infant
- encourage parents to assume increasing responsibility for care of their infant
- assess parental readiness and teach specific care-giving functions
- include parents in stimulation programs
- reassure parents about their ability to care for their baby
- perform ongoing assessment of the family and their coping abilities
- reinforce parents' capability in caring for their infant
- encourage family to verbalize fears and anxieties
- include family in planning infant's care
- hold interdisciplinary meetings—attended by parents, nurses, staff neonatalogists, social workers, physical therapists, respiratory therapists, and home care coordinators—at regular intervals
- utilize techniques to personalize the infant in the eyes of the family:

1. display infant's name on the crib
2. dress the infant in doll clothes or specially made garments
3. place stuffed animals and toys in the crib
4. place mobiles on the crib
5. celebrate monthly birthdays
6. decorate the neonatal intensive care unit appropriately for major holidays
7. keep infant scrapbook containing notes to parents and photographs of infant, family, and hospital staff
8. maintain infant diaries about daily activities, infant weight, feedings, and care

- develop parent-parent support (groups and one-to-one)
- encourage parents to view their newborns as infants and not as patients, especially when they are nearing discharge
- provide for rooming-in, overnight stays, and care-by-parents programs prior to anticipated discharge
- include counseling and parent teaching in discharge planning
- provide regular comprehensive home follow-up of high-risk infants by means of public health nurse, social worker, developmental clinics
- identify appropriate community resources to family, such as infant stimulation programs, developmental day-care centers, parent support groups, sources of financial aid, and clinics for professional and neurological evaluations
- if infant is dying, provide a private room where family can hold infant
- encourage family of a dying infant to visit the neonatal intensive care unit often
- discuss dying infant with family often
- help family of dying infant to express feelings, concerns, and expectations
- establish follow-up support groups for families experiencing infant death

ADOLESCENT PREGNANCY

A large segment of the childbearing population does not fit into the comfortable model of husband/father and wife/mother. While the birth rate for married persons has consistently dropped in the United States over the last 10 years, the birth rate for unmarried adolescents has almost doubled. According to Shearin and Burnett (1976),

Adolescent pregnancy in the United States is a major health problem. Each year over one million adolescents under the age of 20 become pregnant; of these, approximately 500,000 are unmarried. If pregnancy occurs before growth has ceased, the biologic risk of mortality and morbidity is greater. (p. 78)

Thus, fetal and neonatal mortality are more frequent in adolescent pregnancies. This is also a high-risk population for medical and/or social complications because of such factors as late prenatal care, inadequate nutrition, and inconsistent compliance with instructions about health care.

Adolescence is a time of turmoil in which the individual must accomplish many developmental tasks. Perhaps the most difficult of these tasks is the development of a personal identity. This can be very hard for a pregnant teen-ager who must recognize the growing fetus as a person also. Pregnancy during adolescence is frequently an unwanted occurrence and, therefore, a crisis. The main key to reducing complications in adolescent pregnancy is the quality and quantity of prenatal care.

Prenatal Care for Adolescents

Major areas that need careful consideration during the teen-age pregnancy are summarized in Exhibit 4-8. For optimum care of pregnant teen-agers, a health care team approach is useful. Team members may include midwives, nurses, physicians, social workers, psychologists, health educators, and nutritionists; all should have training and experience in the care of teen-agers (Shearin & Burnett, 1976). Early recognition and close supervision of high-risk teen-age pregnancies are essential. Prenatal care team members should establish close communication with a perinatal high-risk center and a special care nursery.

At the Childbearing Childrearing Center, an outreach clinic of the University of Minnesota Hospitals, 115 teen-aged girls were surveyed to determine their preferences in a prenatal care clinic (Zimmerman, 1980). Eleven possible components of prenatal care were listed, and teen-agers were asked to identify the relative value of each component to them. Results indicated that teen-agers have clear preferences regarding their prenatal care. The most impor-

tant was for an ongoing, supportive relationship with their care-giver. Almost as important was education in childbirth preparation, baby care, and the maintenance of good health. The social support of a friend or support group at clinic visits was important, but not as important as consistency of care-giver and the availability of education.

The teen-aged respondents also wanted resource people such as nutritionists and other "experts" on pregnancy and childrearing. These adolescents seemed frightened by the prospect of self-care and felt that their care was best left to the experts. However, their comments showed that they were interested in learning the what and why of their care. It was interesting that most of the respondents wanted a comfortable but "professional" atmosphere in the clinic. They were not looking for a "hip" atmosphere and rock music.

An example of an adolescent pregnancy program that is responsive to these identified needs can be found in Cooper Medical Center's program in Camden, New Jersey. In this program, the team approach is utilized to care for approximately 210 pregnant teen-agers (ages 13 to 18) each year. Services include comprehensive medical care, nursing care, nutritional and social service evaluations, and health education throughout the pregnancy and 1st postpartum year. The teen-agers are helped to explore all options available to them during the pregnancy and following the birth. Referrals are made to vocational training and counseling services, a variety of educational programs, and to day-care centers.

Four registered nurses who work exclusively within the adolescent pregnancy program provide primary nursing care. Consistency in care-givers is arranged by assigning each teen-ager at registration to one of these nurses for prenatal care and follow-up for 1 year postnatally. These nurses are also responsible for the patient education program. At each prenatal clinic visit, a class is offered in one of the following areas:

1. Emotional and Physiological Changes of Pregnancy and Related Comfort Measures
2. Fetal Growth and Development

Exhibit 4-8 Checklist for Adolescent Pregnancy

I. *Determinations: Initial visit*
    Complete blood count
    Complete urinalysis
    Blood type and group
    VDRL
    Culture for gonococcus
    Pap smear
    Chest x-ray
    Sickle cell test
    Nutritional status
    Rubella titer

II. *Discussion points with each visit*   *Suggested schedule*
    1. Anatomy and physiology of pregnancy   1st visit
    2. Sexual activity and venereal disease   2nd visit
    3. Drug-related problems   3rd visit
    4. Nutrition   Each visit
    5. Family planning   4th visit
    6. Childbirth phenomena   5th visit
    7. Infant care   6th visit
    8. Contraception   7th visit
    9. Sexuality and the future   8th visit
    10. Importance of follow-up care   9th visit

III. *Visitation*
    1. Biweekly until 34 weeks
    2. Weekly until delivery

IV. *Educational aspects: Progress report of teacher*
    In school _____
    Homebound _____
    Other _____

V. *Social aspects: Progress report*
    1. Parent/patient
    2. Patient/father of the child
    3. Postdelivery: progress report

VI. *Psychologic aspects*

VII. *Nutritional aspects: Progress report*

VIII. *Nursing report*

IX. *Report of neonatologist or physician who will be present*

X. *Additional problem areas*

Source: Reprinted with permission from "A Checklist for Adolescent Pregnancy," by B. Shearin and A. Burnett. *American Family Physician,* 1976, *14*(1), 79.

3. Labor and Birth
4. The Immediate Postpartum Period and Introduction to Available Social Services in the Community

Pregnant teen-agers are enrolled in those classes appropriate for their stage of gestation. In addition, a 6-week childbirth preparation series, cesarean birth classes, and breastfeeding classes are available. A class offered in the postpartum clinic deals with parenting. The nutritionist holds sessions on nutrition during pregnancy and the 1st year of life, as well as on food preparation and food economy.

Cooper Medical Center's adolescent pregnancy program offers teen-agers consistency and personal involvement in care in the postpartum aspect of the program. According to Susan W. Wallner, Administrative Director (1982),

> The role of the primary nurse goes beyond the clinic setting. In order to assist with the maternal adaptation to parenthood, the primary nurse visits the patient in her home. The first postpartum home visit is scheduled 10 to 14 days postpartum, and subsequent visits are made at 3, 6, and 12 months postpartum. Additional visits are made as required. The nurse does whatever teaching is appropriate regarding maternal and infant care and ensures that both mother and infant are receiving appropriate medical services.
>
> Following the 12 month postpartum period, patients are terminated from the program with encouragement to return for regular care for themselves and their children.

Prenatal Education for Adolescents

Classes in prepared childbirth are a valuable and integral part of routine prenatal care for the teen-ager. Many positive outcomes can be realized from prenatal classes for teen-agers:

> In October, 1979, Booth Maternity Center closed its resident program for teens. However, the Salvation Army's long standing commitment remained strong to respond to the special needs and life styles of young boys/men and girls/women. Thus, a unique Thursday afternoon combination of prenatal medical care plus labor, birth, and parenting preparation classes was initiated to respond to the approximately 100 adolescents who annually deliver here.
>
> Information on nutrition, fetal development, labor and delivery, infant care, well baby checkups, parenting skills, and contraception form the basic curriculum. The style is informal, and group discussion is encouraged. Nutritious snacks of juice and fruit are always available.
>
> Encouraging results have emerged from a study done by Dianne Manning, R.N., and Mary Daniels, Ph.D., of the first fifty-two participants of this innovative program. These participants were compared with those of a matched sample who received care here at Booth before the development of the special clinic/classes. Significant differences were found in the participants of the new clinic in higher numbers of prenatal and postpartum visits and lower numbers of neonatal and intrapartum complications. Over half the mothers in this group (54%) were breastfeeding their babies at the time of the postpartum check compared to 28% of the control group. More young girls/women from the clinic group participated in counseling regarding birth control compared to those in the control group.
>
> While the Thursday clinic/class is extremely important, it is only one aspect of the program offered young parents at Booth. Home visits are made postpartum on a regular basis and each month there are groups and workshops on infant and child development and parenting issues along

with an assortment of reunions, drama presentations, and parties (The Salvation Army, 1981).

Because teen-agers are still adjusting to the body changes of adolescence, their concerns are usually focused on changes that are visible, e.g., stretch marks and weight gain. They need to be assured of their normalcy and encouraged to help themselves look better and feel better. Most teen-aged expectant mothers are not interested in the "birth experience," but rather are concerned about what will happen to them in childbirth. They often have overwhelming fears of labor, and it is wise to ask other teen-aged parents to share their own birth experiences (Johnson, 1979).

Many adolescent girls decide to keep their babies. With an adequate support system, some young mothers are quite capable of caring for their child; many others have a very difficult time with mothering, however. The adolescent needs a great deal of help in decision making from a support person who can be depended on for honesty, consistency, and stability. The crisis of adolescent pregnancy can be a time of learning to plan wisely, making difficult decisions, and—ultimately—becoming more mature and assuming increased responsibility.

In the process of providing support and counseling for the adolescent mother, the father is frequently forgotten. It is often wrongly assumed that he is unconcerned about the pregnant adolescent, her safety, or the well-being of his child. If he wants to be involved, the father should be included in planning alternative solutions regarding the future of the child. Many young expectant fathers find it very difficult to believe that they are about to become fathers. Being involved in the prenatal care, pregnancy outcome planning, and even the labor and birth, helps them face the reality of the situation and the associated responsibilities (Phillips, 1980).

CESAREAN BIRTH

Although there is a great deal of variation among hospitals, cesarean births in the United States now account for approximately 20% of all births. Cesarean birth is a major surgical procedure that entails increased maternal and fetal risks. The morbidity associated with cesarean delivery is greater than that associated with vaginal delivery. Infections constitute the greatest portion of this morbidity. The most common infections are endometritis, urinary tract infections, and wound infections (Marieskind, 1980).

Psychological Integration of the Cesarean Birth

For couples who want to share the birth of their baby and have taken classes to prepare for a family-centered birth, an unplanned cesarean birth can be a cruel blow. Furthermore, it may have a negative effect on the mother's self-concept. Many women report troubled feelings about their cesarean births, such as disappointment, frustration, guilt, depression, failure at not having delivered "normally," feelings of being cheated, feelings of intrusion from the surgical procedure, and alteration in body image. Fathers excluded from participation in cesarean births have reported feelings of isolation, inadequacy, failure, and being cheated. They often feel left out and may have difficulty relating to their baby (Lipson & Tilden, 1980).

Family-Centered Cesarean Birth

Care of parents experiencing a cesarean birth should be family-centered rather than surgery-centered. In an effort to focus on the birth and not the operative procedure, the term *cesarean delivery* or *cesarean birth* should become common usage rather than the more familiar, surgically oriented term *cesarean section*. The rationale is that, although the mother is experiencing an abdominal rather than a vaginal birth, she is still giving birth.

It is essential to provide prenatal and postpartum education regarding cesarean birth and to minimize separation of mother, father, and child at the time of cesarean birth. The cesarean delivery is a birth experience and must be incorporated as such when family-centered care is provided. The goal is a positive birth experience brought about by cooperation of the parents, physicians, and hospital personnel.

Consensus Development Task Force

Because of increasing concern about rising cesarean birth rates, the National Institute of Child Health and Human Development of the National Institutes of Health (NIH) formed a task force to study this issue. The task force, composed of representatives from the many disciplines involved in cesarean birth, held a National Institutes of Health Consensus Development Conference at NIH on September 22 to 24, 1980, at which evidence was presented on the following questions:

1. Why and how have cesarean delivery rates changed in the United States and elsewhere, and how have these changes affected pregnancy outcome?
2. What is the evidence that cesarean delivery improves the outcome of various complications of pregnancy?
3. What are the medical and psychological effects of cesarean delivery on the mother, infant, and family?
4. What economic factors are related to the rising cesarean rate?
5. What legal and ethical considerations are involved in decisions on cesarean delivery?

The NIH Consensus Development Statement on Cesarean Childbirth (1980) includes the following recommendations vital to implementing family-centered cesarean birth:

1. Parent education during pregnancy by health care providers and in childbirth education classes should include information relating to the possibility of a cesarean birth, an explanation of the technical procedures surrounding the cesarean birth, and discussion of choices available to parents.
2. During labor and at the time a decision to perform a cesarean is made,

as time and circumstances permit, a discussion of the indications, procedures, and parental options should take place between the physician or his/her staff and the parents.
3. Information exchange about the entire cesarean birth experience should continue in the postoperative period and at later postpartum visits.
4. In the absence of scientific evidence regarding benefit or risk, the presence at a cesarean birth of the father or surrogate should represent a joint decision among parents, physicians, and hospital representatives.
5. Hospitals are encouraged to liberalize their policies concerning the option of having the father or surrogate attend the cesarean birth.
6. The healthy neonate should not be separated routinely from mother and father following delivery.
7. There is a need for longitudinal developmental followup studies of infants and their parents. These studies should include study populations of sufficient size for meaningful statistical analysis, suitable control groups, and standardized methods of assessment. (pp. 547-548)

Presence of Father or Support Person at Cesarean Birth

In hospitals where family-centered maternity care has been extended to the cesarean birth family, there is no evidence of harm to mother, father, or baby. Research on fathers' presence during cesarean birth has shown no adverse outcome (Marieskind, 1979). Instead of contraindications to the presence of fathers in the operating suite, there is growing evidence that their presence improves the postcesarean behavioral responses of the families (HHS, 1981).

Hospitals should develop a written policy for the presence of the father or support person at a family-centered cesarean birth. The following is an example:

Policy: The presence of a support person at the cesarean birth will be encouraged. The woman, her physicians, and the support person will give written consent and established hospital guidelines will be followed.

Purpose: To provide the woman an opportunity to have a familiar support person in attendance during all the phases of the birth experience. In particular, the father's presence during birth permits him to give support to the mother while facilitating the parent-infant bonding process.

Procedure:

1. Request is made by the woman directly to the physician.
   a. The form "Guidelines for Family-Centered Cesarean Birth" is signed by the woman, all attending physicians, and support person.
   b. One copy of the form is kept by the physician-obstetrician, one forwarded to the hospital, and one retained by the woman. The hospital copy is then placed on her chart and becomes part of the permanent record.
2. The woman and the support person are encouraged to attend expectant family classes and a hospital tour
   a. Class content is to include indications for a cesarean birth, various types and methods of anesthesia, relaxation and other coping methods, a brief description of the surgical procedure, the emotional aspect of cesareans, a general discussion of the postoperative period, and breastfeeding.
   b. A hospital tour is held weekly. Those families desiring alternative times may make arrangements. The hospital tour includes admission to the hospital, proper attire for surgery, infection control, time of entering and leaving the cesarean birth room, activities at the time of delivery, location of the support person in the cesarean birth room, discussion of support measures and feelings of the woman and support persons, immediate care of baby, contact with baby, and immediate recovery period.
3. The support person in the cesarean birth room must follow certain accepted practices.
   a. All persons in the cesarean birth room must wear appropriate attire.
   b. The support person sits beside the woman at the head of the cesarean birth table to offer support.
   c. All attending physicians, in exercising their responsibility for total care of the woman, have the option of asking the support person to leave the cesarean room should any medical and/or surgical complication involving the mother or infant arise.
4. Nursing personnel assist the support person.
   a. They accompany and aid the support person in entering or leaving the cesarean birth room.

b. They observe the support person for signs of fatigue, pallor, etc.

c. They offer nourishment to the support person when necessary.

d. They provide an opportunity for bonding to begin in the cesarean room.

e. Following cesarean birth, they encourage the support person to hold the baby if the infant's condition permits.

5. Nursing personnel and/or pediatrician invite the support person to accompany them as the newborn is transported to nursery.

Many hospitals also require the support person to sign a release form (Exhibit 4-9).

Cesarean Parent Support Groups

Parents who have experienced cesarean childbirth and who support the family-centered cesarean birth experience for themselves and others have formed support groups that help health professionals and the general public to understand family-centered cesarean birth. In order to support cesarean parents throughout their experience, such groups may offer a program of activities with the following goals:

1. to provide emotional support to parents through personal and telephone contact

2. to provide emotional support and greater understanding of cesarean birth through informal discussion groups

3. to encourage cesarean birth education through support of and referral to cesarean birth classes

4. to provide information to cesarean parents, health professionals, and the general public through a program of speakers and films

Sample Protocol for Family-Centered Cesarean Birth

There should be a written protocol for family-centered cesarean birth. The following is an example:

I. There is an agreement between the obstetrics-gynecology department, the surgical department, the anesthesia department, and the hospital executive committee that a support person attend cesarean birth under specified circumstances.

II. Stated guidelines will be followed.
   A. There shall be written agreement between the obstetrics-gynecology department and the anesthesia department for a support person to be present in the operative suite for cesarean birth.

Exhibit 4-9 Sample Cesarean Birth Release Form

I release _____ Hospital, its employees and agents, as well as all attending physicians from all liability of whatsoever nature, whether for personal injuries or in tort or in contract, in connection with or resulting from my presence at the cesarean birth.

I further state that I am in good health, having no communicable diseases or open wound infection.

Date: _____

Signature of Support Person: _____

Signature of Patient (mother): _____

Signature of Physician: _____

Expected birth date: _____

Telephone Number: Home: _____ Business: _____

B. The support person shall be seated at the side of the anesthesiologist in order to be supportive to the mother without interfering with the duties of the attending physicians, anesthesia personnel, or nursing personnel.

III. The support person will wash hands and change into scrub clothes and appropriate head and foot gear before entering the cesarean birth room.

IV. The support person will be accompanied by a hospital representative to the cesarean room and will join the mother.

V. Prior to the cesarean delivery, a form stating the guidelines for the presence of a support person will be signed by the patient, all attending physicians, and the support person.

VI. Nursing responsibilities will include assistance to the patient and support person.

VII. Cesarean birth preparation will be part of the regular expectant family classes. In addition, a cesarean birth film will be available for viewing, as well as a "mini-course" designed for use when a family has not had the opportunity to prepare for a cesarean birth.

VIII. Recovery will take place, so far as possible, with mother, support person, and baby together in the recovery room.

Components of Family-Centered Cesarean Birth

Health care facilities planning a family-centered cesarean birth program should include the following components:

- Preparation for childbirth classes for all expectant families include cesarean birth content.
- Prepared cesarean birth classes are offered to scheduled cesarean families.
- Hospital tours are provided.
- Support meetings are held for parents who anticipate or have experienced cesarean birth.
- Patients may have the option to enter the hospital on day of surgery rather than the evening prior to the scheduled cesarean.
- Cesarean mothers are admitted to rooms with other cesarean mothers or to a private room.
- Hospital rooms for cesarean mothers have electrically operated beds and are close to bathrooms.
- Siblings may visit.
- Cesareans are performed in labor and delivery area rather than in general surgery.
- Regional anesthesia is used instead of general anesthesia whenever possible.
- Minimal abdominal shave and small volume enemas are used to prepare patient.
- Anesthesia screen is lowered so parents can view birth.
- One of mother's arms is freed from restraint for touch contact with father and baby.
- Mirror is available for viewing birth.
- Low transverse ("bikini") incision is used whenever possible.
- An advocate on hospital staff (nurse, physician, or anesthesiologist) describes to parents what is happening during the delivery.
- Presence of support person (preferably father) during the birth is encouraged.
- Baby is delivered into mother's or father's arms whenever possible.
- Baby remains in cesarean room following birth unless immediate nursery care is necessary.
- Father holds his baby and shows him to the mother whenever the infant's condition permits.

- If the infant's condition permits, baby is held against mother's shoulder for skin-to-skin contact.
- If father is not present for birth, he is kept informed.
- If compromised, the infant is transported immediately to the neonatal intensive care unit. Family is kept informed of infant's progress, and father-child contact is initiated as soon as possible.
- Mother recovers in labor and delivery recovery area instead of general surgery recovery area.
- Presence of support person (preferably father) in recovery room is encouraged.
- Parents hold baby in the recovery room, and mother breastfeeds if desired.
- Recovery stay is kept to a minimum.
- Staff helps with early rooming-in until mother can assume responsibility for baby.
- Intravenous lines and catheters are removed as soon as possible.
- Mothers who have attended prenatal classes are encouraged to use relaxation and breathing patterns to relieve recovery discomforts.
- Pain medication is administered promptly.
- Cesarean mothers are encouraged to breastfeed; side-lying position is used initially with infant supported on pillows, or football hold is utilized.
- Comfort tips are taught, e.g., raising the bed to a sitting position to get up, log rolling to turn or change positions, splinting the abdomen with the hands or pillow, abdominal tightening.
- Mobility is encouraged early and often.
- Primary cesarean mothers who seem depressed, frustrated, or fatigued are reassured that many new mothers experience a series of negative emotions at one time or another, even those who give birth vaginally.
- Other cesarean parents visit newly delivered cesarean couples.

- Parents are referred to cesarean support groups.
- In preparation for discharge, staff members do the following:
  1. Have women look at incision every day and explain healing process.
  2. Reassure mother that scar will shrink and fade.
  3. Caution mother that increased vaginal flow may mean excessive activity.
  4. Encourage mother to take lots of fluids and nutritious snacks.
  5. Recommend help at home for the 1st week.
  6. Recommend more rest for quicker recovery.
  7. Discuss sexuality with the cesarean couple.
- Include children (siblings) in postcesarean care.

GRIEF

It is vital for health care professionals to understand the grieving process and their own reactions to profound loss. The feelings of powerlessness evoked in the presence of death and overwhelming grief take an emotional toll. People need humanizing responses in order to recuperate and restore their emotional balance.

Premature Birth

Kaplan and Mason (1960) described the birth of a premature infant as an acute emotional crisis. They outlined three normal psychological tasks that the parents must master to establish a healthy relationship with their premature baby. Parents must (1) prepare for the possible death of the baby (anticipatory grief), (2) acknowledge their failure to deliver a full-term infant, and (3) learn the special needs of the premature baby.

The parents of a premature infant must face the fact that their child is less than perfect at the same time that they must accept the reality of the baby's early arrival. The earlier a pregnancy is interrupted, the greater the likelihood of a strong emotional reaction (Oehler, 1981).

Congenital Anomalies

The parents of a baby born with a defect not only lose their anticipated perfect infant, but also are faced with a bereavement that endures indefinitely (Young, 1977). Oehler (1981) identified several tasks that the staff must perform in caring for families of the defective child; staff members must (1) explain tests, (2) allow time for ventilation of feelings and questions, (3) discuss feelings, (4) help parents prepare explanations for friends and relatives, and (5) refer parents to public health and other community resources, as well as to parent support groups.

Death

Dealing with fetal and infant death is not easy either for families or for their health care providers. When a fetus dies in the antepartum period, the mother often makes excuses for her baby's failure to move. When fetal death has been confirmed, she experiences anger and fear. The baby's father may have an even more difficult time understanding the reality of the fetal death because he has not felt the fetus move as the mother has. There is a time lag for paternal acceptance of both the pregnancy and the death.

When fetal death occurs during the intrapartum period, the purpose of the prenatal period is missing. These parents grieve over the loss of someone whom they have never had an opportunity to know.

Response to infant death is similar for parents and professionals: (1) denial, (2) anger, (3) bargaining, (4) depression, and (5) acceptance, with hope throughout. Factors that affect an individual's ability to deal with death include (1) prior experience or education regarding death, (2) the extent to which expectant parents believe that medical equipment is a safeguard against all complications, (3) availability of a support system, and (4) the interpersonal communication skills of the people involved.

Physical symptoms of grief may range from loss of appetite and fatigue to aching arms. Many mothers talk of their arms "hurting" from not being able to hold their baby. Emotional symptoms of grief span a broad spectrum from guilt and depression to an all encompassing sense of futility.

Although there are many variables in a child's concept of death, it is possible to identify some common childhood reactions to the dying process. Death has the least significance to infants under 6 months of age. Although toddlers cannot conceptualize death, separation creates anxiety for them. Between the ages of 2 and 7, children think in concrete concepts; for example, they may believe that lying very still equates with death while moving around again means life. Early school-aged children find it difficult to differentiate between wishes and what really happens ("I wished he would die . . . and he did, so I killed him."). When dealing with families of dying infants, it is important to include siblings, because they also need help to cope with their grief (Peppers & Knapp, 1980).

Support Groups

Throughout the United States there are volunteer groups of parents who have lost an infant and want to help other families in their time of crisis. These volunteers can speak from experience as they provide reassurance and information concerning the emotions involved in the grieving process. They offer individual visits to bereaved parents, monthly group meetings to share experiences and support each other, telephone or in-hospital visits, resource libraries, inservice seminars for professionals, and training programs for their volunteers.

An excellent example of such a support group is SHARE, a self-help group formed at St. John's Hospital in Springfield, Illinois. Since 1977, St. John's Hospital, area physicians, and community members have been actively involved in meeting the needs of parents who have lost a baby as a result of miscarriage, stillbirth, or early infant death. They provide support throughout hospitalization and follow-up care. The following describes the operation of SHARE:

Orienting Your Staff to the SHARE Concept[1]

Educating Staff to SHARE

SHARE is more than a support group. It is a philosophy of caring for parents who experience fetal/neonatal death. The philosophy encompasses the care that is given from the time of admission until the resolution of grief, providing a variety of ways to respond to these parents. Every person coming into contact with these parents needs some preparation so they can respond to whatever situation they might encounter.

If you are planning to start a group and to integrate a philosophy, get core members in tune with the concepts as early as possible. They can gain this insight by reading articles, poetry, magazines (professional, religious, etc.), newspapers, etc. Other helpful sources are books and articles on related topics such as grief, communication, adoption, infertility, funeral and visitation rites, death and dying, adaptation to change, miscarriage, stillbirth and newborn death. These sources can be very beneficial and will increase their interest and involvement.

Before beginning a support group, there must be an in-service for all personnel who may have contact with these parents—nursing personnel, lab and x-ray technicians, dietary, emergency room and operating room staff, etc. No one group can adequately respond to the needs of the parents without the support of other areas.

Our SHARE program does not have a specific in-service program. We have found it more effective to cover many different aspects over a period of time. An initial orientation program,

coupled with yearly or bi-annual refresher sessions, works the best. This acquaints the staff with the general concept and allows for instruction on new ideas, philosophies and areas of concern. Films, books and articles are excellent discussion materials. The following sheets of suggestions are also helpful tools and serve as good checklists. Core members and facilitators will also need to be made aware of any changes in policies or procedures either by an in-service or a staff meeting.

Nursing Philosophy for Caring for Grieving Parents

Caring and Relating to the Patient and Family That Has Lost a Pregnancy

Policy
The staff will assist the parents experiencing a loss of pregnancy due to an incomplete or complete miscarriage according to the philosophy of St. John's Hospital.

Purpose
To provide a supportive atmosphere for the grieving parents; to assist them in resolving their grief.

Special Instructions
Parents shall be given the following options and allowed to have time alone to discuss and decide, unless directed otherwise by the patient's attending physician:

To baptize the baby.
To know the baby's sex.
To be allowed to see, touch and hold the baby.
To name the baby.
To be involved in the funeral arrangements and encouraged to attend the funeral.
To be offered appropriate referral.

[1]Reprinted with permission from "Starting Your Own SHARE Group," St. John's Hospital of the Hospital Sisters of the Third Order of St. Francis, Springfield, Illinois, 1981.

Specific Guidelines

At the time of miscarriage, offer to the parents:

To baptize the baby.

To know the sex of the baby if it can be identified.

To see the baby, if possible. (An explanation should be made of what they can expect the baby to look like.)

To touch and hold the baby, if they would like.

Note: If the parents should ask what will be done with the baby, reply with "What would you like to be done?"

After the miscarriage, obtain a feeling tone of anticipation for the baby.

Pick up disappointment, anger, fear of future miscarriages, feelings of unfairness, etc.

Explain to them society's reaction:

1. That many relatives, friends, etc., may not understand that the loss of the baby is real and that grieving may last beyond a couple of weeks.

2. They may be told that they can have other babies, but this was the baby they wanted.

Try to encourage communication between spouses.

Husbands may have a difficult time expressing their grief.

Introduce the SHARE concept:

That no parent should have to go through this experience alone.

That the reason for SHARE is the comfort and mutual reassurance that parents who have had this experience can offer each other.

Through local SHARE meetings, members can share their experiences, thoughts, and feelings.

Emphasize SHARE is not a therapy group. Instead, it offers parents the opportunity to ventilate their feelings and to obtain support.

Either spouse may come alone or together.

Give them a SHARE card.

They will be on the newsletter mailing list. If they wish to be taken off the list, they are to let us know.

Documentation:

1. Document on discharge sheet the date of "SHARE" visit.

2. Document on communication sheet that SHARE person saw the patient.

3. Document on daily patient management sheet under patient teaching.

The R.N. should fill out an information card and send to Pastoral Care.

Some hospitals have developed forms that are helpful in gathering information from parents who have experienced fetal or neonatal death. Examples of different forms that have been developed are shown in Exhibits 4-10 through 4-13.

Guidelines for Nursing Staff

Below are some ideas which we have found helpful when caring for a grieving mother. We merely intend them as food for your ideas and thoughts.

Things Which Should Be Optional to a Mother in Grief

Staying on the maternity floor or moving to a different floor

Exhibit 4-10 Memorial Medical Center's Checklist for Parents Experiencing a Loss

Memorial Medical Center's Checklist for Parents Experiencing a Loss

Experiencing Newborn Death, A Stillbirth, Neonatal Death, Miscarriage Gestation:		Memorial Medical Center Springfield, Illinois		
DATE	TIME	✓ TO INDICATE COMPLETION		SIGNATURE
		Saw baby when born and/or after delivery: Mother_____ Father_____ Other_____		
		Touched and/or held baby: Mother_____ Father_____ Other_____		
		Given option of being transferred off the Maternity Dept. Yes_____ No_____		
		Baby transferred to HRNC: Yes_____ No_____ N/A_____		
		Autopsy requested: Yes_____ No_____		
		Autopsy permit signed: Mother_____ Father_____ N/A_____		
		Photo taken: Yes_____ No_____		
		Photo given to Parent(s)_____: on file_____.		
		Named baby: Yes_____ No_____ Name:_____		
		Footprints and souvenir birth certificate made: Yes_____ No_____: Given to Parent(s)_____; on file_____.		
		I.D. bands and/or crib cards; given to parent(s)_____: on file_____.		
		Length of baby_____ Sex of baby_____ Weight of baby lbs_____ oz_____		
		Baptism: Yes_____ No_____		
		Minister notified: Own _____Hospital's_____		
		Baby to SIU Medical School: Yes_____ No_____		
		To have burial: Yes_____ No_____ Funeral: Yes_____ No_____		
		Funeral home notified: Yes_____ No_____		
		Both parents involved: Yes_____ No_____		
		Informed about postponing funeral until mother is able to attend: Yes_____ No_____ N/A_____		
		Given option of having services in hospital chapel if mother's health warrants: Yes_____ No_____		
		Social Services notified: Yes_____ No_____		
		Cashier Department notified to show sensitivity at time of discharge: Yes_____ No_____		
		Information given about SHARE: Mother_____ Father_____		
		Blue SHARE card to Supervisor's Office: Yes_____ No_____		
		COMMENTS:		
		This is not a permanent part of the chart. Send to the supervisors office when patient is discharged.		

Exhibit 4-11 Attendance Sheet for First Visit at SHARE Meeting

SHARE

A Source of Help in   St. Nicholas Hospital
Airing and Resolving Experiences   Sheboygan, Wisconsin
Name _____   Date _____
Address _____   Phone _____

Parish or Church Affiliation _____
We lost a baby by _____ miscarriage, _____ stillbirth, _____ early infant death,
on (date) _____. Length of pregnancy _____
How did you hear about this meeting? _____
Comments you may wish to add: _____
_____
_____
_____

Being involved in the preparation for the funeral

Attending the funeral

Seeing, touching and holding the infant

Photographs of the baby before and/or after death

The monitoring of phone calls from friends and relatives

Disposing of the baby's things

Religious rites (Baptism)

Regular treatments as is the practice for mothers with healthy babies

Not releasing the birth announcement to the media particularly if the baby may not live

Viewing other nursery babies after the death of the infant

Naming the infant even though this practice is not required by law

Things That May Help a Mother during Grief
Being involved in the preparation for the funeral

Attending the funeral

Recognition of the death by people who come in contact with the mother (a simple "I'm sorry" is sufficient)

Allowing hospital personnel who have experienced a similar situation to talk with the mother

Being allowed to mourn, to cry, etc.

Pampering the mother

Handwritten notes and personal letters acknowledging the grief of the mother

Being truthful about the baby's prognosis in a compassionate, sensitive way (the helping person should sit as they listen and relate to the mother)

Referring to the baby by name if the mother wishes to name the child and by sharing even the smallest bit of information about the baby with the mother in order to remind her of the good memories

Exhibit 4-12 Evaluation Sheet for Parents Attending SHARE Meetings

SHARE
St. Nicholas Hospital, Sheboygan, Wisconsin

SHARE meetings are planned to help you, and your ideas and suggestions are welcome. We invite you to share them with us.

Suggestions for presentations or discussions at future meetings?

Ideas for improvement of the meeting format (length of meeting, room arrangement, etc.).

Other?

Would you be interested in attending future SHARE meetings?

128   FAMILY-CENTERED MATERNITY CARE

Exhibit 4-13 SHARE Checklist

ST. JOHN'S HOSPITAL
Springfield, Illinois

SHARE CHECKLIST

CODE: Y = Yes   M = Mother
       N = No   F = Father
       OF = On File

Address _____   Father's Name _____
City _____   Baby's Name _____
State _____ Zip _____   Other Children _____
Home Phone Number _____   _____

LOSS NOW   PREVIOUS LOSS
☐ Miscarriage   ☐ Miscarriage
☐ Stillbirth   ☐ Stillbirth   Week Gestation _____
☐ Newborn   ☐ Newborn

Date	Time	Check ☐ to indicate completion:	Signature
		☐ Saw baby ☐ M ☐ F ☐ Touched baby ☐ M ☐ F ☐ Held baby ☐ M ☐ F , after delivery	
		☐ Given option of being transferred off Maternity Department	
		☐ "First Foto Information Card" given to parent(s): ☐ M ☐ F	
		☐ One picture with gown and blanket ☐ One picture unclothed	
		☐ Instant Photo: Given to parent(s)	
		☐ Did parent(s) name the baby? Name given: _____	
		☐ Baptism ☐ Notification slip sent to Pastoral Care	
		☐ Keepsake Memories Envelope given with: ☐ Complimentary Birth Certificate with Footprints ☐ Crib Card ☐ Bereavement Booklet ☐ Blanket ☐ Bracelet ☐ Photograph ☐ Lock of Hair ☐ SHARE Card ☐ Tape Measure ☐ Footprints/Precious Feet ☐ Seashell	
		☐ Funeral Arrangements made by: ☐ M ☐ F	
		☐ Informed about postponing funeral until mother is able to attend	
		☐ Burial options for miscarriage explained: ☐ Hospital Burial ☐ Private Burial ☐ Cremation	
		☐ Remembrance at Memorial Service explained	
		☐ Miscarriage burial notice completed	
		☐ Autopsy	
		☐ If miscarriage, was sex determined ☐ Yes ☐ No Weight _____ Length _____ Sex ☐ Male ☐ Female	
		☐ Grief process explained to: ☐ M ☐ F	
		☐ Resource information given to parent(s) about: ☐ SHARE group ☐ Newsletter Parent(s) response _____	
		☐ Parent(s) allowed time in making decisions ☐ Need for follow-up	

COMMENTS:

White Copy, *MEDICAL RECORDS*; Yellow Copy, *SHARE FILE*

SHARE CHECKLIST

#1321

*Some Things That Are Not Helpful to a
Grieving Mother*
Being with another mother who has
had a healthy newborn baby

Overcheerfulness

Not preparing the mother for tests and
procedures since she may misin-
terpret them and become frightened

Ignoring the newborn death in conversation

*Things You Can Say Which Are Not
Helpful*
Dispose of the remains

You can have other children

The child would have been abnormal
anyway

He/She is an angel in heaven

It was for the best

You're lucky you're alive

Forget it, and put it all behind you

*Things You Can Say Which Are Help-
ful*
I am sorry

I know this is a bad time for you

Is there anything I can do for you?

Is there someone who would be helpful to you now that I can call?

*(This was prepared by Decatur
AMEND parents. You are welcome to
duplicate the information and pass it
out as handouts.)*

**Suggestions for Those Caring for
Parents Who Have Lost a
Newborn**

- Encourage them to name the
baby—this helps to include the
baby in the parents' lives and
gives appropriate perspective to

the child's existence. Otherwise,
they may try to replace it with
subsequent children.

- Give the parents the crib card
with weight, length, date and
time of birth and the physician's
name. Also give them the infant's
I.D. bands and birth certificate
with footprints.

- Encourage them to keep a memory book to provide a tangible
memory of feelings during the
time of their loss.

- Honor their request or offer to
take a picture of the baby whenever possible.

- Suggest that the parents themselves dispose of the baby's
items, as this assists them in
acknowledging the baby's life
and death.

- Encourage both parents to be
involved in the burial plans and
discussion of autopsy—this
involvement may be necessary to
promote family communication.

- Introduce them to community
resources and other families with
similar experiences who will be
helpful to them during this difficult time.

- If possible, try to make arrangements so the grieving parents can
be together day and night during
the hospitalization period. This
promotes synchrony among couples in the grief process, facilitates communication between
partners and allows the nurse to
facilitate and mediate communication.

- Talk about the loss as this facilitates the parents' incorporation of
this significant life event.

- Include family members in the
discussion of the loss, especially
grandparents. Let them also

view, touch and hold the stillborn or neonate who has died.

- Encourage the parents to think about how they will share the news with siblings. It may be helpful to rehearse this with them or to have them rehearse it with a friend or relative.
- Let them know that they might anticipate the resurgence of grief during holidays and on anniversaries such as the baby's birthday.
- Prepare them for painful things that others may unwittingly say.

(You may want to duplicate this information and hand it out to the core members or staff who will be working with these parents.)

Identification of Grieving Parents

Some hospitals have coding methods to mark the door of a patient whose baby has died. Luther Hospital in LaCross, Wisconsin uses a rainbow with a cloud. This symbol is also placed on the medical record so that physicians will note it in the future when the mother comes for her checkups or for care during future pregnancies.

At St. John's Hospital in Springfield, Illinois, color-coded tape is applied to the clipboard outside the patient's room to signify a woman who does not have a healthy baby. A 4-inch strip of black tape is placed on the clipboard if the infant has died; a 4-inch strip of red tape, if the infant is in the high-risk neonatal center. This method identifies these patients for personnel who enter the rooms.

REFERENCES

The High-Risk Family and Family-Centered Neonatal Intensive Care

American Academy of Pediatrics (AAP). *Standards and recommendations for hospital care of the newborn* (6th ed.). Evanston, IL: The Academy, 1977.

Ayoub, C., & Jacewitz, M. Families at risk for poor parenting: A model for service delivery, assessment, and intervention. *Child Abuse and Neglect: The International Journal*, in press.

Babson, S., Pernoll, H., & Benda, G. *Diagnosis and management of the fetus and neonate at risk*. St. Louis: C.V. Mosby, 1980.

Biggs, J. Recognition of the "at risk" pregnancy. *Obstetrics and Gynecology*, 1982, *11*(2), 71-75.

Brazelton, B. Behavioral assessment of the premature infant: Uses in intervention. *Birth, Interaction and Attachment*, Johnson & Johnson Pediatric Round Table Series, 1982, 6.

Brookwood Medical Center. *Nursery: Family centered maternity care*.

Colman, A., & Colman, L. *Pregnancy: The psychological experience*. New York: Seabury Press, 1971.

Ferrara, A., & Harin, A. *Emergency transfer of the high-risk neonate*. St. Louis: C.V. Mosby, 1980.

Garbarino, J. Changing hospital childbirth practices: A developmental perspective on prevention of child maltreatment. *American Journal of Orthopsychiatry*, 1980, *50*(4), 588-597.

Grant, P. Psychosocial needs of families of high-risk infants. *Family and Community Health*, 1978, *1*(3), 93-97.

Johnson, S. *High-risk parenting: Nursing assessment and strategies for the family at risk*. Philadelphia: J.B. Lippincott, 1979.

Klaus, M.H., & Kennell, J.H. *Parent-infant bonding*. St. Louis: C.V. Mosby, 1982.

Nurses Association of the American College of Obstetricians and Gynecologists. *Standards for obstetric, gynecologic, and neonatal nursing*, Chicago, IL: The Association, 1981.

Wilson, R.W., & Schifrin, B.S. Is any pregnancy low risk? *Obstetrics and Gynecology*, 1980, *55*(5), 653-655.

Adolescent Pregnancy

Johnson, S. *High-risk parenting: Nursing assessment and strategies for the family at risk*. Philadelphia: J.B. Lippincott, 1979.

Phillips, C. *Family-centered maternity-newborn care: A basic text*. St. Louis: C.V. Mosby, 1980.

The Salvation Army. *Listening booth*. Philadelphia: The Salvation Army, Booth Maternity Center, 1981, *4*(8).

Shearin, B., & Burnett, A. A checklist for adolescent pregnancy. *American Family Physician*, 1976, *14*(1), 78-79.

Wallner, S. Personal Correspondence, January 8, 1982.

Zimmerman, E. Teenager's prenatal care preferences. *ICEA Sharing*, 1980, *7*(3), 15, 19.

Cesarean Birth

Lipson, G., & Tilden, V.P. Psychological integration of the cesarean birth experience. *American Journal of Orthopsychiatry,* 1980, *50*(4), 598-609.

Marieskind, H.I. An evaluation of cesarean section in the U.S.A. A report and recommendations for the Office of the Secretary of Health, Education, and Welfare. Washington, DC: U.S. Government Printing Office, 1979.

Marieskind, H.I. *Women in the health system.* St. Louis: C.V. Mosby, 1980.

U.S. Department of Health and Human Services (HHS), Public Health Service, National Institutes of Health. *Cesarean childbirth,* NIH Publication No. 82-2067, October 1981.

Grief

Kaplan, D.N., & Mason, E.A. Maternal reactions to premature birth viewed as an acute emotional disorder. *American Journal of Orthopsychiatry,* 1960, *39*, 539-552.

Oehler, J.M. *Family-centered neonatal nursing care.* Philadelphia: J.B. Lippincott, 1981.

Peppers, L., & Knapp, R. *Motherhood and mourning: Perinatal death.* New York: Praeger, 1980.

Young, R.K. Chronic sorrow: Parents' response to the birth of a child with a defect. *The American Journal of Maternal Child Nursing,* 1977, *2*(1), 38-42.

Chapter 5

Family-Centered
Postpartum Care

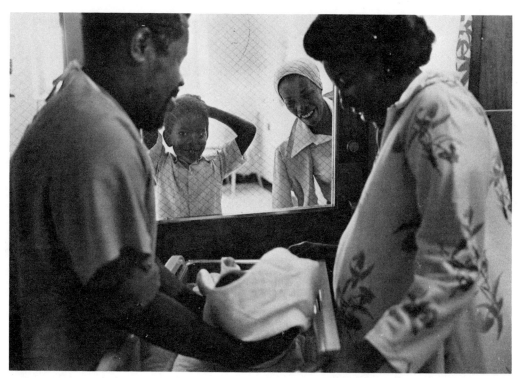

(photo © Alison E. Wachstein, from *Pregnant Moments*, Morgan & Morgan, 1979)

5

The primary goal of postpartum care in the birth facility should be to optimize family beginnings. When both parents feel confident of their ability to care for their infant by the time mother and baby go home and feelings of attachment to the new baby have already developed among family members, the transition to the full responsibilities of parenthood becomes easier.

To meet this philosophical belief, birth facilities are increasingly changing to a staffing pattern by which families are cared for as a unit. Nurses become family nurses, providing complete care for mothers and their babies, and including other family members in the care process. From the time of birth, the family is viewed as the unit of care. This shift in emphasis is often difficult because nurses are accustomed to being postpartum or nursery nurses; with experience, however, most nurses find increased satisfaction in becoming maternity nurses rather than being confined to a functional specialty. The family, too, benefits by the continuity of care they receive during the postpartum period—care that may continue after discharge when the primary care nurse makes herself available via telephone or is able to visit the family at home.

OVERVIEW OF A FAMILY-CENTERED POSTPARTUM PROGRAM

A comprehensive family-centered program is broad in scope and is planned to meet as nearly as possible the needs of the newly formed family. For some families, this means discharge only a few hours after birth; for others, the inclusion of the father, grandparents, other children, and, perhaps, friends in the bonding process and care of the new baby may be the most important component of family-centered care.

Because the ultimate aims of family-centered postpartum care are to encourage the development of family bonds and to prepare family members for their new roles, all policies and procedures should be developed with these goals in mind. Throughout the postpartum period (whether mother and baby are normal or at risk), the mother, father, siblings, baby, and significant others should be together as much as they desire. Whenever possible, babies should be cared for at the mother's bedside, including during the immediate postbirth period. Educational opportunities should be offered to family members to prepare them for the responsibilities of being parents, grandparents, and siblings of a new baby. Discharge planning and referral services should be included as part of the program.

Immediate Care of the Newborn

Increasingly, babies are being cared for while held in the arms of a family member or in a cot or incubator placed at the mother's bedside. The baby is never admitted to the central nursery, but instead, remains with the family until discharge.

135

At the Nurse-Midwifery Unit at Hennepin County Medical Center in Minneapolis, Minnesota, babies never leave their mothers' bedside. Under the Cybele Cluster System concept (Fenwick & Dearing, 1981), single-room care extends throughout the intrapartum and postpartum period. If complications arise, a small central nursery is available for immediate care of the baby. Fairview Hospital in Minneapolis, Minnesota has opened a family unit composed of self-contained apartments where the entire family can stay until mother and baby are ready to go home. The following is a description of this program:

The physical set up of the FCU [Family Care Unit] consists of 14 rooms equipped with private bathrooms, double beds, night stands, a dresser/desk, and a cafe style table for dining. The decor reflects a very home-like theme. There is a central Tub area available for sitz baths and showers. We also have a kitchen set up for patient/family use and have nourishments delivered twice daily. We have our utility rooms set up so patients can retrieve any necessary supplies or linens for themselves or their babies. There is a central lounge and a classroom. There is no newborn nursery.

Our admission criteria speak to the mother and infant who have experienced an uncomplicated delivery (our Cesarean Birth families can be admitted when the mother is ready to assume care for herself and infant) and desire 24 hour rooming-in. The mother is admitted directly from the Labor and Delivery area following a recovery period. The infants are admitted from the Transition Nursery following this period. Both the mother and infant must have physician approval for admission.

The nursing staff serves a primary role of consultant. We have maintained our standards of routine OB checks and infant checks as well as required care plans and nursing documentation. The mother is the primary care giver for herself and infant under the supervision of nursing. The recording of infant feedings, etc. is done by the family.

The educational needs of our patients are met via our Closed Circuit TV Programs as well as two group classes presented daily in the morning and the evening. We encourage family participation in these classes.

To further change the role of the nursing staff, our Housekeeping Department is responsible for all the bed-making, cleaning and stocking on the Unit.

We have no restrictions on visitors regarding scheduling or holding the babies. We encourage the families to monitor their visitors in regard to handwashing before holding the infants as well as being free from illness.

Families are encouraged to eat their meals together if they desire. Several alternatives exist to make meals available to family members. A complimentary breakfast is served to any immediate family with the mother at that time.

One of the most exciting components of this Unit is that we are seeing client as well as nursing needs met. We have made a client-desired birthing alternative available to families seeking a truly home-like setting. An additional benefit is that this Unit gives a high level of job satisfaction for the nursing staff. Being relieved of housekeeping chores and being given the role of primarily consultant and teacher, the nursing staff is enjoying the satisfaction of having time to develop truly individualized plans of care with their patients and watching these plans prepare the family for their transition home.[1]

At Rose Medical Center in Denver, Colorado, the results of 5 years' experience in caring for the babies at their mothers' bedside in the immediate postbirth period have been excellent. No neonatal or maternal complications went unrecognized or were further complicated because the newborn and other family members stayed together during the recovery period (Wexler & Bowes, 1980). Frequent observations of both mother and baby were performed by nurses, and routine procedures were carried out at the bedside. O'Connor's demonstration project on early and extended infant contact included doing procedures such as vitamin K injection, initial hematocrit determination, application of Dextrostix, and vital sign measurements at the mother's bedside. Heat loss was minimized by increasing the temperature in the delivery room, placing the nude baby on the mother's chest before weighing the infant, drying the infant after birth, putting a warmed blanket over mother and baby, and placing a stockinette cap on the baby's head (McKay, 1982). Studies have verified that, with efforts to avoid neonatal heat loss, babies can be left with their mothers without danger of hypothermia (Gardner, 1979; Hill & Shronk, 1979; Phillips, 1974).

Strengthening Family Attachment

The immediate postbirth period is neither the beginning nor the culmination of bonding behavior. It is, rather, a continuation of a process that began during pregnancy. It is important to realize that bonding is not provided but rather facilitated by practices such as skin-to-skin contact, delay of certain procedures, early breastfeeding, or time immediately after the birth for the parents to see and hold their infant. The attachment process is an ongoing one, and the family, not a procedure, is the most important element in promoting bonding (Mahan, 1981). After the initial

postbirth bonding period, complete rooming-in with minimal separation of mother and baby during the waking hours promises the best results for future parenting (Mahan, 1981).

Many birth facilities use assessment forms to evaluate the adequacy of parental bonding behavior, particularly that of the mother. While it is important to assess attachment behavior, the measures used to assess attachment reflect the standards of good parenting held by major consumers of bonding research—the educated, middle- to upper-class heterosexual couples. Although these behaviors are not an essential component of attachment, they could·become part of a general conception of good parenting applied (coercively) to all individuals as bonding programs become more common (DeVries, 1980).

With this caution in mind, assessment of the interaction between parents and child is useful in planning postpartum and discharge care. Most attachment screening tools have been developed for mother and baby, but the father and siblings should be included in the observation of the unfolding of attachment. Many facilities have spaces on the Kardex or the medical record where notes can be recorded about the attachment behavior of each family member.

Efforts are now being made to develop experiences for parents that encourage attachment behaviors throughout the postpartum period. Dean, Morgan, and Towle (1982) developed a simple strategy to help parents focus their undivided attention on their new baby, to reduce their anxiety, and to allow the parents and child to learn about one another. The intervention consisted of a 20-minute teaching session entitled "Know Your Baby Better," devoted to one particular infant and given solely for that infant's parents. Prior to the session, the assigned nurse listed those characteristics of the infant that were either common or likely to provoke anxiety—for the purpose of discussing these with the parents. Medical records were also reviewed to determine if any other variations should be pointed out to the parents.

The atmosphere of the sessions was kept warm and personal. For example, babies were always called by their names. During each ses-

---

[1]By Lynn Esenten, Head Nurse, MIC and Family Care, Fairview Hospital, Minneapolis, Minnesota.

sion, the baby's identifying characteristics were explained with an emphasis on the infant's individuality and uniqueness. As the parents inspected their infant, the nurse called attention to the noted variations and answered questions. In addition, the baby's hearing and vision abilities were demonstrated so that parents would be encouraged to speak to and establish visual contact with their child; reflexes were explained and elicited if they were felt to be anxiety-provoking or reinforcing to parent-infant interaction. At the end of the session, parents were given the sheet that had been filled out during the infant's preliminary assessment.

The "Know Your Baby Better" sessions were carefully evaluated by comparing groups of mothers who had attended them with a control group who had not. Results showed a decrease in anxiety in those who had participated in the intervention session; parents reacted to the session by playing with their babies, talking with them, undressing and examining them, and marveling over their individuality and ability to respond.

Interventions such as this are simple and yet apparently have a marked impact on parental behavior. As a part of family-centered postpartum care, continuing efforts to facilitate attachment behaviors among all family members are necessary. A formal program is not always necessary, but it is important to provide an environment in which the family can be together in privacy in a homelike atmosphere and in which sensitive, interested care-givers can encourage the attachment process.

Rooming-In

The most basic component of a family-centered program is rooming-in, the opportunity for the parents and their baby to be together to the extent they wish during the postpartum period. Rooming-in provides early and prolonged contact between parents and baby. Rooming-in enables the newborn to get to know the parents—to see them, to respond to their voices and touch, and to begin developing patterns of feeding and waking that synchronize with those of the parents. Parents have many opportunities to learn

and practice baby care under the supervision of the birth facility staff.

Rooming-in is not a new concept, having been discussed since before the 1940s. Only with the publication of research findings that have shown the values of rooming-in and the publication of *Implementing Family-Centered Maternity Care with a Central Nursery* (Haire & Haire, 1971), has its use become widespread, however. The Interprofessional Task Force on Health Care of Women and Children (1978) endorsed the concept of flexible and optional rooming-in with a special emphasis on the provision of maximum mother-infant contact within the first 24 hours of the baby's life and with a central nursery where the baby could receive care as desired by the mother.

These endorsements are well grounded, because research supports the desirability of rooming-in. In a 1973 randomized study with carefully matched controls, Greenberg, Rosenberg, and Lind concluded that rooming-in mothers felt more confident and competent in baby care than other mothers and thought they would need less help in caring for their infants at home. In addition, rooming-in mothers could attribute more to their babies' cries. Chateau (1979), in reviewing studies on early stimulation, concluded that "it is reasonable to assume that during the postdelivery sensitive phase of development the infant is also best served by a pattern of maternal behavior that for the most part is genetically determined and that qualitatively and quantitatively differs markedly from the input he receives from others at the time" (p. 56). Chateau observed that it is still very common for individuals (e.g., nurses, midwives, aides) other than the infants' own parents to have full access to them after birth and emphasized the importance of parent-infant contact during the first hour after birth. Many others (Garbarino, 1980; O'Connor, Vietze, Sherrod, Sandler, & Altemeier, 1980; Siegel, Bauman, Schaefer, Saunders, & Ingram, 1980) have reported on the importance of early and extended parent-infant contact in reducing parenting inadequacy and abuse.

The provision of extended parent-infant contact is an inherent part of family-centered postpartum care. Families should be allowed to choose their own patterns of rooming-in, however. For example, some mothers—especially those with children at home—may feel confident in their parenting abilities and prefer a lesser amount of contact with the newborn than the first-time mother. The mother who has had a cesarean delivery or other complication may not at first feel physically able to care for her infant, although in this situation another family member, friend, or staff member may do so. Some mothers may not immediately desire rooming-in, but choose this option later when they are psychologically and physiologically ready to care for their baby. The policy on rooming-in, therefore, should be flexible, allowing for the varying needs of families. It should not be an either/or option, but should be provided to the extent families wish. When parenting inadequacy is of concern, however, it is important to encourage rooming-in.

At Illinois Masonic Hospital in Chicago, Illinois, a nurse makes rounds each morning to find out the daily wishes of the mothers regarding rooming-in. The mothers may choose full or partial rooming-in, or they may elect to have their babies only during feedings. Because mother-baby nursing is practiced at this hospital, the baby can be cared for at the mother's bedside even if the baby spends much of the day in the nursery. (See discussion of mother-baby nursing later in this chapter.)

Although each birth facility must develop rooming-in policies that consider the needs of their clientele and the availability and expertise of nursing staff, the following policy is typical:

Purpose: To provide a flexible program of family-centered care whereby the parents and their baby may be together to the extent they wish.

1. Healthy babies may be cared for at their mothers' bedsides as soon as the parents request. Babies may remain with their mothers throughout the day and night or for any length of time the parents desire.

2. Babies who spent the night in the nursery are taken to their mothers' rooms after weights and temperatures have been determined and other morning care provided.

3. According to the wishes of the mother and the pediatrician, a baby may be examined either in the nursery or in the mother's room. Laboratory procedures generally are done in the nursery and are completed before the baby is taken to the mother's room. If a laboratory test is needed while the infant is in the mother's room, specimens may be drawn there, or the infant may be returned to the nursery, depending on the mother's desires and the laboratory technician involved.

4. All infants are returned to the nursery during regular visiting hours, 7:00 to 8:30 P.M., unless the mother is in a private room and does not expect visitors or unless neither she nor her roommate expects visitors.

5. The nurse explains newborn variations so that the mother will not become alarmed unnecessarily. The nurse also stresses the importance of observation and the necessity for the mother to report promptly any unusual conditions, such as regurgitation or color change. A special form (Exhibit 5-1) is given to the mother to record stools, voiding, and formula intake. The nursery charge nurse on each shift is responsible for charting such information on the baby's hospital record.

6. At least one person is present in the regular nursery at all times to provide uninterrupted supervi-

Exhibit 5-1 Newborn Bedside Record

NEWBORN BEDSIDE RECORD					

Room	Name	Breast-p.c. _____ Formula	Circ. _____

Special Orders

Date	Time	Feeding	Urine	Stool	Comments
					Crib card - kept up to date by mother & nurse not for chart

0739805

Source: Reprinted with permission of St. Lawrence Hospital, Lansing, Michigan.

sion of infants remaining in the nursery. Additional nursery personnel are assigned as needed.

7. If most or all of the babies are at their mothers' bedsides, the major portion of the nursing staff work in the postpartum area. As the babies are returned to the nursery during rest periods or visiting hours, personnel scrub, enter the nursery, and care for assigned babies.

8. Labor and delivery personnel may scrub and assist nursing personnel in the postpartum and nursery areas if they are not needed in labor and delivery. (*Note:* Increasingly more often in family-centered programs, personnel are able to function in all areas of the obstetric unit.)

Physical Facilities

Seldom is there a need for any major alterations in the birth facility's physical set-up to permit rooming-in. Almost every existing maternity facility can be adapted for rooming-in. As stated by the American Academy of Pediatrics, the safety of rooming-in is dependent on good, individual aseptic technique rather than on physical facilities (AAP, 1977).

Practices recommended by the AAP (1977) include the following:

- Rooms should not contain more than four mothers.
- Mothers should be provided privacy.
- Floor space should be at least 120 square feet for each mother's bed, chair, bedside table, bassinet, and cabinet.
- There should be one sink for every two mothers and infants.

- A covered receptacle with plastic liners should be available for soiled diapers and a hamper supplied for used clothing and bedding.
- Clean, long-sleeved gowns should be available for visitors and a hamper placed either inside or outside the unit for discarded gowns.

Visitors

In a family-centered program, the father (or significant other) is never considered a visitor. He is free to come and go as he wishes and to participate in infant care. The father is taught hand-washing procedures and wears a cover gown when handling his baby. He may go to the nursery to bring the baby to the mother's room, although he may be asked to show an identification band or to recite the mother's identification bracelet number before he receives the infant. If the baby is being cared for in the nursery, for example, for jaundice, he and the mother can scrub, gown, and enter the nursery to be with their baby. In some facilities, a father may scrub, don a gown, and enter the regular care nursery during visiting hours to hold up his infant for viewing.

When fathers are with their babies, they are asked to refrain from smoking; fathers who are ill are asked to avoid contact with their babies. Visitation hours for fathers are usually from 7:00 A.M. throughout the day and evening, but there may be no restrictions at all.

Grandparents are commonly welcomed as important family members and are able to wash, gown, hold, and care for the baby. At Hampton General Hospital in Hampton, Virginia, grandparents may visit from 12:00 noon until 8:30 P.M. A similar policy is in effect at St. Lawrence Hospital in Lansing, Michigan. An hour in the evening is designated for grandparents to wash, put on cover gowns, and be in the room with the baby; visiting grandparents are limited to two at a time, however. Some birth facilities also welcome grandparents into the regular care nursery when appropriate for parent support, but limit to two the number of visitors to any one baby.

Sibling visitation is increasingly recognized as an important component of family-centered postpartum care. Ideally, the sibling is included during labor or from the time of birth, joining the family in the celebration of the baby's arrival. Several types of sibling programs have been developed; many of these began by allowing siblings to see the neonate and were liberalized to allow siblings to hold and help with the baby's care. Some facilities have special rooms where mother and older children may visit together; others have children wash, gown, and enter the mother's room to hold the baby. Regulations in some states prevent siblings from visiting the maternity floor. Such regulations should be rescinded, given contemporary knowledge of the detrimental effects of separation anxiety, the mother's oft-reported sadness at being unable to be with her other children, and the lack of evidence that infection increases when siblings visit (Haire & Haire, 1971; Novak, 1981; Umpenhenour, 1980; U.S. Department of Health and Human Services, 1979; Wranesh, 1982).

Wranesh (1982) suggested that siblings be allowed to visit during regular 1-hour visiting periods in the afternoon and evening. Under Wranesh's protocol, staff nurses screen the children, take their temperatures, and teach them to wash and don a cover gown. Information is obtained from the accompanying adult concerning immunizations, recent illness in the sibling or other family members, and exposure to communicable disease (Exhibit 5-2).

At Hennepin County Medical Center, the following policies govern maternity visitation, including sibling visitation:

> Visiting hours have been established and must be enforced to protect the rights of the mothers to have rest, privacy, time to recuperate and to become familiar with the newborn and the care of the newborn. It is important for the parents and siblings to have time together and time to get to know the newborn. Therefore, fathers (or the mother's one special visitor) and the siblings of the newborn have special visiting privileges. Visiting hours

Exhibit 5-2 Pediatric Screening Sheet

COMMENTS AND RECORD OF PEDIATRIC VISITS:

_____
_____
_____
_____
_____
_____

PEDIATRIC SCREEN

Within the last 2 weeks	YES	NO	_Within the last 2 weeks_	YES	NO
Has the child had sniffles?			Has anyone at home had sniffles?		
vomiting?			vomiting?		
diarrhea?			diarrhea?		
sneeze?			sneeze?		
fever?			cough?		
cough?					
rash?					

	YES	NO	_Within the last 3 weeks_	YES	NO
Has the child had chickenpox?			Has the child been exposed to chickenpox?		
measles or measles vaccine?			measles?		
rubella or rubella vaccine?			rubella?		
Clinical evaluation: runny nose			mumps?		
temp.					
cough					

Sibling visit cleared by Pediatric Screen _____, RN, Date _____

Source: Reprinted with permission from "The Effect of Sibling Visitation on Bacterial Colonization Rate in Neonates," by B. Wranesh. _Journal of Obstetric, Gynecologic, and Neonatal Nursing,_ 1982, _11,_ 212.

---

for all other persons are: 1-2 p.m. and 7-8 p.m.

Children under the age of 14 other than siblings may not visit.

The primary visitor (father or one special visitor) and siblings may visit at any time during the day.

The nurse is responsible for enforcing the visiting policies including:

1. Having all babies in the nursery from 1-2 p.m. and 7-8 p.m. Babies on the nurse midwife unit must be in the covered crib with the cover down when visitors are present.
2. Orienting the primary visitor to the procedure for gowning and scrubbing in order to handle the newborn.

3. Noting on the care plan who the primary visitor will be.
4. Noting on the care plan that siblings will be visiting.
5. Orienting siblings to the procedure for gowning and scrubbing in order to handle the newborn.
6. Asking all visitors to leave after 10 p.m., except for primary visitors on the nurse midwife unit who will be staying for the night.

Sibling Visitation

I. A. To promote early integration of newborn into existing family unit.

B. To define policies for sibling visiting.

II. Procedure:

A. Using "Visiting Hours—Maternity" pamphlet, discuss sibling visiting with mother early in the P.P. period.

B. Sibling visiting should be pre-arranged with Nursing Staff.

C. Sibling visiting should be arranged for times other than routine visiting hours so that the family is not interrupted by others.

D. Siblings should report to Team Center.

1. Nurse should screen for any signs of illness.

2. Nurse should instruct children on hand washing and should provide suitable cover gowns before they enter the mother's room.

E. Sibling visiting should take place only in the mother's room, with the baby.

F. Parent(s) should not let children roam unaccompanied throughout the Maternity Unit.

G. No other children under age 12 are allowed on the station and all other visitors must observe regular visiting hours.[2]

At Woman's Hospital in Houston, Texas, siblings are invited to attend a birthing party with their parents, the new baby, and the grandparents. The following procedure is used for the sibling party:

I. POLICY

Any sibling is invited to have a Birthday Party with their new baby. Grandparents (only) are also invited to attend. The party will be held between 8:15 p.m. and 9:00 p.m. any night.

II. PURPOSE

A. To promote family bonding.

B. To decrease sibling rivalry.

C. Enhance the feeling of sibling importance to the family unit.

III. GENERAL INFORMATION

Some patients, but not all, are informed regarding Sibling Parties. Therefore, a special effort must be made by the nurse to make the parties available to all patients.

IV. SPECIAL CONSIDERATIONS

A. Siblings will be screened by a nurse on the unit to exclude:

1. Temperature above 99°F

2. Cough, running nose, sneezing, sore throats

3. Rash or skin lesion of any kind

B. Parents will be questioned regarding siblings' general health in the last 48 hours:

1. Vomiting

2. Diarrhea

3. General malaise

4. Known exposure to communicable disease

C. Parents will be instructed of seriousness of having a sick child visit the newborn, both for their new baby and other newborns in the nursery.

V. EQUIPMENT

A. Paper isolation gown (cut to fit child)

B. Soap and water

VI. PROCEDURE

A. Note on Nursing Care Plan date and number of people to attend Sibling Birthday Party.

B. Give Dietary 24 hour notice by submitting a list of room

---

[2]Reprinted with permission of Hennepin County Medical Center, Minneapolis, Minnesota.

numbers and number of people attending.

C. Supply each group with disposable plates and forks.

D. Distribute Birthday Cakes to each room (which will be delivered by Dietary at 7:00 p.m. along with snacks).

E. Instruct mother to have sibling wash hands and put on cover gown before handling infant.

F. Bring infant to room at 8:15 p.m.

G. Instruct parents that sibling must be closely supervised if he/she is to hold infant.

VII. CHARTING

A. Chart on nurses notes form #1520, instructions given to parents and how infant was received by sibling.[3]

Most birth facilities set aside 1 or 2 hours during the day for nonfamily visitors who may view the babies through the nursery window and visit with the parents. Rooming-in infants are returned to the nursery during these visiting hours. However, if the mother is in a private room and does not expect visitors or if neither roommate in a semiprivate room expects visitors, the infants may remain with their mothers. If visitors arrive unexpectedly, the babies can be taken to the nursery. Alternately, during visiting hours the mother and father (or significant other) may enter the nursery to hold and feed their baby.

Safety

Some birth facilities require that parents who elect rooming-in sign release forms before they participate in the program. More commonly, instructions are given to emphasize safe infant care, or, as at Providence Hospital in Southfield, Michigan, the mother is asked to read and sign infant safety guidelines (Exhibit 5-3).

---

[3]Reprinted with permission of Woman's Hospital, Houston, Texas.

MOTHER-BABY NURSING

Haire and Haire (1971) described the value of caring for the mother and baby as an integral unit, recommending that nursing personnel be assigned whenever possible to give complete care to the same mother and baby throughout their hospital stay. The nurse is responsible not only for the mother, but also for the infant—whether the mother chooses to have the infant at her bedside or in the nursery. Such an arrangement allows continuity and individualization of care. More and more hospitals are embracing this form of care. The most difficult aspect of changing to mother-baby nursing is breaking out of the traditional roles of postpartum or nursery nurses.

In mother-baby nursing, sometimes called couplet care, all routine postpartum and nursery functions are carried out by the primary nurse. Such an arrangement can avoid duplication of services and overlap of responsibility. Each nurse is assigned to care for three to four mother-baby couples and is responsible for giving reports on her mother-baby couples. To simplify reporting and recording, there is often a combined Kardex for mother and baby (Exhibit 5-4); the medicine Kardex and unit charts may also be combined. The Kardex may have spaces for recording what the mother has been taught about care of herself and her baby. It can be used along with a companion standardized hospital form that records blood pressure, other vital signs, medication, and treatments to compose joint reports. At Providence Hospital in Southfield, Michigan, the shift report guidelines shown in Exhibit 5-5 are followed. The report is also tape-recorded.

There are wide variations among family-centered programs in implementing mother-baby nursing. At New Life Center, Family Hospital, in Milwaukee, Wisconsin, the nurse assigned to mother-baby care is responsible for the morning care of the baby and routine care of the mother. This nurse's responsibilities include

• vital signs of infants (preferably in mother's room)

Exhibit 5-3 Providence Hospital Infant Safety Guidelines

The nursing staff at Providence Hospital wants to promote options for family togetherness during your stay here. Fathers may visit anytime from 9:30 a.m. to 10:30 p.m. and at other times by special request. Babies are encouraged to be with their mothers as much as possible, although they may go back to the nursery at any time. Babies must be in the nursery during general visiting hours.

These policies allow family togetherness but they also require parent participation to ensure infant safety.

Therefore, the nursing staff requires that when participating in your baby's care, you agree to:

1. Put the baby in the crib when napping or using the bathroom. Call a nurse if you need help.
2. Return the baby to nursery when you leave your room.
3. Always keep an eye and hand on the baby when he/she is out of the crib.
4. Never leave the baby alone on your bed.
5. Do not take a sleeping pill if you plan to feed the baby at 2:00 a.m. or have your baby in the room at night with you.
6. Ask questions about yourself and your baby, and ask for any help you might need.

The above information has been reviewed with me and I understand and will abide by the above guidelines.

_____

Mother

_____

R.N.

_____

Date

Source: Reprinted with permission of Providence Hospital, Southfield, Michigan.

- bath (demonstration and return demonstration)
- charting on the infant's chart
- checking on any laboratory work that may be needed
- assessment of mothers' and babies' conditions
- physical care
- charting on the bedside chart of the mother and the unit chart

Individual teaching is provided as needed. Any pertinent information regarding the infant's health status is given to the nursery nurse so that the pediatrician can be notified.

At Providence Hospital in Southfield, Michigan, a registered nurse (couplet care nurse) and a nurse assistant (couplet care nurse assistant) compose a Family Care Team. Each Family Care Team is assigned a maximum of six couplets on day shifts and eight couplets on evening shifts. A nurse who is working alone is assigned a maximum of four couplets on day shifts and six on evening shifts. Assignments are made by a family care coordinator according to the needs of the mother and baby. All mothers are covered by couplet care whenever staffing permits, including weekends and holidays. Daily assignment sheets help clarify staff assignments and responsibilities (Exhibit 5-6). Nurses stay on couplet care for several days in a row to provide continuity of care and teaching for their couplets.

In providing couplet care, the nurse

1. performs physical care for assigned mothers and infants.
2. plans, assesses, implements and evaluates nursing interventions to meet learning needs of parents.

Exhibit 5-4 Combined Kardex

Baby   *Mother*

Sex:_____ Weight:_____   Gravida:_____ Para:_____

Blood type:_____   Age:_____ Blood type:_____

Gestational age:_____   Rh:_____

LGA_____ SGA_____ AGA_____   RhoGAM:_____ Slip sent:_____

                                                         Given:_____

APGAR at 1 min. _____   E.D.C._____

        5 mins._____   Birth_____ (date, time)

LeBoyer bath_____   Type of birth:_____

    Bonding_____   _____

Feeding: Formula_____   Diet:_____

    Breast_____   Allergies:_____

    Supplements_____   VDRL_____ Rubella_____

Physician:_____   Physician:_____

Instructions   *Instructions*

Stool changes:_____   Peri care:_____

Cord and circ. care:_____   Breastfeeding:_____

_____   Sibling rivalry:_____

Diapering and room care:_____   Emotional adjustment:_____

_____   Bonding:_____

Bath demo:_____   Formula feeding:_____

Return demo:_____   Activity:_____

_____   Formula prep:_____

Normal appearance, etc.:_____   Breast care:_____

_____   PP exercises:_____

_____   Hand-washing and gowning:_____

_____

_____   Home adjustment:_____

Problem   *Approach*   *Problem*   *Approach*

_____ _____   _____ _____

_____ _____   _____ _____

_____ _____   _____ _____

_____ _____   _____ _____

Miscellaneous (stat meds., lab tests)

_____

_____

_____

_____

_____

_____

Exhibit 5-5 Shift Report Guidelines

OBJECTIVE OF FAMILY CARE SHIFT REPORT: To give pertinent facts relating to care of mothers and infants in the least amount of time possible.

MOTHERS

1. *Name*
2. *Room* Number
3. *Day* Postpartum or Cesarean birth
   a. Reason for C-Birth by postpartum nurse.
   b. If delivery day—report time of delivery.
4. *Diet* other than regular.
5. *Activity* if not ambulatory.
6. *Voiding only* if not voiding; DTV times; or any other problem.
7. **Vital signs* only if outside of normal limits.
8. ***Special tests and procedures* in progress or to be done; doctor orders and nurse orders *other* than routine.
9. *Significant lab tests* in progress or to be done; abnormal results.
10. *I.V.'s,* I.V.P.B., special medications: Heparin, blood or blood derivatives, MgSO$_4$ within 24 hours.
11. *Actual current status,* especially if different from normal and significant health history.

*Normal limits temperature 97-99, *pulse 60-100, respirations 16-24, blood pressure 100-140 systolic, 60-90 diastolic, FHT 120-160.

**F.A.T., O.C.T., Consultations, X-rays, Abnormal results.

INFANTS

1. *Name*
2. *Section* Number
3. *Sex*
4. *Pediatrician*
5. *Breast or bottle*
6. *Lab* work due—also pertinent lab results— e.g., Bilirubin, HGB, HCT
7. *Positive* Coombs or positive ABO
8. *Pertinent facts*—e.g., Bili light, temperature every 4 hours, Karo between feedings, X-ray, consultations, special treatments, day of circumcision.
9. *Important problems*—e.g., slow to feed, lack of bonding, poor breastfeeding, physical problems, keep in.

Source: Reprinted with permission of Providence Hospital, Southfield, Michigan.

3. administers medications and treatments for mother and infant assignment.
4. records appropriate documentation on clinical progress record, graphic sheet, bonding sheets, Kardexes, and Education and Discharge Record of assigned patients.
5. makes rounds and assesses patient needs early in the shift. Consults with physician when he or she is on unit and obtains needed orders at that time.
6. communicates to Coordinator Nurse or Charge Nurse of patient conditions requiring physician's attention. This would include elevated temperatures, lab reports and needed changes in orders. The Couplet Care nurse will contact the physician for needed orders if not communicated in a timely manner.
7. consults with Coordinator Nurse and other Couplet Care nurses on patient needs beyond his/her realm of experience and skill.
8. receives assignment and patient report at beginning of shift from **Coordinator Nurse or Charge Nurse.**

Exhibit 5-6 Daily Staff Assignment Sheet

ROOM	MOTHER	BABY
301[1]		
2		
302[1]		
2		
304[1]		
2		
305[1]		
2		
306[1]		
2		
3		
4		
307[1]		
2		
308[1]		
2		
309[1]		
2		
310[1]		
2		
311[1]		
2		
312		
313[1]		
2		
314		
315[1]		
2		

FAMILY CARE CHARGE NURSE_____

FAMILY CARE NURSE COORDINATOR_____

COUPLET CARE

	Breaks			Breaks Relief	
A					
B					
C					
D					
E					
F					
G					

UNDELIVERED/GYN. PT.

H					

NURSERY ASSISTANT_____

CIRC. & SUPPLY ASSISTANT_____

CLASSES TODAY_____
                    INSTRUCTOR_____ TIME_____

MEETINGS_____
_____

UNIT DUTIES: ____ BLUE ALARM
_____ PANTRY   ____ SOILED UTILITY
_____ SHOWERS   ____ CLEAN UTILITY
_____ TREATMENT RM.   ____ HALL LINEN

Source: Reprinted with permission of Providence Hospital, Southfield, Michigan.

9. reports pertinent data on patients to Coordinator Nurse throughout shift and at shift report.
10. performs appropriate discharge planning with referral to agencies and departments such as Social Service, Pastoral Care, VNA and Public Health.
11. gives report to student nurses and does appropriate problem solving and follow-up with students and/ or instructors.
12. relieves peers and Coordinator Nurse on P.M. shift. Communicates pertinent report when being relieved.
13. makes rounds on assigned infants and all infants in nursery at least every hour.[4]

The role of the nurse assistant in couplet care is

I. To assist the RN in physical care of the mother and infant. Typical duties:
   A. Linen to mothers, bed changes, bath if indicated.
   B. A.M. baths for infants—crib changes
   C. Assist with ambulation, teach pericare and hygiene
   D. Treatments and instruction— including sitz bath, pericare, peri lamp, enema
   E. Routine testing—TPR, I + O [intake and output], urine S + A [sugar and albumin], protein
   F. Transport infants to and from nursery
   G. PRN infant needs—Karo H_2O, temps q 4 hours, feedings
   H. Circulation and surveillance of entire nursery on regular (q 1 hour at least) rounds

II. To promote family togetherness while carrying out responsibilities under the direction of the RN.
   A. Teaching and assisting parents.
      1. feeding and changing— basic infant care
      2. scrubbing and hygiene technique
      3. listening
      4. check on infants who remain with parents after scheduled feeding times.
   B. Observation and return demonstration of techniques

III. To assist in maintaining the physical environment.
   A. Keep rooms neat—bedside H_2O, trash, linen
   B. Keep nurseries neat—assist nursery N.A.
   C. PRN errands—lab, x-ray
   D. Unit duties as assigned on daily assignment board
   E. Transferring and discharging patients

IV. To assist the RN with other tasks as directed.[5]

Nursery Coverage

Usually, at least one nurse is needed in the regular care nursery to provide continuous coverage for babies who are receiving phototherapy or other treatment, whose mothers have gone home, or whose mothers are unable to care for them or choose not to do so. Separate Kardexes and charts are kept for nursery babies. The following are the responsibilities of the well baby nurse:

1. Taking report on new admissions with mother-baby nurse from

[4]Reprinted with permission of Providence Hospital, Southfield, Michigan.

[5]Reprinted with permission of Providence Hospital, Southfield, Michigan.

labor and delivery and/or transition nursery.

2. Updating census board in well baby nursery.
3. Giving patient care for the following:

    - babies being adopted
    - babies whose mothers have been discharged
    - babies under phototherapy (bili-lights)
    - on 11 to 7 shift babies that are "in for feeds"

4. Assisting with feedings of first day cesarean babies if the baby is not being cared for at the mother's bedside.
5. Following up bilirubin levels and redraws on babies under bili-lights.
6. Requesting mother-baby nurse assistant to take bili-light babies out to feed prn and requesting time baby needs to be back under lights [*Note:* In some facilities, such as Family Hospital's New Life Center in Milwaukee, Wisconsin, babies receive phototherapy treatment in their mothers' rooms. The mother-baby nurse therefore would oversee care of the baby.]
7. Weaning babies with unstable temperatures to open crib.
8. Reporting unusual problems to the mother-baby nurse and acting as a resource person to mother-baby nurse.
9. Communicating to the mother-baby nurse when assistance is needed in the nursery.
10. Being in the nursery during visiting hours.
11. Following up ABO set-ups and PKUs on all newborns.
12. Assisting with circumcisions.

13. Signing off new orders and discharge orders and updating Kardex.

When there are no boarder babies or babies under the phototherapy lights, the well baby nurse becomes a mother-baby nurse. When there are an increased number of "in for feeds" on 11-7, one of the mother-baby nurses becomes #2 well baby nurse. If one baby is in the well baby nursery, a nurse must be in the nursery.[6]

Postpartum Nursing Schedule

Flexibility is important in planning mother-baby nursing care. A suggested postpartum procedure follows:

1. Following admission to the postpartum room, the mother is oriented to family-centered care and visiting hours for fathers and others, as well as to hand-washing, infection control, and safety responsibilities.
2. The admission nurse determines when the infant and the mother are stable and ready to participate fully in family-centered care. The nurse consults with the physician if there are any concerns.
3. A flexible patient care schedule is maintained throughout the day. For example, a mother may prefer a shower and linen change in the afternoon or evening rather than in the morning.
4. A team work concept is fostered. Team members must keep each other informed. Care plans are developed through joint team conferences and should include teaching plans, approaches and expected outcomes, along with discharge plans individualized to the family.

Source: Adapted from Sutter Memorial Hospital, Sacramento, California.

---

[6]Adapted and reprinted with permission of University Hospital Medical Center, Salt Lake City, Utah.

The following is a suggested but by no means rigid daily schedule:

6:45 A.M.   Report from night shift staff
7:00 A.M.   A.M. care and preparation of mothers for breakfast
7:30 A.M.   A.M. care, vital signs, assistance to pediatricians in the nursery, mothers' treatments PRN (e.g., perilight, shower, linen change); nurses' coffee break
9:15 A.M.   Infants to mothers; teaching ad lib (e.g., infant feeding, breast care, infant bath)
10:00 A.M. Discharges
12:00 P.M. Lunch; nurses' lunch
12:30 P.M. Treatments (e.g., perilight)
1:00 P.M.   Teaching
2:00 P.M.   Finish day routines; charting/care plans; teaching
2:40 P.M.   Report from day shift staff
3:00 P.M.   Vital signs (mothers and infants); treatments (e.g., perilight, ambulation of cesarean mothers); teaching (e.g., baby bath demonstration if baby born on P.M. shift of the previous day)
5:00 P.M.   Dinner; nurses' dinner
5:30 P.M.   Infant feeding; observation of mother-infant interaction (because demand feeding is practiced, flexibility in planning observation periods necessary so that mother-infant interactions can be assessed)
6:15 P.M.   Infants to nursery for visiting hours unless no visitors are expected
6:30 P.M.   Regular visiting times; babies in nursery; nurse charting (mother and infant); vital signs and treatments PRN
8:00 P.M.   Infants return to mothers
10:00 P.M. Infants return to nurseries for the night unless mother wishes to have baby remain with her; other babies brought out for demand feedings according to the mother's wishes; evening care; charting
10:45 P.M. Report
11:00 P.M. to
7:00 P.M.   Infants weighed

Financial Considerations

Vestal (1982) reported cost savings with couplet care. Prior to the implementation of mother-baby care, 20 full-time equivalents (FTEs) were hired to staff the postpartum unit and 18 to staff the newborn nursery. With mother-baby care, a savings of at least six FTEs in direct care-givers was possible. Exhibit 5-7 reveals the cost savings described.

THE 4-40 WORK SCHEDULE

Several hospitals visited by the authors used a 4-40 workweek (four 10-hour days per week). On the day staff, the nurses worked 7:00 A.M. to 5:30 P.M. The evening staff arrived at 1:00 P.M. and worked until 11:30 P.M. The night staff arrived at 10:30 P.M. and worked until 9:00 A.M. Holidays and vacation days were scheduled in terms of hours rather than days; for example, five holidays based on an 8-hour day

Exhibit 5-7 Determining Staffing Requirements for Family-Centered Postpartum Care

Average daily census
  Projected average daily census of postpartum unit
  18 mother/infant dyads
  5 mothers and 5 babies in each unit that cannot receive dyad care
  Total = 46 patients
Patient Acuity
  Patient acuity is low, approximately 1.5/6.0, requiring 4 nursing care hours per 24 hours per patient
Staffing patterns
  7:00 A.M. to 3:00 P.M. shift requires minimum of 5 FTE in family center, 2 FTE in nursery
  3:00 P.M. to 11:00 P.M. shift requires minimum of 4 FTE in family center, 2 FTE in nursery
  11:00 P.M. to 7:00 A.M. shift requires minimum of 3 FTE in family center, 2 FTE in nursery
  Total staff need (to include weekend off and benefit time) = 32

Source: Reprinted with permission from "A Proposal: Primary Nursing for the Mother-Baby Dyad," by K. Vestal. *Nursing Clinics of North America* 1982, 17(1), 7.

(five-day workweek) meant a total of 40 hours, or four 10-hour days off for holidays.

Overlap time was used for care planning conferences, in-service programs, staff meetings, parent teaching, committee work, or unit and hospital projects. Where mother-baby or couplet care was practiced, the overlap time was particularly useful in early mornings. In those instances, while night staff cared for babies in the nurseries, day staff was free for early A.M. care of mothers. By the time night staff went off duty at 9:00 A.M., mothers and babies were together again, unless a baby remained in the nursery. After 9:00 A.M., all nurses could be involved in mother-baby care. The nursery could be closed until needed again at visiting hours or for night care.

As long as 10 years ago, Kent (1972) reported improved patient care and increased job satisfaction with the 4-40 workweek. Most nurses interviewed by the authors about 4-40 staffing were very positive. They all appreciated the benefits of full-time employment while, at the same time, having 3 full days a week to themselves.

EVALUATION OF NURSING CARE

Whatever staffing pattern is chosen, continuous evaluation of nursing care is essential. A valuable part of a quality assurance system can be patient feedback. Daily checklists on nursing performance that are completed by patients at Woman's Hospital in Houston, Texas, are useful in ongoing audits of patient satisfaction with nursing care (Exhibit 5-8). Other forms for eliciting patient feedback on nursing care are used at Sutter Memorial Hospital in Sacramento, California (Exhibit 5-9) and St. Lawrence Hospital in Lansing, Michigan (Exhibit 5-10). Patient responses on such forms can also be useful when care is being planned.

CONTROL OF INFECTION

The possibility that family-centered maternity practices would increase infection rates has always been a concern. When it first became common for women to give birth in hospitals rather than at home, hospitals established rigid procedures because of this fear. As Wooden and Engel (1965) pointed out, however, these practices and the use of a large central nursery were designed to meet the needs of the obstetric patient with complications, not the healthy mother and baby. In fact, Wooden and Engel observed that epidemic infections can often be best controlled by keeping mothers and babies together and out of the congregate nursery.

A classic study reported by Wooden and Engel (1965) compared data from a hospital in which a family-centered approach was used with data from a control hospital in which conventional methods were used. The rates of puerperal infection for the two hospitals were the same, and the neonatal infection rates were both within the accepted norms. Wooden and Engel concluded that close contact of the infant with the outside world through the father is unlikely to increase the incidence or dissemination of neonatal infection; in fact, such contact may be advantageous because it exposes the infant gradually to the father's bacterial flora and can therefore aid in the infant's acquisition of immunity.

Haire and Haire (1971) summarized the evidence indicating that the central nursery, not contact with parents, is one of the chief sources of staphylococcal contamination. Nursery personnel, not parents, are usually responsible for spreading *Staphylococcus* infections. The logical conclusion to be reached from these studies is that the infant's time in the nursery should be limited rather than the time spent with the parents. In the *National Nosocomial Infections Study Report* (U.S. Department of Health and Human Services, 1979), it was concluded that family-centered practices are no more likely to result in maternal or neonatal infections than is traditional obstetric and newborn care.

The most important elements in preventing infection appear to be careful hand-washing and screening of those in contact with mother and baby for infectious disease. The AAP (1977) stated that "most of the common infectious agents responsible for colonization and disease in the nursery are transmitted from infant to infant by the hands of nursery personnel. Therefore scrupulous attention must be paid to hand-

Exhibit 5-8 Checklist for Evaluation of Nursing Care

Nurse_____ Patient_____ Room_____

POSTPARTUM	Poor	Fair	Good	Excellent
7-3				
Provided Emotional Support	1	2	3	4
Food	1	2	3	4
Answered Call Light Promptly	1	2	3	4
Medications on Time	1	2	3	4
Knowledge of Baby	1	2	3	4
Explanation of Procedures	1	2	3	4
Communication	1	2	3	4
Answered Baby Related Questions	1	2	3	4

Nurse_____ **3-11**

	Poor	Fair	Good	Excellent
Provided Emotional Support	1	2	3	4
Food	1	2	3	4
Answered Call Light Promptly	1	2	3	4
Medications on Time	1	2	3	4
Knowledge of Baby	1	2	3	4
Explanation of Procedures	1	2	3	4
Communication	1	2	3	4
Answered Baby Related Questions	1	2	3	4

Nurse_____ **11-7**

	Poor	Fair	Good	Excellent
Provided Emotional Support	1	2	3	4
Food	1	2	3	4
Answered Call Light Promptly	1	2	3	4
Medications on Time	1	2	3	4
Knowledge of Baby	1	2	3	4
Explanation of Procedures	1	2	3	4
Communication	1	2	3	4
Answered Baby Related Questions	1	2	3	4

My day would have been better if (Please comment)

Source: Reprinted with permission of Woman's Hospital, Houston, Texas.

washing" (p. 112). The Nurses Association of the American College of Obstetricians and Gynecologists (NAACOG, 1981) similarly stated that "handwashing before and after contact with each patient, even when gloves are used, is the most important means of preventing the spread of infection" (p. 1). The hand-washing procedure recommended is to lather the hands and vigorously rub them together for at least 15 seconds, rinse well and dry with a paper towel, and use the towel to turn off the faucets.

Each birth facility must establish its own policies regarding infection control. It appears, however, that rigid nursery procedures to reduce the spread of *Staphylococcus* infection are unlikely to produce better results than conventional nursery techniques (Gezon, 1960).

Included in general infection control policies are the following areas:

- employee health
  a. Each employee is to have a physical examination when hired and annually thereafter. Tuberculosis screening is done on a yearly basis. Routine nose and throat, hand, and stool cultures are of questionable value and are therefore not recommended (NAACOG, 1981).

Exhibit 5-9 Family-Centered Perinatal Services Questionnaire

The Perinatal Center constantly endeavors to better serve the health and personal needs of those using our services. Please help us to evaluate how we are doing by answering the following questions. Place a check in the appropriate box after each question and return this to the nurse before you are discharged. Thank you for your time and consideration.

1. Did the hospital personnel caring for you introduce themselves?
   [ ] Usually   [ ] Sometimes   [ ] Seldom

2. Were the nurses supportive during your labor?
   [ ] Usually   [ ] Sometimes   [ ] Seldom

3. If a machine was used to monitor your baby's heart rate (fetal monitor), was its purpose explained to you?
   [ ] Yes   [ ] No   [ ] Wasn't used

4. Did your support person feel welcome during your hospital stay?
   [ ] Yes   [ ] No

5. Do you feel that you and your family received personal attention during your stay?
   [ ] Yes   [ ] No   [ ] Sometimes

6. Were you and your family taught proper handwashing techniques while caring for your baby?
   [ ] Yes   [ ] No

7. Were the nurses helpful with breast or bottle feeding?   [ ] Yes   [ ] No

8. Did the nurses give you instructions on diapering your baby?   [ ] Yes   [ ] No

9. Did you observe a baby bath demonstration?   [ ] Yes   [ ] No

10. Were you taught how to take your baby's temperature?   [ ] Yes   [ ] No

11. Was your baby in your room as often as you wanted?   [ ] Yes   [ ] No

12. Is this your first baby?   [ ] Yes   [ ] No

13. If this is your first baby, do you feel that the skills you practiced in the hospital have prepared you for going home with your baby?   [ ] Yes   [ ] No

14. Would you use this hospital again or recommend it to a family member or friend?
    [ ] Yes   [ ] No

I would really like to say:

_____

_____

_____

_____

Source: Reprinted with permission of Sutter Memorial Hospital, Sacramento, California.

Exhibit 5-10 Patient Evaluation of Family-Centered Maternity Care

St.Lawrence
HOSPITAL

PATIENT EVALUATION OF FAMILY CENTERED MATERNITY CARE

Thank you for being a participant in the Family Centered Maternity Care at St. Lawrence Hospital. Our hospital constantly endeavors to make our care as satisfactory as possible. Please help us to evaluate our care by answering the following questions and by giving us your comments. When you have completed your questionnaire, give it to the ward clerk before leaving the hospital. Please feel free to express your honest opinion, for only by knowing your views, can we provide you with the services which will make you most comfortable. Please circle the answers and add your comments.

1. Were you and your family treated with courtesy and understanding?　　　always　usually　sometimes　never

2. Is this your first baby?　　　yes　　no

3. What nursing assistance was most helpful to you during labor?

   _____

   _____

4. Was there anything that would have made your labor and delivery more enjoyable?

   _____

   _____

5. How long do you think the baby should be with you in recovery?　_____

6. Was the length of time the baby was in recovery:　too long_____about right_____
   not long enough_____

7. Did you feel free to have your baby either in your room or in the nursery as you desired?　　　always　usually　sometimes　never

8. Did you get adequate rest while in the hospital?　　　always　usually　sometimes　never

9. We would appreciate any comments concerning the father's participation in caring for the baby:

   _____

   _____

Exhibit 5-10 continued

10. Did you receive all the information you felt
    you needed for either your care or the care
    of the baby: yes   no

    If not what information would you have desired?

    _____

    _____

11. What nursing assistance was <u>most</u> helpful to
    you in feeding your baby?

    _____

12. What nursing assistance was <u>least</u> helpful to
    you in feeding your baby?

    _____

13. Do you have any suggestions concerning
    coffee hours?

    _____

14. Did you visit with your other children?   yes   no
    What was their reaction?

    _____

15. Are there any additional comments you wish to
    make concerning any aspect of your hospital
    experience? Please use the back of this page
    if necessary.

    _____

    _____

    _____

    _____

    _____

    _____

    _____

    _____

Source: Reprinted with permission of St. Lawrence Hospital, Lansing, Michigan.

b. Employees with the following illnesses should not work: communicable disease, upper respiratory or throat infection, skin abscess(es), herpes simplex, herpes zoster, scabies, lice, diarrhea, or fever of unknown origin (NAACOG, 1981). Employees who have been ill with sore throats are to have throat cultures before returning to work.

c. Female nursery personnel susceptible to rubella should be identified and given an opportunity for immunization if they are of childbearing age.

• employee infection control measures

a. Employees should change from street clothes to clean scrub clothes at the beginning of each shift. Rings are to be limited to plain wedding bands.

b. When leaving the obstetric unit, employees should wear a clean, securely fastened cover gown or laboratory coat over scrub clothes. Other employees entering the rooming-in unit should cover their uniforms with a clean cover gown.

c. Physicians should cover their street clothes with either a clean cover gown or a clean laboratory coat.

d. Personnel are never to go from one mother to another, one infant to another, or from a mother to an infant without first washing their hands for 15 seconds.

e. Housekeeping and dietary personnel are not allowed in the room while the baby is with the mother. (In some birth facilities, this policy also applies to laboratory personnel.) Courtesy carts are not to be taken into the room if the baby is present.

f. If obstetric and clean gynecological or medical-surgical patients are cared for on the same unit, separate personnel are assigned to each type of patient. Medical-surgical patients are not assigned to rooms with antepartum or postpartum patients.

• rooming-in policies to promote infection control

a. The father is taught and expected to follow principles of antisepsis, e.g., strict friction hand-washing and wearing a cover gown while handling the baby. He may wear a short sleeve cover gown if he rolls up his sleeves and washes his arms to the elbows.

b. The mother is instructed to wash her hands thoroughly before caring for her baby.

c. Parents are asked not to visit between rooms or walk in the halls with their babies except when transporting them to and from the nursery.

d. There is no exchange of equipment between bassinets by mothers or nursing personnel. Bassinets are restocked with ample supplies (diapers, shirts, blankets, linen, soap, disposable wash cloths, bath basin, bulb syringe) before they are taken to the mothers' rooms in the morning.

e. Babies are returned to the nursery during visiting hours unless the mother and (if applicable) her roommate do not expect visitors. Parents may enter the nursery during visiting hours, wash and gown, and care for their baby.

f. Visitors with signs of cold or flu or who come from homes where other children have signs of cold or flu are not permitted on the postpartum floor. The mother should be instructed in this regard for the safety of her baby and others.

Detailed policies for the control of infection in the nursery appear in *Standards and Recommendations for Hospital Care of Newborn Infants* (AAP, 1977). The most important aspect of infection control in the nursery is hand-scrubbing at the beginning of the shift and hand-washing between babies.

Most hospitals employ the cohort system; infants born during the same time period are kept together. After the babies of each cohort are discharged, the nursery is thoroughly cleaned.

Isolation procedures are required for newborns with

- pustular lesions
- purulent discharge
- diarrhea
- mother with hepatitis
- mother with ruptured membranes for 24 hours or more at the time of delivery or with foul-smelling amniotic fluid
- foul or unusual odor
- mother with unexplained febrile illness at the time of birth
- delivery outside the obstetric area
- mother with herpes simplex II

Babies with congenital rubella syndrome or those born to mothers with chickenpox should be transferred immediately to an isolation area in the pediatric unit (NAACOG, 1981).

If a mother develops an infection that persists, she may be either transferred from the obstetric floor or placed in isolation. In some birth facilities, mother and baby are separated when the mother develops an infection or even when her temperature rises (which not uncommonly occurs without evidence of maternal morbidity). The baby has in all likelihood already been exposed to the mother's organisms, however; furthermore, if the mother is breastfeeding, the baby is receiving immunity benefits from the milk. Therefore, the need to separate mother and baby should be carefully evaluated. In many instances, when morbidity is not serious, 24-hour rooming-in with the mother taking precautions, such as careful hand-washing, masking, and gowning, may be preferable to separation.

FAMILY POSTPARTUM EDUCATION

Major goals of the postpartum period are to educate family members so that they feel comfortable caring for the new baby and to ensure that the mother understands the changes in her body and practices self-care. A central role, therefore, of the postpartum nurse is that of parent educator. Gorman and Kennedy (1980) pointed out the advantages of having on the staff a nurse whose main role is to educate the parents of newborn infants. That person should be an experienced pediatric nurse who understands the importance of educating and supporting parents and who has counseling skills in the areas of child development, family life, and personal relationships. More commonly, however, teaching is an ongoing responsibility of all nurses caring for mothers and babies.

Teaching begins during the immediate recovery period when the mother is taught about postpartum procedures, the need for blood pressure determinations, evaluation of fundal height and firmness, and assessment of the lochia flow. Rest and reassurance about her condition and that of her baby are important to the mother in the early postpartum period when she is still "taking-in" and is not yet ready to assume responsibility for her own or her baby's care. When she reaches the "taking-hold" phase (Rubin, 1961), she is ready to try mothering behaviors and is ripe for teaching and opportunities to practice baby care.

Teaching Methods

Both formal and informal educational opportunities are important. The gathering of a group of parents is not only time-efficient, but also provides an opportunity for discussion, the exchange of ideas, mutual problem solving, and group support. Another teaching strategy that can help parents learn the fundamentals of care, although it should be followed by staff demonstrations and assistance, is the use of educational TV.

One-to-one opportunities to teach occur frequently during the postpartum stay. Small amounts of information can be learned and practiced in this way so that parents build a base of knowledge that will fortify them when they go home with their baby. Furthermore, teaching can be done when parents are ready rather than according to a schedule. For example, the opportunity to practice a baby bath can be planned for a time when the father is present. As with all aspects of family-centered maternity care, flexibility and sensitivity to the family's needs are the keys to effective teaching.

Most birth facilities have well-developed teaching plans covering areas such as physiological changes in the mother, nutrition, sexuality, exercise, emotional changes, and infant care and feeding. The advantage of written plans is that staff members communicate similar information to parents, lessening the confusion that occurs when conflicting advice is given.

Because parents vary in their level of knowledge and skills, parental self-assessment and nursing assessment through history taking and interviewing can help determine teaching needs. At Family Hospital in Milwaukee, Wisconsin, parents are asked to indicate areas in which they feel competent on a postpartum teaching checklist (Exhibit 5-11).

Worcester Hahnemann Hospital in Worcester, Massachusetts, has a comprehensive postpartum patient education plan that concentrates teaching efforts on individually assessed needs:

Purpose:

To assist mothers and fathers to develop confidence and acquire skills in the care of their newborn infant.

Organizational objectives:

1. To reinforce teaching by nurses during direct patient contact.
2. To make newborn and postpartum health information readily available to all maternity patients.

Exhibit 5-11 Postpartum Teaching Checklist

In order to better provide teaching which is of importance to you, the New Life Center Staff has developed the following checklist. Please indicate areas in which you do *not* need teaching by checking the appropriate box.

Peri Care	
Breastfeeding	
Nutrition While Breastfeeding	
Formula Preparation	
Diapering	
Cord Care	
Circumcision Care	
Bath Demonstration	
Rectal Temperature	
Use of Bulb Syringe	
Normal Newborn Characteristics	
Family Planning	
Self-Breast Examination	
Postpartum Exercises	
General Postpartum Instructions	
Additional areas in which you would like instruction:	

Your Signature_____

Source: Reprinted with permission of Family Hospital, Milwaukee, Wisconsin.

3. To standardize information given to parents regarding basic newborn and postpartum care.

Learner objectives:

Orientation

1. Mother will seek reinforcement and instruction in areas of concern.
2. Given Postpartum Instruction Sheet [Exhibit 5-12], mother will, with assistance from the nurse, identify strengths and/or weaknesses by checking appropriate areas of concerns.
3. Mother will utilize contents of crib appropriately.
4. Parents will inform family and friends of the maternity visiting privileges and encourage them to comply.
5. Mother will demonstrate proper method of opening bottle and attaching nipple while maintaining sterility and verbalize understanding of one use only for each bottle.
6. Parents will cleanse hands each time before handling baby utilizing correct hand washing technique.
7. Given appropriate information, mother will verbalize understanding of hospital routine.
8. Mother will request modification of routine if desired and if it is applicable.

Bonding

1. Mother verbalizes concerns which she may have regarding the physical appearance of her infant.
2. Given the information regarding variation in the normal neonate, mother verbalizes an understanding of such variation as it applies to her infant.

3. Parent and infant exhibit appropriate physical and social responses as a result of mutual stimulation.

Diapering

Mother will demonstrate proper technique and understanding of hygiene in cleansing and diapering newborn.

Bottle Feeding

1. Mother will meet infant's nutritional needs by feeding at appropriate intervals (every 3-4 hours) and in appropriate quantity (graduating from 1 to 4 ounces).
2. Mother will demonstrate proper bottle feeding technique, including:
   a. proper positioning of the infant
   b. proper placement of the nipple in the infant's mouth
   c. elimination of air from the nipple
   d. burping during and after the feeding.

Breastfeeding

1. Mother will establish good lactation with a minimum of emotional trauma.
2. Mother will breastfeed infant on demand and gradually increase feeding times determined by infant needs (5 to 15 minutes).
3. Mother will demonstrate proper technique including:
   a. correct placement of the baby on the breast, with the nipple well back in the infant's mouth.
   b. correct method for removing infant from the nipple
   c. nursing from both breasts at each feeding.
   d. burping infant between breasts and at the end of the feeding.

4. Mother will list two measures that will prevent or reduce the occurrence of complications such as nipple cracks, fissures or bleeding.

Jaundice

When given appropriate written material and explanation, mother will verbalize knowledge of the cause, effect and treatment of jaundice in the newborn.

Mothers' Class

1. Mother will demonstrate procedure or discuss importance of bathing infant from the cleanest to the dirtiest area.
2. Mother will relate importance of never leaving the infant unattended.
3. Mother will describe signs or symptoms of illness that should be reported to the physician.
4. Mother will explain how to take a rectal temperature.
5. Parents will transport their infant from the hospital to their home in a crash tested car seat.
6. Mother will demonstrate or verbalize correct method of self-breast examination.

METHODS AND EVALUATION

Methods

1. During initial interview mother will assess her needs and check the areas in the first column of the Postpartum Instruction Sheet [Exhibit 5-12].
2. Staff person demonstrating or instructing each of the checked listings will initial appropriate box.
3. Teaching on a one-to-one basis will be an ongoing process throughout the mother's hospi-

talization and will be performed by all twenty four hours of nursery and postpartum staff, the Nursing Mothers Counselor staff and volunteer personnel. Initial material covered on Instruction Sheet.
4. Mothers' Class in a group setting will be held in the Patient Solarium on Monday, Wednesday and Friday. Following mother's attendance, her assigned nurse places her initials on the Instruction Sheet denoting areas covered in the class.
5. The Instruction Sheet remains in each room (on the inside of the bathroom door) so that both nurse and mother are aware of progress and are able to plan together for additional learning required.

Evaluation

1. Person witnessing return demonstration or hearing the mother verbalize understanding of a listed item signs third column with her initials.
2. Need for further teaching will be noted in the last column and noted on chart and patient care plan—sign as completed.
3. Document and sign all teaching on patient's chart.
4. Instruction Sheet will be reviewed and discussed by patient and nurse on the morning of discharge and reinforcement given where needed.[7]

Providence Hospital in Southfield, Michigan, has a family education record consisting of two parts, one dealing with maternal care and the other with infant care. It concisely summarizes

---

[7]Reprinted with permission of Worcester Hahnemann Hospital, Worcester, Massachusetts.

Exhibit 5-12 Postpartum Instruction Sheet

INSTRUCTIONS: Assess teaching needs with patient. Nurse who instructs patient and nurse who receives return demonstration, initial respective columns. Need for further teaching should be noted if necessary.

	Need for Instruction	Demonstra. or Instruction	Return Demo. or Demo. of Understand.	Evaluation of Knowledge & Progress Recommendations
A. *Self Care*				
1. Fundus (Uterus) and Lochia (Flow)—Amount, Color				
2. Perineum Care —cleansing, sitz baths, sprays and ungts., hemorrhoids				
3. Breast Care—non nursing—supportive bra				
4. Rest				
5. Hygiene —daily bathing frequent handwashing				
6. Nutrition —well balanced diet extra fluid if nursing				
7. Elimination —Urinary Intestinal				
8. Exercise —Abdominal and perineal				
9. Family Planning —Contraceptive info.				
B. *Infant Care*				
1. Handling, positioning, safety.				
2. Diapering—stools, cleansing, prevention of diaper rash.				
3. Care of Genitalia Female Circumcised Male Uncircumcised Male				
4. Cord Care —keep dry, alcohol				
5. Infant bath —sponge, tub				
6. Infant behavior —sleeping, crying, activity, spitting up				

Exhibit 5-12 continued

7. Prevention of Infection
—Handwashing—mother,
  father and others before
  handling baby—after
  diaper change
  Gowning of father and
  others.

8. Breastfeeding
—Technique of nursing,
  length and frequency of
  nursing, nipple care,
  breaking suction.
  Supply and demand.
  Colostrum milk,
  engorgement, burping,
  supportive bra, breast
  pads, use of breast
  pump or hand
  expression.

9. Bottle Feeding
—Technique, positioning,
  burping, amt. and
  frequency of feedings,
  preparation of formula.

10. Jaundice

11. PKU
—Technique for obtaining
  urine spec. verbal and
  written

C. *Patient aware of need for*
regular health care.
  1. Follow-up for self and
     infant

2. Self-breast exam
3. Pap Smear
4. Infant Immunization

Source: Reprinted with permission of Worcester Hahnemann Hospital, Worcester, Massachusetts.

assessment of the knowledge of the baby's primary care-giver and objectives for learning. In addition, there is space for individual learning objectives (Exhibit 5-13).

Dismissal and Home Follow-Up

When a mother and her baby go home, written information can reinforce the teaching program. At Prentice Women's Hospital and Maternity Center in Chicago, Illinois, new mothers are given a list of telephone numbers of organizations they can call for help, such as La Leche League, a cesarean group, a parent support group dealing with death of infants and children, a parental stress hot-line, Parents Anonymous, Spanish Family Services, the Public Aid Central office number, and hospital numbers (including the postpartum floor). At Lansing General Hospital, Osteopathic in Lansing, Michigan, each

Exhibit 5-13 Family Education Record

Providence Hospital
Southfield, Michigan

FAMILY EDUCATION RECORD

PART I — MATERNAL CARE

LEARNING OBJECTIVE The post partum woman will	Dates	Initials	Assess.	SO Present	LEARNING OBJECTIVE	Dates	Initials	Assess.	SO Present
1. Administer peri care using front to back technique, sitz bath, topical medications.					7. Recognize signs of infection, including fever, odor, pain, bleeding, urinary problems.				
2. Carry out breast care including support, nipple care, monthly examination.					8. Verbalize importance of follow-up examination with physician.				
3. Engage in appropriate activity, understanding limitations, need for rest.					INDIVIDUAL LEARNING OBJECTIVES				
4. Discuss the involutional process, lochial changes, healing, nutritional needs.									
5. Know chances of pregnancy based on selection or non-selection of family planning method.									
6. Explore emotional adjustments including depression, sibling reactions, handling advice, relationship with mate.									

ASSESSMENT CODE:
V — Verbalizes or demonstrates understanding
R — Repeat, follow-up needed
P — See clinical progress record
N/A — Not applicable

R.N. Signatures	Initials

653-14-R-10-80 784-5023

Exhibit 5-13 continued

ASSESSMENT CODE:
V — Verbalize or demonstrate understanding
R — Repeat, follow-up needed
P — See clinical progress record
N/A — Not applicable

PART II — INFANT CARE

LEARNING OBJECTIVE The Primary Care Giver will:	Dates	Initials	Assess.	SO Present	LEARNING OBJECTIVE	Dates	Initials	Assess.	SO Present
1. Conduct infant bath with safe technique, proper equipment, cord care, diapering.					8. Verbalize understanding of formula and supplement preparation: sterilization techniques, equipment, reading labels.				
2. Administer circumcision care including: applying ointment, 2X2s, observing for infection.					9. Recognize signs of infection including: Fever, demonstrates taking temp, diarrhea, feeding problems, infection of cord.				
3. Verbalize understanding of infant elimination, bowel patterns, urination as indication of adequate intake.					10. Verbalize importance of taking infant for follow-up check and immunization.				
4. Verbalize understanding of infant behavior: emotional needs, coping with crying.					11. Verbalize importance of using infant auto safety seat.				
5. Feed infant comfortably exhibiting knowledge of positioning, reflexes, burping.					INDIVIDUAL OBJECTIVES:				
6. Demonstrates suctioning of mucous from infant's mouth and nose with bulb syringe.									
7. Exhibit knowledge of lactation process: supply and demand, pumping breasts, community support.									

Source: Reprinted with permission of Providence Hospital, Southfield, Michigan.

mother is given a discharge instruction record when she is discharged (Exhibit 5-14). It provides an easy reference and a summary of important information.

Many birth facilities provide for telephone follow-up of families, usually by the primary care nurse, who is already known to the family and appreciates their special needs. Telephone contact is usually made between 48 and 72 hours after discharge in order to assess the new mother and baby in the home environment, to provide an opportunity for the mother to share her feelings with a supportive health professional, to answer questions concerning routine care of mother and baby, and to make referrals to a physician, clinic, or community resources if necessary. The form shown in Exhibit 5-15 is used at Family Hospital in Milwaukee, Wisconsin, as a guide during the telephone follow-up.

COMPONENTS OF A FAMILY-CENTERED POSTPARTUM PROGRAM

The following components of family-centered maternity care are emphasized in the postpartum period:

1. attachment

   - Parent-infant attachment is assessed.
   - Efforts are made throughout the postpartum period to facilitate the development of attachment behaviors.
   - Appropriate planning, intervention, and evaluation are done if attachment behavior appears lagging.

2. rooming-in

   - Rooming-in is available throughout the postpartum period to the extent desired by parents.

3. visitation

   - The father or significant other may visit and care for the baby.

   - Grandparents and siblings have specified visiting hours when they may wash, gown, and hold the baby.
   - Parents may enter the regular nursery during visiting hours or, if visitors are not expected, the baby may remain in the mother's room.
   - When circumstances warrant, grandparents may gown, wash, and enter the regular care nursery to provide support for the parents.

4. mother-baby nursing

   - One nurse is assigned the care of a mother-baby couple.
   - The nurse is responsible for complete care of assigned mother-baby couples, including teaching, charting, reporting, and implementing the nursing process.
   - Scheduling is flexible according to family needs.
   - Family evaluation of care is solicited.
   - Infection control policies minimize mother-infant separation whenever possible.

5. teaching

   - Informal and formal teaching features flexibility, sensitivity to parental teaching needs, and attunement to individual learning styles.

6. discharge

   - Parents are given discharge instructions.
   - Parents are given the birth facility telephone number and told they may call on a 24-hour basis.
   - The primary care nurse makes a follow-up telephone call or home visit after discharge.
   - Referral to community sources of assistance is initiated when appropriate.

Exhibit 5-14 Discharge Instruction Record

Lansing General Hospital, Osteopathic
LANSING, MICHIGAN
PHONE 372-8220

DISCHARGE INSTRUCTION RECORD

IF AN UNUSUAL PROBLEM ARISES—CONTACT YOUR PHYSICIAN

SCHEDULE OF APPOINTMENTS	
WHEN	WHO
1.	
2.	

☐ CALL DR _____ FOR APPOINTMENT

MEDICATION — (A) NAME   (B) DOSAGE   (C) TIME(S) TO TAKE   (D) SPECIAL INSTRUCTIONS.

☐ PRESCRIPTIONS GIVEN
☐ NO MEDICINES REQUIRED

2. DIET

TYPE _____

☐ HAS COPY OF DIET   ☐ UNDERSTANDS DIET
☐ RECEIVED INSTRUCTIONS FROM DIETICIAN

3. ACTIVITY

☐ NO RESTRICTIONS   ☐ RESTRICTIONS (SEE BELOW)
☐ MAY RETURN TO WORK/SCHOOL
☐ BATHING
☐ CAR RIDING
☐ CAR DRIVING
☐ CLIMBING STAIRS
☐ LIFTING
☐ SEXUAL ACTIVITIES
☐ HOUSE/HANDIWORK
☐ SEE SPECIAL INSTRUCTIONS

4. SERVICES REFERRAL

AGENCY _____

5. ALCOHOL RISK

☐ HAS BEEN CAUTIONED THAT ALCOHOL MAY INTERACT WITH PRESCRIBED MEDICATION

DISCUSSED ☐ YES ☐ NO ☐ NOT APPLICABLE

DATE _____

FORM NO. 3570 MR 600

6. SPECIAL INSTRUCTIONS (EQUIPMENT NEEDED — DRESSINGS — DIET — ACTIVITY, ETC.)

☐ NO   ☐ YES   ☐ NOT APPLICABLE

7. SYMPTOMS TO REPORT TO PHYSICIAN

I HAVE BEEN INSTRUCTED, UNDERSTAND AND CAN USE THE ABOVE INFORMATION

PATIENT OR SIGNIFICANT OTHER'S SIGNATURE

NURSE'S SIGNATURE _____ DATE _____

DISCHARGED AT	TIME	DATE
TRANSPORTED BY	☐ HOME ☐ BASIC NCF ☐ SKILLED NCF	
TO:	☐ HOME CARE PROGRAM ☐ OTHER HOSPITAL	
WITH WHOM	BY WHOM	

Source: Reprinted with permission of Lansing General Hospital, Osteopathic, Lansing, Michigan.

Exhibit 5-15 Telephone Follow-Up Report

family hospital — Milwaukee, WI
Continuing Care Program
New Life Center

TELEPHONE FOLLOW-UP REPORT

646-028 10/77

ADDRESSOGRAPH

I.

Mother's Name _____ Age _____ Gr _____ Para _____
Address _____ City _____ Zip _____
Phone _____ Obs. _____
Father's Name _____ Age _____ Address as above: ☐ Yes ☐ No
Baby's Name _____ Sex _____ Birthdate _____
Ped _____ Brst _____ Bottle _____
Family Care Nurse _____
Date Mother Admitted _____ Dischg _____ Date baby dischg _____
Nursing Referral Made at Discharge: ☐ Yes Where: _____ ☐ No

II. Problems with delivery, post partum stay, baby: ☐ No ☐ Yes (see Kardex)

III. Identification of problem areas at time of phone call: **X** = problem present; **0** = no problem

MOTHER		BABY	
1. General Health (Wt. loss, fatigue, diet, lochia, etc.)		1. General Health (Skin, cord, weight, condition of circ., etc.)	
2. General Emotional State (Reaction to infant, depression, has she been able to be out of the house?)		2. Feeding Habits (Times, amounts, vitamins? solids?)	
3. Family Situation (Father's involvement, sibling rivalry)		3. Sleeping Habits (Where? How Long?)	
4. Financial Situation		4. Bowel Patterns	
5. Six Week Visit Scheduled to OB?		5. Visit of Ped. Scheduled?	

IV.

Description of Problems Above	Possible Solutions Discussed

(OVER)

Exhibit 5-15 continued

V. Further Follow-Up Indicated: ☐ Yes ☐ No

Reason(s) for Follow-Up:

Follow-Up Accepted by Mother: ☐ Yes ☐ No

Kind of Follow-Up Indicated:

Return Phone Call: _____ Date: _____
(*record below*)

Home Visit _____ Date _____

VNA Referral _____ Made By _____

Health Dept. Referral _____ Made By _____

Nurse _____ Date _____

REFERENCES

American Academy of Pediatrics (AAP). *Standards and recommendations for hospital care of newborn infants.* Evanston, IL: The Academy, 1977.

Chateau, P. Effects of hospital practices on synchrony in the development of the infant-parent relationship. *Seminars in Perinatology,* 1979, *3*(1), 45-60.

Dean, P., Morgan, P., & Towle, J. Making baby's acquaintance: A unique attachment strategy. *The American Journal of Maternal Child Nursing,* 1982, *1,* 37-41.

DeVries, R.G. Bonding: Institutional conceptions of infant attachment. Paper presented at the Pacific Sociological Association meeting, 1980.

Fenwick, L., & Dearing, R. *The Cybele cluster: A single room maternity system for high- and low-risk families.* Spokane: Cybele Society, 1981.

Garbarino, J. Changing hospital childbirth practices: A developmental perspective on prevention of child mal-

treatment. *American Journal of Orthopsychiatry,* 1980, *50*(4), 588-597.

Gardner, C. The mother as incubator—After delivery. *Journal of Obstetric, Gynecologic, and Neonatal Nursing,* 1979, *8,* 174-176.

Gezon, H. Some controversial aspects in the epidemiology of hospital nursery staphylococcal infections. *American Journal of Public Health,* 1960, *50,* 473-484.

Gorman, C., & Kennedy, C. The parent-educator nurse. *American Journal of Maternal Child Nursing,* 1980, *5,* 277-279.

Greenberg, M., Rosenberg, J., & Lind, M. First mothers rooming-in with their newborns: Its impact upon the mother. *American Journal of Orthopsychiatry,* 1973, *43*(5), 783-788.

Haire, D., & Haire, J. *Implementing family-centered maternity care with a central nursery.* Bellevue, WA: International Childbirth Education Association, 1971.

Hill, S., & Shronk, L. The effect of early parent-infant contact on newborn body temperature. *Journal of Obstetric, Gynecologic, and Neonatal Nursing,* 1979, *8,* 287-290.

Interprofessional Task Force on Health Care of Women and Children. *Joint position statement on the development of family-centered maternity/newborn care in hospitals.* Chicago: The Task Force, 1978.

Kent, L.A. The 4-40 workweek on trial. *American Journal of Nursing,* 1972, *72*(4), 683-686.

Mahan, C. Ways to strengthen the mother-infant bond. *Contemporary OB/GYN,* 1981, *17,* 177-187.

McKay, S. *Humanizing maternity services through family-centered care.* Minneapolis: International Childbirth Education Association, 1982.

Nurses Association of the American College of Obstetricians and Gynecologists (NAACOG). *Infection control for the obstetric patient and the newborn infant.* NAACOG Technical Bulletin No. 9. Chicago: The Association, 1981.

Novak, J. Sibling preparation and participation. *Cybele Report,* 1981, *2*(3), 3-4.

O'Connor, S., Vietze, P., Sherrod, K., Sandler, H., & Altemeier, W. Reduced incidence of parenting inadequacy following rooming-in. *Pediatrics,* 1980, *66*(2), 176-182.

Phillips, C. Neonatal heat loss in heated cribs vs. mothers' arms. *Journal of Obstetric, Gynecologic, and Neonatal Nursing,* 1974, *3,* 11-15.

Rubin, R. Basic maternal behavior. *Nursing Outlook,* 1961, *9*(11), 683-686.

Siegel, E., Bauman, K., Schaefer, E., Saunders, M., & Ingram, D. Hospital and home support during infancy: Impact on maternal attachment, child abuse and neglect, and health care utilization. *Pediatrics,* 1980, *66,* 183-190.

Umpenhenour, J. Bacterial colonization in neonates with sibling visitation. *Journal of Obstetric, Gynecologic, and Neonatal Nursing,* 1980, *9,* 73-75.

U.S. Department of Health and Human Services, Bureau of Epidemiology. Alternative birth centers: Assessment of the risks and recommendations for operation. *A National Nosocomial Infections Study Report,* 1979.

Vestal, K.W. A proposal: Primary nursing for the mother-baby dyad. *Nursing Clinics of North America,* 1982, *17*(1), 3-9.

Wexler, P., & Bowes, C. Puerperium: Care in family-centered hospital settings. *Clinical Obstetrics and Gynecology,* 1980, *23,* 1087-1092.

Wooden, H., & Engel, E. Infection control in family-centered maternity care. *Obstetrics and Gynecology,* 1965, *25,* 232-234.

Wranesh, B. The effect of sibling visitation on bacterial colonization rate in neonates. *Journal of Obstetric, Gynecologic, and Neonatal Nursing,* 1982, *11,* 211-213.

Education for Parenting

(photo © Alison E. Wachstein, from *Pregnant Moments*, Morgan & Morgan, 1979)

6

As an ongoing part of antepartum, intrapartum, and postpartum care, parent education is often anticipatory, informal, and focused on a parent couple or small group. Complementing informal education is a more structured program of perinatal education that may be organized and offered by birth facility staff or by community childbirth educators. Sometimes the talents of both groups are combined in a cooperative program of childbirth education. Such an approach recognizes that the educational team is not limited to health care providers within perinatal care settings, but "includes the cooperative interrelationships of hospitals, health care providers, and the community in an organized system of care so as to provide for the total spectrum of maternity/newborn care within a particular geographic region" (Interprofessional Task Force, 1978, p. 4). At Rose Medical Center in Denver, Colorado, for example, the parent education program includes community childbirth educators and members of the nursing staff. Payment is on a hourly rate and all childbirth educators receive the same salary. At Hennepin County Medical Center, Minneapolis, Minnesota, non-nurse childbirth educators also work on the perinatal education team with midwives and nurses.

As birth facility staffs have increasingly involved themselves in parent education programs, largely because of the recommendations of the Interprofessional Task Force on the Health Care of Women and Children (1978), the survival of community childbirth education has been threatened. Birth facility-based classes are often recommended or required by physicians for their patients who wish to participate in family-centered care options offered at that facility. In addition, childbirth educators who are on the staff of a birth facility have easier access to their fellow team members for communication and referral. Furthermore, nurses are often more readily accepted as "experts" in obstetrics than are childbirth educators who may not be nurses and whose classes are often taught without facility sponsorship.

When expectant parents can no longer choose among different methods of childbirth preparation, however, a monolithic system that can lead to decreased sensitivity to family needs may develop. It is also possible that many expectant parents (e.g., the poor, the educationally disadvantaged, minority groups) will remain underserved, since most classes are geared to the vocal middle-class family for whom birth facilities compete. Oftentimes, when classes are offered in-house, it is tempting to espouse a philosophy of care that reflects what is done rather than one that clearly presents options. It is important to recognize that there are distinct advantages to providing childbirth education programs that utilize the unique skills of both experienced birth facility staff members and community childbirth educators.

THE CHILDBIRTH EDUCATOR

The Nurses Association of the American College of Obstetricians and Gynecologists (NAACOG) in its publication *Guidelines for Childbirth Education* (1981) defined childbirth education as "the process designed to assist parents in making the transition from the role of expectant parents to the role and responsibilities of parents of a new baby which includes the period from the time of conception to approximately three months after birth" (p. 1). The NAACOG guidelines outline the role of the childbirth educator in establishing and maintaining appropriate channels of communication with other team members, including the mother, father, physician, nurses, and other health care professionals (Exhibit 6-1).

Teacher Preparation

Before an educational program is established, those responsible for the program must prepare themselves adequately for working with families in a teaching/counseling role. A knowledge of obstetrics, while important, is only one aspect of the educator's role; communication skills, sensitivity to family needs, understanding of the educational process, and parent advocacy are also vital. There are national training programs for childbirth educators that can serve both the beginning and the advanced teacher. Organizations that have or are developing certification programs for childbirth educators are listed in Appendix F.

Local training programs and workshops are often available, sometimes through community colleges or continuing education programs. The complexities of the teaching process and the relative inexperience of most aspiring childbirth educators make it important for them to seek further education before they assume their teaching role. The competencies identified by NAACOG as necessary for the childbirth educator can be used as a checklist for evaluation of learning needs.

NAACOG's childbirth education survey revealed that childbirth educators represent a variety of backgrounds, and that childbirth education encompasses a variety of educational packages depending on the purpose and circumstances of the program. In an attempt to provide national guidelines within a framework of diversity, it was felt that the most valid approach would be to identify competencies for practice, rather than to specify credentials for entry into practice. A competency is a cognitive, affective, or psychomotor skill. The competencies presented are divided into three sections:

> Section A identifies the *competencies in educational process* that are essential for the childbirth educator entering practice in any setting.
> Section B identifies the overall *content competencies* necessary for entry into practice from which the childbirth educator will choose depending on the purpose and scope of any given program.
> Section C identifies the *continued competencies* necessary for maintaining and expanding knowledge and skills beyond entry into practice.

Section A—Competencies in Educational Process

A childbirth educator entering practice is able to:

1. Conduct a consumer needs assessment to determine program goals and strategies.
2. Adapt a childbirth education program to the identified needs by:
   A. Stating program goals
   B. Writing observable, measurable learning objectives
   C. Selecting from a range of teaching strategies those

Exhibit 6-1 Childbirth Educator's Role in Relation to Childbirth Team Members

The childbirth educator's role with the various team members:

	MOTHER	FATHER	PHYSICIAN	NURSE	SOCIAL WORKER	NUTRITIONIST
ANTEPARTUM	Is a resource person. Teaches relaxation, breathing, comfort measures. Assesses physiologic and psychologic states	Establishes role of coach. Helps develop team concept and effort. Assesses ability to work with partner and cope with stress.	Communicates any unusual findings relative to mother's status or father's ability to cope. Encourages parents to locate physician who will care for the infant.	Clarifies questions of antepartal procedures not requiring direct medical input. Communicates class performance. Predicts area where support of nurse is needed for mother and father. Communicates any concerns parents may have that might influence early parenting. Refers parents who may need assistance or followup at home.	Refers parents who may require the use of community resources during pregnancy.	Refers for special diet counseling.

	MOTHER	FATHER	PHYSICIAN	NURSE		
INTRAPARTUM	Properly trained parents are able to function with sufficient independence so that they require only intermittent support from the labor staff. Occasionally, the labor-coach may be unable to be present during labor and the childbirth educator acts as coach. Whether paid or voluntary, the labor coach is not a hospital employee and does not relieve the hospital staff of its responsibility for monitoring the safety of mother and baby. Likewise, the coach has no authority to dictate medical or nursing intervention deemed necessary for the safety of the mother and/or the baby.					

	MOTHER	FATHER	PHYSICIAN	NURSE	SOCIAL WORKER	NUTRITIONIST
POSTPARTUM	Follows-up to assess early parenting adjustment.	Follows-up to obtain feedback on delivery experience.	Solicits feedback on individual performance. Encourages parents to maintain well baby followup.	Solicits feedback of any concerns mother expresses postpartally. Solicits feedback on individual couple performance. Solicits feedback about postpartum adjustment. Solicits information about newborn status. Solicits information regarding parents' ability to cope with newborn at home.	Refers parents/infant who may require community resources after delivery.	Refers for mother/infant diet counseling for lactation or infant nutrition.

Source: Reprinted with permission from *Guidelines for Childbirth Education,* by the Nurses Association of the American College of Obstetricians and Gynecologists. Washington, DC: The Association, 1981.

appropriate to the specific group

D. Planning for the use of evaluation techniques during and after the program

3. Use the principles of adult education to implement the program by:
A. Recognizing the role of the adult learner in the educational process
B. Assuming the role of teacher in adult education
C. Applying the principles of group process
D. Creating a milieu for learning and problem solving
E. Fostering a positive self-concept and independence in learning
F. Allowing for flexibility within the stated program goals
G. Demonstrating skills in using a variety of teaching strategies

4. Incorporate evaluation data in the short- and long-range development of the program by:
A. Collecting data on learner progress throughout the program (process evaluation)
B. Collecting data on learner performance at the end of the program (outcome evaluation)
C. Validating evaluation data with other members of the childbirth team for the purpose of program improvement
D. Using evaluation data as a basis for deciding whether to continue the existing program or modify it for future presentation, by comparing evaluation data outcomes with goals and objectives of the program

Section B—Content Competencies

A childbirth educator *entering* into practice is able to:

1. Communicate clearly the scientific basis for maternity care, including:
A. Physical and psychosocial adjustments—antepartum and postpartum
B. Anatomy and physiology of reproduction
C. Fetal growth and development
D. Labor and delivery process
E. Nutrition in pregnancy and lactation
F. Family planning
G. Theoretical basis for prepared childbirth
H. Advances in medical technology
I. Potential medical/nursing intervention, including Cesarean birth and anesthesia
J. Normal variations of the newborn
K. Infant nutrition and care, and parenting skills
L. Body conditioning exercises

2. Demonstrate acceptance of:
A. Childbirth as a normal process
B. Diversity in family lifestyles
C. Parents' feelings, attitudes, rights, and responsibilities
D. Contributions to all childbirth team members

3. Accurately demonstrate self-help tools for use during labor, including:
A. Relaxation techniques
B. Breathing techniques
C. Positioning for comfort and efficiency of labor

D. Physical relief measures (counterpressure, mouth care, effleurage, etc.)
4. Prepare the support person to assume an active role as coach during labor by:
   A. Fostering independence and self-confidence in ability to perform within the limits of the support person's role
   B. Encouraging the development of a communications network between parturient and coach
   C. Providing concrete activities to be carried out during labor
   D. Enhancing the spirit of cooperation among all members of the childbirth team wherever possible
   E. Personally supervising practice sessions for the purpose of identifying those coaches performing appropriately, those requiring assistance, and those who will not be able to perform under stress
5. Provide anticipatory guidance for the postpartal period including:
   A. An accurate picture of the involutional process
   B. Common feelings of both mothers and fathers after delivery
   C. Parenting skills that foster positive parent/infant interaction
   D. Options for infant nutrition and any necessary prenatal steps to be taken
   E. Infant care techniques
   F. Response to learner requests for information

These competencies in Sections A and B are considered *minimal* for entrance into practice as a childbirth educator.

Section C—Continued
Competencies for Practice

For continued competence, it is expected that the childbirth educator will be able to present evidence of maintaining and expanding knowledge and skills by participation in professional development activities that will accomplish one or more of the following:

1. Increased knowledge of the scientific basis of maternity care and impact of advancing technology
2. Increased knowledge of the health care system as it affects childbirth education practices
3. Increased awareness of societal evolution and its impact on childbearing and the family
4. Expanded values clarification and appreciation
5. Additional or improved self-help tools to be used during labor
6. Improved skills as an educator[1]

Because of rapid changes in the field and the continual refinement of knowledge, childbirth educators have the responsibility to keep their skills up-to-date by reading, attending workshops and seminars, and participating in evaluation activities that provide information about the adequacy of their teaching and their ability to respond to family needs. The well-informed childbirth educator not only subscribes to professional journals, but also reads books written both for providers and for consumers.

[1]Reprinted with permission from *Guidelines for Childbirth Education* by Nurses Association of the American College of Obstetricians and Gynecologists. Washington, DC: The Association, 1981, pp. 4-6.

Facilitating Classes

The overriding temptation in a teaching situation is to provide information to a captive audience rather than to recognize and use learners' own resources as a basis for their further self-education and learning. Although lecturing has a place in childbirth classes, it must be remembered that only about 10% of lecture content is retained and that the best learning occurs when participants are actively involved in the process. Therefore, childbirth classes should include a variety of teaching approaches and should use all the senses of the learner. Furthermore, attention to the integrity of the forming family unit is far more important than any specific set of methods and techniques.

An atmosphere in which participation and discussion are possible should be created, but this does not mean that everybody *must* be involved in the same way. Forced participation may drive some class members away; therefore, the opportunity for involvement should be provided, but individuals should be allowed to decide how much they wish to interact with other class members. For some, just being in class is a major step, and they should not be frightened away by pressure to "join in" if it makes them uncomfortable.

COMPREHENSIVE CHILDBIRTH EDUCATION PROGRAMS

In the infancy of childbirth education, a community-based class in prepared childbirth was usually the only class option. Now, however, the many and varied learning needs of expectant and new parents have been recognized, and comprehensive parent education programs offer many educational alternatives. In addition to preparation for childbirth classes, such programs typically offer sibling and grandparent classes, classes for pregnant teen-agers, and, often, parenting and/or father discussion groups. At Sutter Memorial Hospital in Sacramento, California, the parent education program is considered an integral component of the family-centered program and includes many educational options for expectant families and new parents.

The Parent Education Program not only complements, but is an integral component of a Family Centered Care Program in the Maternity Department. By providing assistance through education programs, and information about use of available community resources, the parent(s) and/or expectant parent(s) will be able to prepare for childbirth and parenting with increased awareness and satisfaction in choices and decisions they must make.

Providing information, counseling and education during pregnancy, parent involvement programs, and parent discussion/education groups before, during and after the birth of a child, meets a basic need of the family in transition to parenthood. This is especially important for those families experiencing a maternal/fetal complication, or a psycho-social crisis in their life.

At Sutter Memorial Hospital [one of the Sutter Community Hospitals], several types of classes/services are currently being offered:

Early Pregnancy Classes—focusing on the physiological and emotional changes, nutrition and hygiene, recognition of danger signals, body mechanics and exercise, and healthy ways to cope with discomforts of pregnancy.

A series of 3 classes. A fee of $18.00 (for Sutter patients) or $24.00 (for all others) is charged.

Maternity Tour and Orientation—focusing on description of Family Centered Care, physical location of maternity services, hospital procedures, and the sequence of events surrounding the childbirth experience.

Tour held every week. Is *not* a requirement for father's participation in delivery.

Lamaze Prepared Childbirth—focusing on the preparation of the expectant mother for the childbirth experience, and her support person as an effective coach, using chest breathing and relaxation techniques. Also prepares couples for possible complications of labor.

A series of 6 classes. A $36.00/$41.00 fee is charged.

Cesarean Birth/Special Pregnancy Classes—focusing on the physical, intellectual and emotional preparation of the pregnant woman and her support person for a Cesarean birth experience, including information on the high-risk obstetrical patient and her support person, procedures she'll most likely experience, such as amniocentesis, ultrasonography, non-stress test, Oxytocin-Challenge Tests (OCT's), etc., as well as emotional aspects of a high-risk pregnancy. This class is a requirement for the support person planning to stay with mother throughout the Cesarean birth.

A series of 3 classes. A $18.00/$21.00 fee is charged.

Teen Pregnancy Class—focusing on sequence of events surrounding childbirth, equipment and procedures, policies and services available. Intended to complement pregnancy minor's programs in community.

This class is offered on a PRN basis. There is no charge.

Lamaze Refresher—focusing on the Lamaze Review preparation of the expectant mother and her support person who have experienced a Lamaze Prepared Childbirth with a previous pregnancy within the last two to two and one-half years.

A series of 3 classes. A fee of $18/$21 is charged.

Individual/High-Risk Counseling Program—focusing on the medical obstetrical-neonatal problem facing the family, methods utilized to manage the problem, reduction of anxiety created by the condition, and utilization of hospital and community resources.

Prenatal Classes in Spanish—available on a PRN basis including an Early Pregnancy series, as well as a Prepared Childbirth series.

Same length and charges as in English classes.

Bradley Classes—focusing on nutrition, labor and delivery process, decision-making, husband-coached childbirth.

Homestyle Orientation—focuses on preparing the expectant woman & her support person for a Homestyle birth in regard to policies and procedures. It also focuses on the physical surroundings of the hospital maternity unit.

Lamaze Refresher Homestyle—focusing on the Lamaze review with a special preparation in the homestyle experience for the expectant mother and her support person who have had a Lamaze prepared childbirth with a previous pregnancy within the last two to two and a half years. It includes the homestyle orientation.

Infant CPR—focusing on preparing parents or others who are going to care for the newborn to learn the techniques of giving infant CPR.

Mothers Are People Too—a support group of new mothers who meet monthly to share concerns about the new role of mothering.

The prime focus is on the mother as an individual.

During hospitalization in the Family Centered Care Program the family receives individual instruction by nursing staff on *Basic Infant Care Skills,* including feeding, bathing, dressing, diapering, holding and communicating with the newborn, as well as postpartum care of the mother.[2]

The Parenting Program at Booth Maternity Center in Philadelphia, Pennsylvania, offers group activities and individual support and counseling monthly to 450 Booth families who are expecting a new baby and/or who have children under 3 years of age. The program, funded by the United Way, private foundations, and individual contributions, is primarily based at Family House, a custom-designed facility adjacent to Booth Maternity Center. The goal of the program is to facilitate optimal family relationships throughout the early childrearing years.

Prenatally, the Parenting Program at Booth offers childbirth preparation classes, including a special class for teen-agers. Postpartally, parents benefit from a community-based parent-to-parent support system (called Booth Buddies), parent-child groups, activity days, special events, and "topic nights." A network of resources, such as specialized counseling, peer support, and semimonthly group sessions, is available to help families who have experienced fetal or neonatal death. Families who have given birth to children with abnormalities or who are confronted with social or emotional issues that interfere with the parent-bonding process are offered counseling, peer support, and help in obtaining information.

A publication called *Listening Booth,* issued monthly to Booth families, summarizes the upcoming activities of the program. The offerings range from play groups, stepparent support groups, assertiveness training, yoga, classes for single parents, teen parent-child groups, toy making, and grandparent groups to recreational activities (e.g., picnics, jumping in the leaves in the fall, and egg dyeing in the spring). Child care is provided during most Family House functions.

Establishing a Program of Parent Education

Programs such as Booth Maternity Center's Family House program may represent utopia for those just beginning to establish an educational program, but the scope of any program is limited only by the energies and imaginations of those who conduct it. Traditionally, most programs begin with a basic series of preparation for childbirth classes, which may be oriented toward a particular method of childbirth, such as Lamaze, Bradley, or Read (see Appendix 6-A for resources). Serious preparation and groundwork are required to devise a curriculum that will most nearly meet the learning needs of the population served. Also, a network of communication concerning the purpose of the classes must be established with health care providers and among the community at large.

Those who are establishing or expanding a program of parent education should:

- determine the needs of the population being served. If childbirth preparation classes are already offered in the community, there might be a greater need for refresher classes, early pregnancy classes, fathering discussion groups, or an outreach program for single, poor, or other disadvantaged groups.
- contact members of the medical and nursing community, preferably on a personal basis, to explain the purposes of the educational offerings, the course content, and the logistics of the classes.
- contact other groups, such as LaLeche League, public health nursing services, and community parenting groups, to explain the program.
- maintain contact with these groups once classes have been established to elicit feed-

---

back about the adequacy of couple preparation and needs for shifts in teaching emphasis.

- provide yearly reports to community and professional groups about the number of class participants, new teaching staff, addition of audiovisual aids, program changes, continuing education activities.

- locate comfortable facilities with carpeting, freedom from distraction, toilets, good lighting and ventilation, sound-proof room. Schools, churches, libraries, university facilities, and one's own home are possibilities. Hospitals may have good classroom space, but there may be constant interruptions from the public address system or the atmosphere may be sterile.

- establish a liaison system (Exhibit 6-2) with birth facilities to provide for communication about couples' special needs.

- arrange for publicity about classes via
  - radio and TV
  - newspaper articles
  - speeches to community groups
  - film nights for the community to show current films and explain the educational program
  - open house orientation to the birth facility for prospective or pregnant couples
  - distribution of printed information through maternity shops, libraries, laundromats, grocery stores, physicians' offices, clinics.

- develop a registration brochure (Exhibit 6-3).

- develop information forms for class participants. In abbreviated form, this information may be included on the registration form, or the form may be completed prior to or during the first class session.

Exhibit 6-2 Childbirth Education Liaison Form

Dear Childbirth Instructors:
Please use this form to help us evaluate and assist the couples in your class when they come to the Birth Center.

Couple's names _____
Number of classes attended _____
Instructor _____

Please circle all that apply: #1 is the lowest level; #5 is the highest level

Anxiety level	1	2	3	4	5
Partner's interest	1	2	3	4	5
Ability to work with partner	1	2	3	4	5
Interest in classes	1	2	3	4	5
Independence	1	2	3	4	5

Any special problems or comments that you wish to make:
_____
_____
_____

Your comments will be kept confidential. They will not be shared with the patient nor will they become a part of her chart.

Thank you for your input.

Source: Reprinted with permission of Santa Cruz Community Hospital, Santa Cruz, California.

Exhibit 6-3 Family-Centered Preparation for Childbirth at University of Utah Medical Center

FAMILY-CENTERED PREPARATION FOR CHILDBIRTH
AT UNIVERSITY OF UTAH MEDICAL CENTER

University of Utah Hospital offers a LaMaze based series of classes designed to prepare couples for the experience of childbirth. Basic anatomy and physiology, labor and delivery, breathing and relaxation and hospital procedures are taught, with films and other visual aids to enhance discussion. Classes are limited to 10 couples.

CLASSES

Family-centered preparation for childbirth classes are offered in the evenings as a six-week, 18-hour series. For couples who have taken a LaMaze or Bradley series of prenatal classes with a previous pregnancy, a three-week, nine-hour series is offered bimonthly. Dress is casual and comfortable.

COST

The classes are free to couples planning to deliver at University of Utah Hospital. There is a $20 non-refundable fee for couples delivering elsewhere. Make checks payable to University Hospital.

REGISTRATION

You must register during the fifth or sixth month of pregnancy to ensure enrollment and completion of classes. To enroll, complete the attached form and take it (with fee, if applicable) to the information desk in the main lobby of University Hospital, or mail to:

Head Nurse, 5 East
University of Utah Hospital
50 North Medical Drive
Salt Lake City, Utah 84132

You will be notified of class location and time about **three** weeks before classes begin.

QUESTIONS/CANCELLATIONS

For further information, call **581-2328** and leave a message with the answering machine. We will return your call. Since there is often a waiting list for enrollment, please call if you must cancel. Congratulations! We look forward to meeting you in class. You will be notified of the date of your class about three weeks before classes begin.

RETAIN THIS PORTION FOR FUTURE REFERENCE
Detach and fill out completely

Preparation for Childbirth (6 weeks) ☐
Refresher Course (3 weeks) ☐

Mother-to-be
Name _____
           last   first   middle

Address _____ City _____ Zip_____

Telephone: Home _____ Work _____

Age _____ Date baby expected _____

Name of physician
or nurse-midwife _____

No. of previous pregnancies _____ Blood type and RH factor _____
    High School   College
    1 2 3 4   1 2 3 4   Degree_____ Major_____

Occupation _____

Breast feeding ☐
Bottle feeding ☐   Do you smoke? _____

How did you learn about the classes? _____

Father-to-be (or support person — the structure of the classes makes it necessary that you have someone with you)

Name_____ Age_____
              last   first

    High School   College
    1 2 3 4   1 2 3 4   Degree_____ Major_____

Occupation _____Do you smoke? _____

For office use:

Date received _____

Date of classes _____

Notified: Date _____   Mail ☐   Phone ☐

Source: Reprinted with permission of The Prenatal Education Program in the Nursing Department at the University of Utah Medical Center, Salt Lake City, Utah.

- develop a teacher's record that can be used to plan class sessions that meet student learning needs, to establish priorities in working with individual women/couples, and to assess information that should be relayed to intrapartum care providers. Journal entries after each class session can serve the same purpose.

- encourage observation of classes by medical and nursing staff, inviting them personally and requesting their feedback after observation.

- arrange for class helpers who may be nursing students, educators-in-training, or class "graduates." The ratio of instructors to students should be adequate to provide not only group instruction but also individual help. A ratio of one instructor per five couples is a realistic one if individual attention is a priority.

- develop the class content and method of instruction.

- select and/or develop media and teaching aids to meet the needs of the class.

- develop an evaluation system through activities such as
  - student evaluations of class and teacher effectiveness (Exhibit 6-4)
  - birth reports submitted by participants after birth (Exhibits 6-5 and 6-6)
  - informal feedback from obstetric staff
  - instructor participation in labor observations of couples taught
  - tape or video recordings of class sessions that allow teachers to review their teaching and to assess their ability to communicate, listen, use touch, adjust to silences, and use their body as a visual aid
  - mutual observation of classes by teachers who provide each other with feedback and stimulate new teaching methods
  - teacher meetings to discuss ways to increase effectiveness.

Exhibit 6-4 Sample Childbirth Class Evaluation

(to be completed after final class session)

Please help us make our classes better by sharing your feelings about the class that you have taken.

1. Which class meeting did you think was the most important? _____

2. Which class meeting did you think was the least important? _____

3. Which class meeting did you enjoy the most? _____

4. Which class meeting did you enjoy the least? _____

5. What teaching aids did you find the most helpful (e.g., books, films, slides, hand-out sheets)? _____

6. What would you have liked to learn, but did not? _____

7. How did you learn about the class? _____

8. What suggestions do you have? _____

9. Do you feel the instructor was effective? _____

10. If so or if not, why? _____

Exhibit 6-5 Sample Birth Report

To graduates of preparation for childbirth classes:
We are interested in finding out what happened during your labor and birth and in your evaluation of the childbirth preparation classes. Please complete the following questionnaire and return it to your teacher. This will help us to improve the classes to meet the needs of pregnant couples. We are asking you to complete this questionnaire within the first few days after birth because events will still be fresh in your mind.

****

QUESTIONNAIRE FOR MOTHER

Date: _____

Age: _____   Name: _____

Number of children: _____

When did you first visit a doctor or midwife for this pregnancy? _____

Date and time of birth: _____

Dates you attended birth classes: _____

Please circle the numbers of the preparation for birth classes that you attended: I II III IV V VI VII VIII

Please circle the numbers of preparation for birth classes that your support person attended: I II III IV V VI VII VIII

Did you attend the hospital tour? _____

Was the hospital tour helpful? _____

In what way? _____

Type of birth (vaginal, cesarean, forceps) _____

If you had a cesarean birth, but also experienced labor, please answer those questions that pertain to your birth experience. In addition, please complete a Cesarean Birth Questionnaire [Exhibit 6-6].

LABOR:

How did the labor start? _____

When did you go to the hospital? _____

How far were you dilated when admitted? _____

How far apart were your contractions when you were admitted? _____

Did you feel prepared for the beginning of labor? (knew signs, when to call the doctor or hospital, etc.) _____

Was there anything in particular you found helpful during labor? (position, effleurage, etc.) _____

How was your support person helpful to you during labor? _____

Medications and Treatments:

Did you have any medication? _____

What? _____

At what point? _____

Effectiveness? _____

Did you have an anesthetic? _____

What type? _____

When? _____

Effectiveness? _____

Did you have any other type of treatment (x-rays, electronic fetal monitoring, intravenous, stimulation of labor, etc.)?

_____

Did you have an episiotomy? _____

Exhibit 6-5 continued

RELAXATION:
Were you able to relax well? _____fairly well? _____
   not very well? _____not at all? _____
   throughout labor? _____most of the time? _____
   until _____.
What interfered most with your ability to relax? _____

What helped most? _____

Did you find relaxation helpful? Please explain: _____

BREATHING:
What type of breathing were you able to use and when? _____

Did you feel the breathing was very effective? _____
   somewhat effective? _____helpful only (when) _____
   not helpful? _____
What were your expectations as to the help the breathing would be? _____

Please check the appropriate boxes for the amount that you practiced:

	not at all	less than 1 day a week	1–2 days a week	3–4 days a week	5–6 days a week	Every day	Practiced with support person
Exercises							
Relaxation							
Breathing							

BIRTH:
Pushing
   Did you have an urge to push? _____
   The pushing stage (2nd stage) lasted for _____mins.
   Were you able to push effectively? _____
Was this birth experience satisfying to you? _____
Would you repeat this type of experience if you have more children? _____
Did the baby's father participate in the birth? _____
If not, where was the father during birth? _____
Rate the medical care you received during labor and birth:
Excellent _____ Good _____ Adequate _____ Poor _____
Comments: _____
Rate the nursing care you received during labor and birth:
Excellent _____ Good _____ Adequate _____ Poor _____
Comments: _____

BREASTFEEDING:
Are you breastfeeding? _____ If you are breastfeeding, how long do you plan to continue? _____

Exhibit 6-5 continued

CLASS EVALUATION:
The class that I consider the most important and that benefited me the most was _____
The area of instruction that benefited me least was _____
_____

What did you learn in the class that was most useful to you? _____
_____

Ways in which I feel the classes could have better prepared me for the total experience of childbirth are: _____
_____

How would you rate the quality of audiovisual materials used?
Excellent _____ Good _____ Fair _____ Poor _____
How would you rate the quality of instruction given you?
Superior _____ Excellent _____ Good _____ Fair _____ Poor _____
Please rate how useful the childbirth classes were to you during labor and birth: of great use _____
    moderate use _____ little use _____
What suggestions would you make for improving our classes? _____
_____
_____

Thank you!

****

QUESTIONNAIRE FOR FATHER

                                        Date: _____
Age: _____   Name: _____
Your occupation: _____
How many years of education have you completed? (Check all that apply.)
    Grade school _____
    High school _____
    College _____ Number of years _____
    Degree(s) obtained _____
Ethnic background _____
Do you have other children? _____ If yes, how many? _____
    Ages: _____
    Were you present at their births? _____
    Describe your experience(s), please: _____
_____

Did you attend classes for the labor/birth? Yes _____ No _____
    How many classes did you attend? _____
    Where? _____
Did you attend a hospital tour? Yes _____ No _____

LABOR:
How much time did you spend with your partner while she was in labor?
    _____ none of the time
    _____ 1/4 of the time
    _____ 1/2 of the time
    _____ all of the time
If you were with your partner during labor, why was it important for you to be there? What did you do? How were you
    received by staff? Doctor? What did they do for you? _____
_____
_____

Exhibit 6-5 continued

If you were not with your partner during labor, why weren't you? _____
_____

Rate the *labor* experience for yourself. (Place an X at the appropriate position on the scale.)

| −4 | −3 | −2 | −1 | 0 | +1 | +2 | +3 | +4 |

Very bad   Not good,   Very good
experience   not bad   experience
                                   experience

    If you rated the labor experience below 0, why? _____
_____

BIRTH:
Did you attend the birth? _____ Yes _____ No
During the pregnancy, did you plan to attend the birth?
    _____ Yes _____ No _____ Undecided
If you attended the birth, why was it important for you to be there? *What did you do? How were you received by the staff?*
    Doctor? What did they do for you? _____
_____
_____

If you did not attend this birth, why not? _____
_____

Rate the *birth* experience for yourself. (Place an X at the appropriate position.)

| −4 | −3 | −2 | −1 | 0 | +1 | +2 | +3 | +4 |

Very bad   Not good,   Very good
experience   not bad   experience
                                   experience

If you rated this below 0, why? _____
_____

CLASS EVALUATION:
Have you attended a preparation for birth class before? _____
Please circle the numbers of the preparation for birth classes that you attended: I II III IV V VI VII VIII
Did you feel the childbirth classes were
    _____ Well prepared
    _____ Not well prepared (Please explain below.)
    _____ Increased my interest and knowledge
    _____ Discouraged my interest (Please explain below.)
The person who presented the program:
    _____ Answered questions clearly
    _____ Did not offer opportunity to ask questions
    _____ Did not answer questions clearly
    _____ Spoke loudly and clearly enough for understanding
    _____ Was difficult to hear
    _____ Appeared competent and knowledgeable about subject matter

Thank You!

Exhibit 6-6 Sample Cesarean Birth Report

QUESTIONNAIRE FOR MOTHER

Date: _____

Name: _____   Date of Birth: _____

Place of birth: _____   Instructor: _____

Number of vaginal births: _____Number of cesarean births: _____

PREVIOUS CESAREAN:

If you had a previous cesarean, what was the reason, as you understand it? _____

_____

How do you feel about your previous cesarean? _____

_____

PRESENT CESAREAN:

What was the reason for this cesarean birth? _____

_____

Was this cesarean birth scheduled? _____

Did you remain awake and aware during this cesarean? _____

Did the baby's father remain with you? _____

Did you attend prenatal classes? _____

Were you prepared for your cesarean birth? _____

Did you use breathing techniques for your labor? _____

How did you feel when you learned of your need for cesarean? _____

After the birth, when did you hold your baby(ies) for the first time?

    1. Within 1/2 hour after birth _____

    2. 1/2 to 5 hours after birth _____

    3. 6 to 11 hours after birth _____

    4. 12 to 24 hours after birth _____

    5. More than 24 hours after birth _____

How long did you hold your baby(ies) the first time?

    1. Less than 10 minutes _____

    2. 10 to 30 minutes _____

    3. 31 to 60 minutes _____

    4. Longer than 1 hour _____

How are you feeding your baby?

    1. Breastfeeding exclusively _____

    2. Breastfeeding plus one or two bottles a week _____

    3. Breastfeeding plus daily bottles _____

    4. Bottle feeding exclusively _____

How do you feel about this birth experience, given the circumstances?

    1. Very pleased and enthusiastic _____

    2. Pleased _____

    3. Not very pleased _____

    4. Very upset and displeased _____

Did you obtain enough information about cesarean birth in your birth preparation classes?

    Yes _____ No _____

Ways in which the classes could have better prepared me for the cesarean·birth experience are: _____

_____

Exhibit 6-6 continued

QUESTIONNAIRE FOR FATHER PRESENT AT CESAREAN BIRTH

Date: _____

Name: _____   Age: _____

Date of cesarean: _____   Hospital: _____

Reason for cesarean: _____

Physicians: _____

How did you see your role (why were you there)? _____

_____

What were your thoughts during the cesarean? _____

_____

What were your thoughts before your baby was born? _____

_____

After your baby was born? _____

_____

When did you hold, touch your baby? _____

_____

Describe your feelings when you first saw your baby. _____

_____

What was the attitude of the staff (support, helpfulness, rejection, indifference, etc.)? _____

_____

Did you feel that you were prepared for this experience? _____

Please explain. _____

_____

Thank you!

ANTEPARTUM EDUCATION PROGRAMS

A great variety of classes may be offered. In addition to the commonly available classes in childbirth preparation, special types of classes may be offered according to community needs. For example, Rose Medical Center in Denver, Colorado, offers a monthly two-class series for families expecting a multiple birth, these classes are designed to help parents experience multiple births as a positive event, to promote discussion among parents about their concerns over a multiple birth, to provide information about the medical aspects of multiple birth, and to prepare these parents for possible cesarean birth or premature birth. Classes may be offered for adoptive parents (Lockhart, 1982) to provide information on infant care and the emotional aspects of adoption before and after the baby's arrival. Many perinatal education programs, however, are unable to include such highly individualized classes.

Early Pregnancy Classes

Early pregnancy classes are planned for women (or couples) in the first months of pregnancy or, in some cases, prior to pregnancy. Early pregnancy classes are occasionally single meetings, but a series of classes is more commonly provided. The latter approach is preferable, since information need not be "crammed" into a single long session, class attendees are offered more discussion time, and participants have the opportunity to become acquainted—providing a possible source of support that will extend throughout pregnancy and beyond.

The following is a description of a series of early pregnancy classes:

> *Who:* Expectant mothers or women anticipating pregnancy and their support person who wish to learn about their pregnancy in the early stage.
>
> *What:* Information about nutrition, the physical and emotional changes of pregnancy, fetal development, feeding options, being a consumer of health services, relaxation, and body toning exercises; a tour of the maternity facilities.
>
> *When:* Four classes from 7 to 9 P.M. on Tuesday evenings beginning the first Tuesday of each month.

Classes are small and informal so that participants can share their concerns with instructor guidance. Participants are asked to wear clothes in which they can comfortably exercise.

The class curriculum typically includes

I. Session I
   A. Introduction
      1. Getting acquainted
      2. Assessment of knowledge base of participants
   B. Body awareness
      1. Feelings about changing body
      2. Physical changes of pregnancy
      3. Exercises: walking, posture, body mechanics, stretching, pelvic floor, muscle toning
   C. Introduction to relaxation: progressive relaxation
II. Session II
   A. Self-care: nutritional intake, substance abuse, avoidance of teratogenic agents
   B. Medical visits: care components, communicating with health care provider, contracting for birth options
   C. Newborn feeding options
   D. Exercise/movement/relaxation
   E. Changing emotions during pregnancy

III. Session III
   A. Fetal development
   B. Diagnostic tests
   C. Exercise/movement
   D. Relaxation and visualization as an enhancement to prenatal attachment process
   E. Sexuality during the childbearing year
IV. Session IV
   A. Childbirth film
   B. Tour of maternity facilities
   C. Consumerism during the childbearing year, including discussion of "The Pregnant Patient's Bill of Rights and the Pregnant Patient's Responsibilities"
   D. Enhancing communication between the unborn baby and family members
   E. Description of preparation for childbirth programs

Preparation for Childbirth Classes

Classes to prepare expectant parents for their baby's birth may be oriented toward a particular method of childbirth (Bradley, Read, Lamaze) or may be eclectic in focus. They typically cover anatomy and physiology, nutrition, labor and birth information, use of breathing patterns and relaxation methods, comfort measures, emotional adjustments, and the role changes that accompany pregnancy. Childbirth classes are typically couple-oriented. The woman is not required to bring the baby's father, however; she may bring a friend or relative to provide support.

Preparation for childbirth classes may be described as follows:

> *Who:* Expectant mothers and the support persons of their choice who wish to prepare jointly for labor, birth, and the early weeks of parenting.
>
> *What:* A series of eight classes to help parents-to-be understand the emotional demands of pregnancy; gain insight into their expanding roles

as they relate to each other and their children; become intelligent consumers of health care while maintaining their confidence in the health care system; obtain information about pregnancy, childbirth, infant care, and parenting; and learn body-toning exercise, breathing patterns, relaxation methods, and comfort measures for labor.

When: Wednesday evenings from 7:00 to 9:30 P.M. beginning the first Wednesday of each month.

Class size is often limited, so early registration is important. Participants wear loose-fitting, comfortable clothes and bring two pillows and a blanket or sleeping roll to class sessions. Women should plan to begin class during their 7th month of pregnancy.

The following is a typical class outline:

I. Session I
   A. Introduction
      1. Group warm-up and get acquainted
      2. Course overview
      3. Philosophy and principles of childbirth preparation
   B. Childbirth film
   C. Introduction to exercises: body mechanics, pelvic tilt, tailor sitting, pelvic floor exercises
   D. Pregnancy charts: body changes during pregnancy, placental transfer of drugs and other agents that may be teratogenic
II. Session II
   A. Nutritional assessment: pattern of food intake, weight gain, implications of nutrition in pregnancy outcome
   B. Exercise review and introduction of stretching exercises, leg-strengthening exercises, abdominal toning, flexibility exercises
   C. Pelvic anatomy
      1. Position and presentation of fetus

2. Problems related to positions, including breech exercise for breech presentation
      3. Change of fetal position (posterior to anterior) by use of pelvic tilting and abdominal massage (Andrews, 1980)
   D. Introduction to relaxation
III. Session III
   A. Exercise review
   B. Labor overview with emphasis on early phase
   C. Breathing for early labor
   D. Relaxation: practice and introduction to visualization
   E. Group discussion of emotional changes and adaptations during pregnancy
IV. Session IV
   A. Review relaxation and breathing pattern
   B. Touch relaxation
   C. Discussion of active labor and breathing pattern demonstration with return demonstration
   D. Back labor: management principles
   E. Medical procedures and problems during late pregnancy
V. Session V
   A. Hospital tour and discussion
   B. Breathing pattern and relaxation review
   C. The use of medications during labor: advantages and disadvantages, timing, doses, alternatives to medication
   D. Discussion of transition phase of labor and breathing pattern demonstration with return demonstration
   E. Role playing of transition with discussion of helper strategies
VI. Session VI
   A. Review of relaxation and breathing patterns working in small groups
   B. Induction of labor: how labor differs and management strategies

C. Normal birth slides, including *Birth Atlas* slides
D. Cesarean birth and cesarean prevention
VII. Session VII
A. Relaxation and breathing review
B. Film
C. Second stage labor (McKay, 1981; Noble, 1981)
D. The normal newborn: care and characteristics, including feeding choices
VIII. Session VIII
A. Sharing of another couple's birth experience (or that of two couples, one having a vaginal birth and the other a cesarean birth)
B. Review of second stage labor and discussion of family-infant attachment
C. Parenting: role playing of stresses of new parenting, discussion by experienced parents of adjustment to newborn, sources of community support
D. Infant safety, including car seats

Birth Refresher Classes

Couples who have previously attended preparation for childbirth classes (particularly in the past 2 to 3 years) may opt for refresher classes instead of the full series. The content is much the same as the preparation for childbirth series, except that the women's experience is used as the knowledge base and there is greater emphasis on sibling participation and reactions to the upcoming birth. A tour may or may not be included as part of the class series.

The classes may be described as follows:

Who: Expectant mothers and their support persons who have in the past 3 years attended preparation for childbirth classes during a previous pregnancy.
What: Review of content learned in preparation for childbirth classes, including exercises, breathing, relaxa-

tion, and comfort measures, with an update of information about birth facility policies and practices. An optional tour is included. Sibling participation in pregnancy and childbirth is discussed; during the last session, a separate class and hospital tour are provided for children.
When: A three-session class series, beginning the first Wednesday of each month from 7:00 to 9:00 P.M.

Classes are typically limited to 10 couples. Registration is advised by the 7th month of pregnancy, and classes begin during the 8th month. Dress is casual and comfortable. Couples bring two pillows and a blanket or sleeping roll for comfort during practice.

Birth refresher classes typically cover the following:

I. Session I
A. Introduction
1. Icebreaker: discussion of previous birth experiences
2. Review of philosophy of prepared childbirth
B. Film and discussion of "what's new"
C. Exercise review with return demonstration
D. Relaxation review
II. Session II
A. Labor overview and discussion of variations as experienced by class participants
B. Review of breathing patterns for labor
C. Relaxation and visualization as preparation for labor
III. Session III
A. Review of second stage labor
B. Cesarean birth
C. Update: birth facility practices, options for childbirth, medications, family-centered care
D. Sibling preparation
E. Optional birth facility tour

At Hampton General Hospital in Hampton, Virginia, parents are given the following suggestions for sibling preparation:

> The amount of preparation for a new baby in the family and the time it is begun should depend on whether your child is the type who likes to look forward to things or gets too impatient if told about things too soon.
>
> The following suggestions are offered to help in the preparation of your children for this important event.

1. Remember to present the new baby from your child's point of view. The experience is really not going to be quite as wonderful as we tend to make it sound. (In the sibling class we discuss the fact that though babies are cute and nice to have around, they can also be a lot of trouble. They cry a lot, mess their diapers, wet and smell bad. They demand a great deal of Mother's attention because they must be fed, bathed, diapered, etc. If, when all this is going on, the child feels left out or jealous, we encourage him to go to Mom and Dad and talk about it.) Remember your affection and attention have belonged to this child exclusively and this is not easy to share!

2. Even reasonably secure children are going to feel displaced by the new baby. If a move to a new room, bed, etc. is necessary, try to accomplish this as early as possible in the pregnancy, so the child will have less reason to feel "shoved out" when the new baby arrives.

3. Let the child help to get things ready for the new baby, and remember to include purchases for the child also on shopping expeditions.

4. Show the child picture books about new babies, and if possible, visit in a home where there is an infant, so that he realizes this is not going to be an instant playmate.

5. Talk to the child about the advantages of either sex and the unpredictability of this so he won't have his heart set definitely on one or the other.

6. Attend the Sibling Orientation Program in the hospital in order to acquaint the child with where Mom will be when the time comes for the baby to be born. The visit will be remembered, if only vaguely, and can be very reassuring. The hospital becomes part of his world, not some mysterious faraway place.

7. The child should be told about the possibility of Mom going to the hospital while he is at nursery school, in the middle of the night, etc., and that this is part of the unpredictability of a baby's birth. He needs to know who will be caring for him at that time as well as during the remainder of the hospital stay.

8. You may want to have your child brought to the hospital by a friend or relative immediately after the birth to share in the joy and excitement. They may be allowed to join the rest of the family in the birthing room and even hold the new baby right away.

9. Most hospitals now allow children to visit Mom and the new baby while they are still in the hospital. The child should be brought for these visits whenever possible.

10. It's a good idea to have a present (a new doll is ideal) to give to your preschooler when you bring the new baby home from the hospital.

11. It's easy to get lost in friends' excitement over the new baby when they come to call. Whenever possible, encourage them to include the older child in the excitement as well.

12. Father can help a great deal by spending time with the older child *first* when he gets home from work.

13. Mothers too should remember to spend precious "alone" time with each child as often as possible.

14. Remember that jealousy is a very common, normal phenomenon! Most children naturally want to be the best, come first, and be loved most by their parents. This may be expressed indirectly by too much concern and affection for the baby, refusal to go to school, extra demands for Mom's attention, naughty behavior, not eating, not sleeping, loss of toilet training, etc. Or, it may be expressed quite openly by a preschooler's physical attacks on the baby. For this reason it is best *never* to leave them alone together!

15. Your school age child will probably adjust much more easily to a new baby since his world has already expanded to include attachments and activities outside the family. However, be careful not to *impose* on his increased maturity by turning him into a constant babysitter or by giving him responsibilities concern-

ing the baby that are beyond his capabilities.[3]

A list of books for children that may be helpful in preparing them for the birth of a sibling appears in Appendix 6-B.

Cesarean Birth Preparation Classes

As the number of cesarean births has dramatically increased and fathers are present more often during their baby's cesarean delivery, it has become necessary to prepare parents for cesarean birth. Although most preparation for childbirth classes discuss cesarean birth, couples anticipating cesarean delivery benefit by attending classes specifically designed for them. Such classes may be described as follows:

Who: Expectant mothers and their support persons who have already experienced a cesarean birth or who anticipate a cesarean birth.

What: Information on the indications for cesarean birth, prenatal testing procedures, surgical and hospital procedures, feelings related to cesarean birth, ways to increase comfort or cope with discomfort, signs of labor, and the supportive role of the father in cesarean birth.

When: Three classes from 7:00 to 9:00 P.M. on Monday evenings, beginning the first Monday of each month.

The curriculum generally includes the following:

I. Session I
   A. Introduction
      1. Getting acquainted
      2. Discussion of any previous cesarean births
   B. Emotional aspects of cesarean birth: body image and functioning, failure vs. success, grief and loss

---

[3]Reprinted with permission of Hampton General Hospital, Hampton, Virginia.

C. Maternal nutrition
D. Introduction to relaxation
II. Session II
A. Indications for a cesarean birth
B. Economic factors
C. Vaginal birth after cesarean*
D. Fetal maturity and well-being tests
E. Pre-, intra-, and postoperative care and procedures
F. Body-conditioning exercises
G. Relaxation review
III. Session III
A. Hospital procedures to facilitate bonding after cesarean birth
B. Ways to speed recovery
C. Breastfeeding after cesarean birth
D. Physical and emotional adjustments
E. Sharing of personal experiences, feelings, and support group services by cesarean support group couple

Teen-age Birth Preparation Classes

Catano (1979) defined and described the following teaching approaches in reaching pregnant teen-agers:

1. standard prenatal classes designed to include the basic information presented in all prenatal classes but tailored to the age and interest levels of adolescents.
2. informal discussion groups as part of a clinic attendance program. This requires that all pregnant teen-agers' appointments be scheduled in blocks of time (10 each hour) on the same days (i.e., Tuesday and Thursday afternoons).
3. one-to-one outreach teaching in clinic waiting rooms. A teacher approaches girls individually as they wait for an appointment and establishes a dialogue about childbirth, pregnancy, and other concerns.

4. one-to-one or very small group teaching in the teen-ager's home.
5. drop-in center. Emphasis is on social interaction and contact in a convenient, centrally located place where pregnant girls can gather.
6. peer education. This involves training a teen-aged mother (who is a role model) as a resource person.
7. "big sister" approach. Often, with pregnant girls (or new mothers), a one-to-one relationship with someone who cares is the most effective approach. Girls can be matched with women who are themselves mothers and mature adults.
8. residences for single mothers. These residences may offer pregnancy and birth classes in addition to providing shelter for teen-aged mothers.
9. regular or special schools that provide for continuing education during pregnancy. These programs include postpartum assistance for infant day care, maternal and paternal education, and vocational training.

Birth classes for teens may be described as follows:

Who: Pregnant teen-agers and their support persons who want to learn about pregnancy, birth, and infant care.

What: A series of seven classes about physical and emotional changes in pregnancy, food for mother and baby, exercises to prepare for labor and birth, care of new babies, and birth control measures.

When: Seven classes from 3:00 to 5:00 P.M. on Monday afternoons beginning the first Monday of every second month.

The following class outline is typical:

I. Session I
A. Introductions
B. Reproductive system and changing body image

---

*Vaginal birth after cesarean (VBAC) classes are becoming increasingly common to prepare women who previously had cesarean deliveries to give birth vaginally. The format is similar to preparation for childbirth classes, but there is greater emphasis on the implications of the previous cesarean(s).

C. Physiology of menstruation
D. Conception
E. Heredity
F. Introduction to relaxation
G. Relating to others

II. Session II
A. Pregnancy: body change
B. Parenting alternatives (relinquishing or parenting the baby)
C. Emotional responses
D. Interpersonal relationships
E. Exercise/movement/relaxation

III. Session III
A. Exercise/movement/relaxation
B. Nutritional intake, substance abuse
C. Diet: before, during, and after pregnancy
D. Consideration to cultural eating habits
E. Cesarean and cesarean prevention
F. Avoidance of teratogenic agents
G. Labor breathing demonstration and return demonstration

IV. Session IV
A. Labor and birth
B. Signals of possible danger
C. Early signs and beginning of labor
D. Patterns of labor
E. Relaxation
F. Breathing patterns for labor

V. Session V
A. Postpartum period
B. Physical changes in the body
C. Emotional changes
D. Family planning
E. Birth control
F. Family relationships
G. Relaxation: practice and introduction to visualization

VI. Session VI
A. Medical problems
B. Contagious diseases
   1. Venereal disease
   2. German measles
C. Dangerous drugs
D. Sickle cell anemia
E. Exercise/movement/relaxation

VII. Session VII
A. Infant and child care
B. Feeding
C. Bathing
D. Handling
E. Teething
F. Clothing
G. Immunization
H. Common illnesses and first aid
I. Exercise/movement/relaxation

Birthing Room Orientation

Birth facilities that offer couples the opportunity to have their baby in an alternative birth center or a birthing room often have a special orientation class to emphasize the special features of the experience. Policies and procedures are explained, and a tour of the facility is provided. Classes may be described as follows:

Who: Expectant women anticipating a normal healthy birth and support persons who plan to be present during labor and birth.

What: A two-class series with discussion of policies and options, the roles of support persons, family responsibilities, and newborn care. A tour of the facilities and the opportunity to meet staff members are included. For those who desire, an individual session with a member of the staff can be arranged in order to review individual preferences for labor and birth, to determine postpartum visiting arrangements, and to answer questions.

When: The first and third Monday of each month from 7:00 to 9:00 P.M. The optional third session is made by individual arrangement.

Where: Birthing room or alternative birth center lounge area.

Cost: There is no cost to those planning on giving birth in the birthing room or alternative birth center.

Couples who wish to use the birthing room or alternative birth center should preregister by the 7th month of pregnancy and participate in the orientation series by the 8th month. Class size is often limited to 10 couples. Participation in a regular series of childbirth preparation classes or a refresher course is generally required for families using the birthing room or alternative birth center.

Mount Zion Hospital in San Francisco, California, has established the following orientation procedure for couples who wish to use the alternative birth center:

Class I: Tour of facilities, meet staff and other registrants, policies related to Alternative Birth Center

A. Meet in Center room if possible; create comfortable, relaxed setting.

B. Round-table introduction (reason for interest in center, other children, and types of delivery).

C. Purpose of Center:
   1. Provision of home-like atmosphere in safe environment for mother and infant, without regimentation and instrumentation, except as specified in the stated policies (I.V. if anemic). Family will remain as "one," and the newborn will not be separated from mother unless absolutely necessary.
   2. Review and discuss criteria for admission, high-risk conditions requiring move to labor and delivery, criteria for early discharge of mother and infant.

D. Informed consent: Explanation and signature.

E. Explain Family Summary/Preference Sheet and fill out [Exhibit 6-7].

F. Pass out birth certificate forms.

G. Tour of Alternative Birth Center, discuss individualized potential,

---

Exhibit 6-7 Alternative Birth Center Family Summary/Preference Sheet

The purpose of this form is to have on record necessary pertinent information concerning the mother's prenatal course, childbirth preparation and the family's individual plan, if any, for delivery and support aspects.

Names: _____   Obstetrician: _____
Address: _____   Pediatrician: _____
Mother's Birth Date: _____   Due Date: _____   Blood Type: _____
Other Children: _____   No. Pregnancies: _____   Feeding: Breast _____   Bottle _____
Medications other than vitamins: _____

Admission Criteria Check List: *Family Plan for Use of Center:*
_____ Obstetrician's form   Support person(s) _____
_____ Pediatrician's form
_____ Informed consent   Sibling participation (yes/no) _____
_____ Childbirth Education   Immediate rooming-in (yes/no) _____
        Method _____   Early discharge (yes/no) _____
_____ Mt. Zion orientation   Circumcision (yes/no) _____
_____ Prenatal record here   Antepartum Visit: _____
Preadmission (yes/no) _____   24-hour home visit _____
Insurance: _____   72-hr visit (home or ped. ofc) _____
_____   Pictures or films _____
Report of home visit and details of family plan (siblings, episiotomy, etc.)

Source: Reprinted with permission of Mt. Zion Hospital and Medical Center, San Francisco, California.

visit labor and delivery suite, newborn nursery, postpartum unit.

Class II: Roles, other children, breast care, postpartum care and policies

A. Introduce anyone not present in Class I. Summarize first session and respond to questions.
B. Discuss roles of support persons, nurse advocate, physicians (obstetrical and pediatric).
C. Discuss policies regarding participation of other children, reasonable number of persons present during labor, visitors, what to bring to hospital (small familiar objects, own sheets if desired, clean clothing, food).
D. Discuss prenatal breast care for those anticipating breastfeeding, having someone at home to help if early discharge is planned, postpartum visits by Center nurse, antepartum visit (optional).
E. Collect Family Summary/Preference Sheets and Birth Certificate Information.
F. Review signs of labor, whom to call and when to come to the hospital.
G. Refer to support groups in area.
H. Discuss infant care.

Class III: Antepartum Home Visit (Optional)

A. Purpose of this visit is to establish better individual rapport with participant, review individual preferences and family plan for the birth experience in the Center, assure postpartum arrangements.
B. Discuss any individual questions and review overall understanding of material from Classes I and II.[4]

4Reprinted with permission of Mt. Zion Hospital and Medical Center, San Francisco, California.

Birth Facility Tour and Orientation

A tour may be offered for expectant families that have not yet decided which birth facility they wish to use, have chosen not to attend childbirth classes, or have enrolled in refresher classes but are not familiar with the birth facility. Such a tour may be described as follows:

Who: Expectant parents and family members who anticipate giving birth at _____ Hospital (or birth center).
What: A tour of the labor, birth, nursery, and postpartum areas to familiarize families with our facilities. A discussion of hospital policies will also be included.
When: First and third Tuesdays of each month from 7:00 to 9:00 P.M. Second and fourth Saturdays of each month from 10:00 A.M. to 12:00 noon.

Those planning to tour should register at least 1 month prior to their baby's birth, as the number of participants may be limited.

The following is a sample tour itinerary:

1. introduction of staff
2. admission area and admission procedures
   • nursing station
   • labor room, e.g., how to work the bed, location of bathroom for father and other family members
   • parents' lounge
   • equipment, e.g., fetal monitor, intravenous apparatus, suction, blood pressure measurements
3. delivery area
   • equipment, including operation of delivery table, draping, positioning
   • policies concerning support person presence in delivery room
   • immediate care of newborn in delivery room, including family attachment
4. birthing center
   • policies and procedures

- explanation of equipment, e.g., operation of bed
- kitchen
- sibling area
- family lounge
5. recovery area
   - care
   - policy on presence of family members
6. admission nursery
   - care of newly born
   - transfer to mother's room or intermediate care nursery
7. intermediate nursery
   - daily care, including demand or scheduled feeding
   - rooming-in policies
   - care for jaundiced baby and other commonly used procedures, e.g., PKU testing
8. newborn intensive care
   - explanation of equipment and care
   - visitation policies
   - family support
9. postpartum
   - family-centered care policies
   - visiting for family members and friends
   - educational programs
   - discharge

Birth facility tours evoke many feelings in expectant parents—fear about hospitals, worry about the baby's health, and concerns about the treatment they should anticipate. The reality of the upcoming birth suddenly "hits home," and there are often questions that need to be answered. Therefore, tour groups should be kept small and an opportunity offered during the tour and afterwards to discuss couples' reactions and feelings.

Discussion Groups for Expectant Fathers

Fathers benefit from an opportunity to meet and talk with each other about their experiences during pregnancy and their changing roles and relationships. For fathers not inclined to become involved in discussion groups, birth facilities may offer an orientation class so that fathers can participate in family-centered options without attending a full series of classes. Increasingly, however, fathers are involving themselves in childbirth preparation, including discussion groups to prepare themselves for parenthood. Men experience a number of psychological and physical changes during pregnancy and are preparing at this time for the most mature role of their lives—just as their partners are.

Expectant father discussion groups may be described as follows:

Who: Expectant fathers.
What: The opportunity to meet and discuss with other men what it means to be preparing for fatherhood, a process that begins in the 1st weeks of pregnancy and increases in intensity during the 9 months of gestation.
When: 7:00 to 9:00 P.M. weekly for 4 weeks beginning the third Thursday of each month.

The following is an outline of the material usually covered in these discussion groups:

Session I
Goals
   To stimulate expectant fathers to be more aware of their developing role
   To enhance the couple's relationship
   To assist men in adjusting to a major life transition—a transition to a man's most mature role
Session II
Men are on a continuum between being partnered with a pregnant woman and being a "pregnant male"
Session III
Men's versus women's preparation for pregnancy

Session IV
Men in the American culture
Session V
The potential of men to be sensitive to the cues of infant children: to mother
Session VI
"Real" and ideal fathers
Session VII
Psychological adjustment during pregnancy for the male
Session VIII
The Couvade Syndrome and physical adjustment during pregnancy
Session IX
Men's motivations to fathering
   Changes in roles of fathers over recent decades
   Androgeny
Session X
Coping with pregnancy and getting the most from it.[5]

Sibling Classes

Hospital Get Acquainted Classes for Siblings

Classes for children of expectant parents give them an opportunity to feel more comfortable with the hospital setting, to become familiar with the visiting routine after birth, and to ask questions about the hospital and about becoming a brother or sister. Children may be divided into groups by age. Usually planned as a "fun" class, it often includes features such as a film, a party, and a hospital tour. Sibling classes for older children (8 to 15 years) may be scheduled in conjunction with expectant parents' classes, or parents may be asked to accompany their younger child (2½ to 7 years) during their get acquainted party and tour. Parents who accompany their children may need to be reminded that this is a children's class and they should not ask questions or otherwise detract from the children's experience.

---

[5]Reprinted with permission from Terry Jones, M.A., M.Ed., Portland, Oregon.

The following description applies to a typical hospital get acquainted class for siblings:

Who: Children between the ages of 2½ and 15 years whose families are expecting a baby.

What: A hospital tour and class for brothers-to-be and sisters-to-be. If other children in the family feel part of the experience of having a new brother or sister, their bonds with the expected baby will be strengthened both before and after the baby is born. A tour of the labor and birth areas, the postpartum floor, and the nursery are provided; special activities, including a film, are planned following the tour. Tour groups are divided into two age groups: ages 2½ and 7 years and ages 8 to 15 years.

When: From 6:30 to 8:30 P.M. during the fifth class of each expectant parent class series and during the third class for parents taking the refresher course. For children whose parents are not enrolled in classes, the sibling class is offered on the first Sunday afternoon of each month from 1:00 to 3:00 P.M.

The following class outline is not designed to prepare children for the birth itself, but to give children a reassuring introduction to the birth facility:

1. Children are greeted at the door, helped to put pediatric gowns over their clothes, and given a doctor's/nurse's scrub cap and mask to wear. Name tags are made and put on gowns. Explanations are given about what will happen.
2. Children go on tour; their parents may stay behind either to attend an expectant parents' class or to view a film and discuss sibling adjustments to the upcoming birth. An alternative format includes the parents in the birth facility tour. The tour includes labor rooms, birthing rooms, the babies (by using a step-up stool in front of the

nursery windows), a private room and semiprivate room on the postpartum floor, and the family meeting room where children visit their mother and the new baby after birth. If visitation occurs in the mother's room, this can be explained. Details are pointed out to the children, such as what babies look like (e.g., size, color) and how they behave (e.g., sleeping, crying).

3. A film such as "Nicholas and the Baby" or a slide series taken at the birth facility are shown. Slides have an advantage in that, after the tour, the environment looks very familiar and what was seen on tour is reinforced. Included in the slide series are the outside of the hospital; a mother and father being "checked into" the birthing room (or labor area); mother comfortably in bed; the new baby; father giving the first bath (Leboyer); baby being weighed; footprints being taken; Mom, Dad, and child with the new baby in the birthing room; several pictures of new babies; children visiting the nursery with a new toy that is put in the baby's bassinet by the nurse; children visiting their mother in her room; mother on the telephone to the child at home; family going home from the hospital; baby's bath at home; baby being diapered, sleeping, crying, feeding (breast and bottle); child holding baby securely. As pictures are shown, there is the opportunity for discussion about the hospital, sibling visits to the hospital, telephone calls, and what babies are like.

Each facility must determine the extent of orientation for children in its own program. For example, at Woman's Hospital in Houston, Texas, the tour also includes the fetal monitoring equipment, oxygen equipment, and fingerprinting. Children are offered the opportunity to taste infant formula. At Prentice Women's Hospital in Chicago, Illinois, children hear a recording of the fetal heartbeat.

Young children may listen to stories, color pictures, and learn to hold a baby (using a doll and supporting the head); they are encouraged to talk about their feelings and ideas about what it will be like to have a new baby in the family. Older children are also shown baby care, including safety, diapering, feeding, and holding. Because older children are verbal, increased emphasis is placed on discussion.

This get acquainted class is intended for children who will not be present for the birth but who will see the new baby soon afterwards. As such, it is designed as a reassuring peek at where the birth will probably take place, where the parents will be when the baby is born, where the baby will be, where they will visit, and what the new baby will be like. Complications such as cesarean birth or discussion of vaginal birth are not included because it complicates the children's program and is not the primary purpose of the get-acquainted session.

Volunteers can be used to aid the teaching staff. At Hampton General Hospital in Hampton, Virginia, the regularly scheduled nurse on duty fulfills this function, staying with the parents, showing the film (or slides), and answering parental questions. Volunteers are used as tour leaders and as helpers for handling "problem" children or helping them make trips to the bathroom, etc. The number of volunteers needed is determined by the size of the tour group, but at least two volunteers for 10 young children is a realistic number.

Children and their parents may gather together for refreshments after the session. Certificates may be awarded, buttons that say "I am a prepared brother or sister." distributed, and balloons given for participation. Children are reminded that they can bring a small, washable toy for the nursery nurse to place in the baby's bassinet (so they can give the new baby his or her first toy) and are told that the nurses look forward to seeing them again when their new brother or sister is born.[6]

Depending on the size of the group, two to six dolls will be needed and should include both boy and girl dolls and represent different ethnic groups. Buttons and certificates and balloons can

---

[6]The program discussed here was modeled after the sibling program offered at Hampton General Hospital, Hampton, Virginia.

be ordered. Several books can be purchased for use in class. Gift packs prepared by the nursery staff using items furnished as samples from companies (diapers and lotion) can be given to each child. Xeroxed coloring pictures and crayons (crayons can usually be contributed by volunteers) are used for younger children. Also needed is a supply of pediatric gowns in different sizes, doctors and nurses scrub hats, disposable masks for the children to keep, and name tags. Finally, slides or a film and the basic class script need to be available.

Children at Birth

Each couple must decide whether their older children are to be present at birth, during labor, or immediately after the baby is born based on their own values and on the policy of the birth facility. Part of the process, therefore, of educating children to be present at birth involves discussion with the parents. This may take place during birth facility orientation, during refresher classes, or in individual consultations. The parents must explore their own attitudes if their children are to be present at birth and to work out any differences of opinion that may exist between them. They must discuss, for example, whether they envision birth as an intimate matter or a family affair, whether they are comfortable with the mother's nudity in front of the children, whether they are willing to accept their child's behavior (which may not be ideal) during labor and birth, and whether the mother will feel she can express discomfort or verbalize pain in the presence of her children. If the child wants to be present, the parents must decide whether to include the child as an active participant during labor and birth (for example, fanning the mother, holding her hand, or giving her ice chips).

The child must have a support person whom the child knows and likes. The support person may stay at home at night with the child until labor accelerates or may take the child along with a sleeping bag and overnight things to the hospital. The support person sees that the child has books, games, and cards for amusement and that snacks are brought from home. The child is encouraged by the support person to come and go from the birthing area as desired.

Parents who want their children to be present at birth need to consider all these details carefully. A book such as *Birth Through Children's Eyes* (Van Dam Anderson & Simkin, 1981) can help parents understand more about children's experiences. Children can look at birth picture books with their parents and can be told that they may hear noises such as grunting and groaning, that their mother may make faces, that there will be blood, that stitches may be used, and how the baby will look (e.g., color, vernix, cord). Parents can practice breathing and relaxation in front of their children so that this will be familiar behavior.

Classes for children who are to be present at the birth of a sibling should be designed according to the age of the children, the number of children in the class, and the knowledge level of the children. These classes generally have the following components:

1. introduction
   - How old are the children?
   - Do they want a boy or a girl?
   - What names have been chosen for the baby?

2. assessment of child's knowledge base (Perez, 1979)

   - What does the child think will happen during labor . . . and birth?
   - What has the child done to prepare for the birth? Has the child seen any movies? What was the child's reaction?
   - Does it hurt to have a baby?
   - How does the baby get out of the mother's body?
   - What part of the baby comes first?
   - What does the mother look like when she is pushing the baby out?
   - Does the child want to be present when the baby is born?
   - What does the child want to do during birth: for example, help, watch?

3. information about labor process

- labor:

  Mom's uterus, inside her belly, feels like a big hard rock during labor. These are contractions. They help everything to open up inside so that the baby can come out. During labor these may hurt Mom some or make her feel not too good. Mom and Dad will have to breathe a special way, think, and work very hard. This is a time when everyone should try and be very quiet and still.

  Special jobs children can do at this time are getting ice or juice, helping time contractions, kissing and hugging their mother, fanning her.

  The doctor or nurse will check with their fingers the birth passage (where the baby is going to come out), called the vagina, to see if they can feel the baby's head. They put on special gloves so that no hand germs or dirt get on the baby or into Mom before the baby is born.

- pushing:

  Mom has to push the baby out of the birth passage. Her face may even get red. She may make funny noises because she is working so hard.

  Mom's water bag in which the baby swims might leak fluid, or the doctor may make a little hole in it to make the fluid come out a little faster.

- crowning:

  When the baby's head starts to peek out, it doesn't look like a baby's head at first. It looks like a bump of head (show picture). Mom may be blowing out while the baby's head is born, which sounds like someone blowing up a balloon. Everything happens fast now.

  It seems a little funny for everyone to be looking at Mom's naked bottom, but having a baby is a different kind of time. The nurses may wash Mom's bottom with a special soap that is washed off after the baby is born. The doctor or midwife may do an episiotomy, which is a cut to make Mom's birth passage bigger. This usually doesn't hurt Mom.

- birth and placenta:

  When the baby's head comes out, it may be very blue and still (show picture). The doctor will use a bulb syringe to suck the mucus out of the baby's nose and mouth.

  It is very important to dry the baby and keep the baby very warm. A heater will be put over the baby to help do this.

  The baby will get pink as soon as he/she starts to breathe. The baby may not cry right away.

  The baby's funny blue food cord is still attached to the baby's belly button and the other end is still inside Mom. This food cord has to be clamped and cut. This doesn't hurt the baby. Sometimes dads help do this. (Show picture of placenta or have a placenta for children to see.) Sometimes there is a little blood when the cord is cut and the placenta is delivered.

The nurse will put some purple medicine on the baby's cord near his/her belly. The baby goes home with the clamp and the cord. It will come off later when the cord falls off.

• episiotomy

Mom may have to be sewn where the birth passage was made bigger. The doctor or midwife will give Mom a shot to numb the area so it won't hurt her.

• holding the baby

You can wash your hands and then you'll be able to touch and hold your new brother or sister. He or she may cry— which is what babies do a lot of the time—or may look at you or may sleep.

• care of Mom and the baby

The nurse checks Mom's belly and the birth passage for bleeding. She also checks the baby.

The baby will be weighed and measured and drops may be put in baby's eyes an hour or two after birth.

Mom may breastfeed the baby now and everyone can take turns holding the baby.

4. Tour and a movie or slides

Visual aids needed during class include a doll that gives birth, a cord clamp, a real or play placenta, movie or slides, books to read, Doptone, dye used on the baby's cord, mucus trap and catheter, bulb syringe, and scissors.[7]

Grandparents Class

Grandparents are increasingly involved in family birth; they are often the support persons for children who are present for birth. Because the family-centered approach was not available when they became parents, they, too, need education about the options available to today's families and the philosophy behind family birthing experiences. For grandparents who may not be present for birth, preparation helps them to support the new family and to understand "how things are done today."

Grandparent classes may be described as follows:

Who: Expectant grandparents who will be with the family during birth or who want to learn more about contemporary childbirth classes.

What: A class that explains to grandparents about family-centered care, options available during childbirth for today's families, and the role of today's grandparents. A hospital tour and a film on family-centered childbirth are included.

When: 7:00 to 9:00 P.M. the third Thursday of each month.

---

[7]The class described here was modeled in part after the preparation classes offered at Providence Hospital's Family Birthing Center in Providence, Michigan.

The following is a typical outline for grandparent classes:

I. Opening
   A. Introduction and explanations of interest in attending the class
   B. Overview slides on family-centered care
   C. Discussion of options available to expectant families (e.g., birthing room, alternative birth center, preparation for childbirth, Leboyer birth, rooming-in)
   D. Father involvement during childbirth
   E. Changing role of grandparents as a result of mobility and retirement; importance of grandparent support of the new family unit

II. Tour
   A. Labor and birth areas: explanation of technology used during the birth process; emphasis on decreased technology in alternative birth center or birthing rooms; medications typically used; complications, including the reasons and management; policies related to family participation during labor and birth, including role of grandparents
   B. Nursery area: explanation of nursery care, including intensive care nursery, and family-centered options
   C. Postpartum area: family visitation policies, educational programs, discharge from birth facility

III. Wrap-up
   A. Refreshments
   B. Discussion of tour
   C. Normal newborn care, family attachment, feeding[8]

---

[8]This outline was modeled after the Grandparents' Program at Woman's Hospital in Houston, Texas.

Breastfeeding Class

Because breastfeeding is increasingly the chosen method of infant feeding, many educational programs are providing one or two sessions that deal exclusively with this topic. Breastfeeding instruction in the intrapartum period does not take the place of thorough antepartum instruction, when there is time for questions to be answered and for the expectant mother to develop self-confidence in her ability to breastfeed. The participation of fathers in breastfeeding classes is important, for fathers will be instrumental in providing support for their partners. With an increased understanding of the process involved, fathers will be able to help prevent problems and will feel more a participant in the feeding process.

Breastfeeding classes may be described as follows:

Who: Pregnant women who have chosen to breastfeed and their partners.

What: A two-class discussion group that will provide information about breastfeeding, including preparation during pregnancy, and that will help develop confidence in the ability to breastfeed. Sources of community support will be discussed.

When: The third and fourth Tuesday evening of each month from 7:00 to 8:30 P.M.

The following outline of a breastfeeding class is typical:

I. Introduction
   A. Experience of participants with breastfeeding (either personal, through observation, or what others have told them)
   B. Reasons for decision to breastfeed

II. Role of partner support

III. Advantages and disadvantages of breastfeeding

IV. Physiology of lactation

V. Preparation during pregnancy and breast care (washing, breast support, nipple toughening, nutrition)

VI. The art of breastfeeding, including nipple care, nursing time, nursing positions, burping, infant's growth, maternal nutrition, introduction of solids and supplementation

VII. Recognization and treatment of problems, including engorgement, sore nipples, inverted nipples, infection, medication, fatigue, maintenance of milk supply

VIII. Breastfeeding and couple relationships

IX. Weaning

X. Hospital and community sources of support for breastfeeding

Newborn Care and Consumerism

Families expecting their first baby can benefit from a short series of classes on newborn care. This may be offered late in pregnancy, usually the last month. Although preparation for childbirth classes may include information on newborn care, the time devoted to this topic is often limited because of the many other topics that must be covered.

The following is a typical description of a newborn care and consumerism class:

Who: Expectant families who want to learn basic baby care.
What: Class on caring for a new baby, including cardiopulmonary resuscitation; choosing a pediatric care provider; making purchases with consideration of cost, safety, and durability.
When: Wednesday evenings from 7:00 to 8:30 P.M. for two sessions beginning the third Wednesday of each month.

A typical class outline is as follows:

I. Introduction and overview

II. Choosing a pediatric care provider
   A. Questions to ask
   B. Referral sources
   C. Prenatal interview with chosen care provider
   D. Typical pediatric care

III. Choosing a method of feeding
   A. Breastfeeding: advantages, disadvantages, and preparation during pregnancy
   B. Bottle feeding: advantages, disadvantages, and preparation during pregnancy
   C. Combining the two approaches

IV. Immediate care of the newborn, including drying, warming, suctioning, vital signs, assessment, use of vitamin K, cord care, prophylactic eye ointment, Dextrostix, tests for metabolic dysfunction

V. Ongoing newborn care: rooming-in, feeding patterns, daily routine

VI. Infant care: bathing and diapering a newborn (demonstration and return demonstration)

VII. Getting to know your newborn baby: normal characteristics, parent-infant attachment behaviors, description (modified) of Brazelton assessment

VIII. Safety: baby-proofing the home, automobile safety, poison prevention

IX. Cardiopulmonary resuscitation (optional): discussion, demonstration, return demonstration[9]

Mother Support Classes

Although both parents benefit from postpartum parenting classes, the mother more often

[9]This outline was adapted in part from class content at Rose Medical Center, Denver, Colorado.

assumes the major responsibility for child care and is more likely to experience the frustrations and isolationism of parenting. Support groups are often informally organized through childbirth education parent groups; more and more frequently, birth facilities are offering a series of informal and ongoing discussion groups that are held during the day and to which babies are invited.

Support classes may be described as follows:

> *Who:* Mothers who have children between the ages of 1 week and 2 years.
> *What:* A support group for mothers who meet with a trained leader to discuss their concerns, to share ideas, and to learn baby crafts and activity and stimulation ideas.
> *When:* 10:00 A.M. to 11:00 A.M. the first Thursday of each month.

Class material is presented according to the expressed needs of participants. Although some specific activity or topic for discussion may be scheduled, the basic class format is informal. Rose Medical Center of Denver, Colorado, offers the following topics in its "Being a Mom" class:

1. discussion topics

   * motherhood
   * new baby
   * postpartum blues (emotional highs and lows)
   * birth experiences
   * special needs of cesarean mothers
   * changes in lifestyle: new family relationships, new responsibilities, other children at home, sexuality, isolation
   * going back to work

2. sharing ideas

   * baby care tips
   * shopping hints

   * babysitting cooperative
   * play groups
   * helpful books

3. baby craft activities

   * newborn mobile
   * play blocks
   * picture books
   * baby stimulation activities

LOGISTICS OF CHILDBIRTH EDUCATION CLASSES

The childbirth educator, in organizing classes and time, can enhance the learning experience for participants by

* limiting class size (usually to a maximum of 10 couples) to permit individualized instruction. A trained helper, who may be a teacher in training, an interested class graduate, or a student in the health care professions, can assist. The teacher must review the teaching plan with the helper and ensure that the helper knows how to demonstrate relaxation and breathing patterns effectively and how to help couples as they learn. A helper who is to serve as a group discussion leader should have group facilitation skills.
* having a well-developed outline of the content for the entire class series, with specific goals and objectives for each class session.
* being familiar with the subject matter so that the need to refer to notes is minimal.
* knowing the community resources available, the obstetrical care options available from various health providers, and the options available at community birth facilities.
* planning classes to avoid extended periods of sitting; alternating discussion with exercise, audiovisuals, breaks, and experiential activities.

- contacting each couple by telephone prior to the first class to answer any questions and to learn of any background information that may influence the pregnancy or birth experience (for example, whether one partner or the other has a child by a previous marriage).
- arriving well before each class session (at least ½ hour in advance) to greet couples and to provide an opportunity for a private conversation if a couple has personal questions or concerns.
- arranging the room to facilitate interaction among class participants. Often, couples bring bed rolls and pillows; in some cases, bean bags, mats, or comfortable chairs are available. A seating arrangement with couples in a circle on the floor or seated around a table may be conducive to discussion.
- learning couple names. Name tags worn each class session help everyone learn the names of other members. A list of participants (with telephone numbers and due dates) can be distributed during the first or second class session. The instructor's and helper's names and telephone numbers should also be included.
- emphasizing comfortable attire.
- explaining basic "rules" early in the first class (for example, no smoking, library checkout policies, availability of the teacher for private consultation, location of bathrooms).
- maintaining a class library with up-to-date written material at different levels of reading ability and written in languages spoken by class participants.
- providing each couple with a packet of materials:
  - summary of exercises, breathing, and relaxation
  - labor reports written by class graduates covering a variety of labor and birth experiences (including cesarean birth, vaginal birth after cesarean (VBAC),

  induced birth, birthing room birth, forceps birth)
  - information on infant products (e.g., car seats) and infant safety
  - summary of commonly used medications, including their uses and side effects
  - *The Pregnant Patient's Bill of Rights and the Pregnant Patient's Responsibilities* (ICEA, 1977)
  - selected resources, such as *Bonding— How Parents Become Attached to Their Baby* (Young, 1978), *Unnecessary Cesareans—Ways to Avoid Them* (Young & Mahan, 1980), *Humanizing Maternity Services Through Family-Centered Care* (McKay, 1982), *Labor and Birth—A Guide for You* (Todd, 1981), ICEA position papers on electronic fetal monitoring and ultrasound, and information sheets on issues of concern (e.g., newborn jaundice, circumcision).

Care should be taken not to overload packets with free literature provided by formula companies, whose subtle message is often aimed at getting parents to buy formula. All pamphlets should be carefully read and evaluated before distribution.

- providing a nutritional break. This not only encourages interaction among class participants, but also provides information about good nutrition. The teacher can bring snacks the first night; if the couples are financially able, the responsibility can then be rotated each session. Couples can be called on in class to explain why they chose the food they did and to describe its nutritional value (the teacher can help with this activity)
- keeping a record or journal to jot down notes about individuals and couples—their special learning needs and concerns they express that merit follow-up by the teacher or discussion with the couple's health care providers.

REFERENCES

Andrews, C. Changing fetal position. *Journal of Nurse-Midwifery*, 1980, *25*, 7-12.

Catano, J. *Teenage pregnancy: A resources kit*. Nova Scotia: Prepared Childbirth Association of Nova Scotia, 1979.

International Childbirth Education Association (ICEA). *The pregnant patient's bill of rights and the pregnant patient's responsibilities*. Minneapolis: The Association, 1977.

Interprofessional Task Force on Health Care of Women and Children. *Joint position statement of the development of family-centered newborn care in hospitals*. Chicago: The Task Force, 1978.

Lockhart, B. When couples adopt, they too need parenting classes. *The American Journal of Maternal Child Nursing*, 1982, *7*, 116-118.

McKay, S. *Humanizing maternity services through family-centered care*. Minneapolis: International Childbirth Education Association, 1982.

McKay, S. Second stage labor—Has tradition replaced safety? *American Journal of Nursing*, 1981, *81*, 1016-1019.

Noble, E. Controversies in maternal effort during labor and delivery. *Journal of Nurse-Midwifery*, 1981, *26*, 13-22.

Nurses Association of the American College of Obstetricians and Gynecologists. *Guidelines for Childbirth Education*. Washington, DC: The Association, 1981.

Perez, L. Nurturing children who attend the birth of a sibling. *American Journal of Nursing*, 1979, *4*, 215-217.

Todd, L. *Labor and birth: A guide for you*. Minneapolis: International Childbirth Education Association, 1981.

Van Dam Anderson, S., & Simkin, P. (Eds.). *Birth through children's eyes*. Seattle: Pennypress, 1981.

Young, D. *Bonding—How parents become attached to their baby*. Minneapolis: International Childbirth Education Association, 1978.

Young, D., & Mahan, C. *Unnecessary cesareans: Ways to avoid them*. Minneapolis: International Childbirth Education Association, 1980.

Appendix 6-A

Teaching Resources for Parent Educators

There is a wide variety of resources now available for childbirth educators, and their quality is excellent. For childbirth educators who are establishing classes and have limited financial resources, basic materials will be sufficient until other aids can be purchased or made. Basic materials include a pelvis and doll, the Maternity Center Association's pregnancy charts and *Birth Atlas* (both available in slide or poster format), and several basic books on the birth process. Many visual aids can be inexpensively constructed. The following is a list of useful resources and places where visual aids may be obtained.

Periodicals

American Baby
575 Lexington Avenue
New York, NY 10022

APRS Federal Monitor
Box 6358
Alexandria, VA 22306-0358

The American Journal of Maternal Child Nursing (MCN)
555 West 57th Street
New York, NY 10019

Birth, Issues in Perinatal Care and Education
110 El Camino Real
Berkeley, CA 94705

Briefs (from the Maternity Center Association, NYC)
Charles B. Slack, Inc.
6900 Grove Road
Thorofare, NJ 08086

Childbirth Educator
352 Evelyn Street
Paramus, NJ 07652

Genesis
1411 K Street, N.W.
Suite 200
Washington, DC 20005

ICEA News
P.O. Box 20048
Minneapolis, MN 55420

ICEA Review: Review of Current Perinatal Issues
P.O. Box 20048
Minneapolis, MN 55420

ICEA Sharing: Newsletter for Teachers
P.O. Box 20048
Minneapolis, MN 55420

Journal of Nurse Midwifery
Elsevier North Holland, Inc.
52 Vanderbilt Avenue
New York, NY 10017

JOGN Nursing
Medical Department
Harper & Row Publishers, Inc.
East Washington Square
Philadelphia, PA 19105

Mothering Magazine
Mothering Publications
P.O. Box 2208
Albuquerque, NM 87103

Perinatal Press
The Perinatal Center
Sutter Memorial Hospital
52nd and F Street
Sacramento, CA 95819

Practicing Midwife
156 Drakes Lane
Summertown, TN 38483

───────────── ∽　∾ ─────────────

Major Sources for Teaching Aids

Childbirth Graphics
P.O. Box 17025
Irondequoit Post Office
Rochester, NY 14167

Beautifully illustrated posters, slides, books, Jamie (A Birthing Doll), Maternity Center Association charts, Childbirth Picture Book Flip Chart, cloth pelvis model.

Educational and Scientific Plastics
Holmsthorpe
Redhill
Surrey RH 12 PF, England

Life-sized plastic female pelvis and other models.

International Childbirth Education
  Association (ICEA)
P.O. Box 20048
Minneapolis, MN 55420

Comprehensive audiovisual catalogue of movies, slide presentations, and videos, books, audiotapes.

Maternity Center Association
48 East 92nd Street
New York, NY 10028

Pattern for knitted uterus, pregnancy charts and slides, *Birth Atlas* charts and slides, literature.

Midwest Parentcraft Center, Inc.
627 Beaver Road
Glenview, IL 60025

Series of six laminated and mounted charts with life-sized uterus and baby depicting birth.

National Foundation March of Dimes
1275 Mamroneck Avenue
White Plains, NY 10605

Materials on nutrition, prenatal care. Many are available in Spanish. Local chapters often supply these materials.

Special Supplemental Food Program for
  Women, Infants, and Children (WIC)
U.S. Department of Agriculture
Food and Nutrition Service
Washington, DC 20250

Nutritional materials for use in Women, Infants, and Children (WIC) programs, publications list, materials on breastfeeding, nutrition and birth defects, infant nutrition.

U.S. Department of Health and Human
  Services
Administration for Children, Youth, and
  Families
P.O. Box 1182
Washington, DC 20013

Information on prenatal care, infant care, fathering, child development, one-parent families, automobile safety, child safety, child abuse, day care, and more.

U.S. Food and Drug Administration,
    Office of Consumer Affairs
Consumer Communications (HFE-88)
5600 Fisher Lane
Rockville, MD 20857

Materials on childbirth drugs, fetal monitoring, fetal health.

Suggested Books for Children

A Baby Sister for Frances by Russell Hoban
(New York, Harper & Row, 1964)

Berenstain Bears' New Baby by Stanley and
Janice Berenstain
(N.Y.C., Random House, 1974)

Big Brother Billy
(Kansas City, Mo., Hallmark Cards, 1977)

Billy and Our New Baby by Helene Arnstein
(New York, Human Sciences Press, 1973)

Go and Hush the Baby by Betsy Byars
(N.Y.C., Viking Press, 1971)

Hi, New Baby by Andrew Andry and Suzanne
Kratka
(New York, Simon & Schuster, 1970)

Hush, Jon! by Joan Gill
(Garden City, N.Y., Doubleday, 1968)

A New Baby by Terry Berger
(Milwaukee, Raintree Pubs., 1974)

A New Baby Is Coming to My House by
Chihiro Iwasaki
(N.Y.C., McGraw-Hill, 1970)

Nicky's Sister by Barbara Brenner
(N.Y.C., Alfred Knopf, Inc., 1966)

Nobody Asked Me If I Wanted a Baby Sister by
Martha Alexander
(New York, Dial Press, 1971)

On Mother's Lap by Ann Herbert Scott
(N.Y.C., McGraw-Hill, 1972)

Peggy's New Brother by Eleanor Schick
(New York, Macmillan, 1970)

Peter's Chair by Ezra Jack Keats
(New York, Harper & Row, 1967)

She Came Bringing Me That Little Baby Girl
by Eloise Greenfield
(Philadelphia, Lippincott, 1974)

Sometimes I'm Jealous by Jane Werner
Watson, Robert E. Switzer, and J. Cotter
Hirschberg
(Racine, Wisconsin, Golden Press, 1972)

Someone Small by Barbara Borack
(N.Y.C., Harper & Row, 1969)

That New Baby by Peggy Mann
(N.Y.C., Coward, McCann and Geoghegan,
Inc., 1967)

We Are Having a Baby by Vicki Holland
(New York, Scribner's, 1972)

Questionnaire on Family-Centered Maternity Care

Date _____

Facility Name: _____

Address: _____

_____

Phone: _____

Your Name: _____

I. *PHILOSOPHY:*

1. What is your Family-Centered Care philosophy statement?
   (Please attach to questionnaire if pre-printed.)

   _____

   _____

   _____

   _____

2. Does your facility have a planning committee for maternal and infant care services?

   _____

3. Are consumer representatives on this committee? _____

II. *PHYSICAL FACILITIES:*

1. Total number of facility beds _____
2. Annual birth census _____
3. Number of obstetrical beds _____

4. Types of accommodations?
   (Please check those which apply)   Yes   No   Cost/Day

   a. Diagnostic-Admitting Room for Labor
   b. Conventional Delivery Rooms
   c. Newborn Intensive Care Nursery
   d. Newborn Nursery
   e. Individual Labor Rooms
   f. Individual Labor Rooms with Windows
   g. Recovery Rooms
   h. Cesarean in Delivery Room
   i. Cesarean in Operating Room
   j. Family Waiting Room
   k. Early Labor Lounge
   l. Birth Room
      Please describe Birth Room briefly (i.e., Free-standing, Home-like, Labor Room Birth, located within the Labor and Delivery Unit). Approximate square footage, etc.

      _____
      _____
      _____
      _____
      _____
      _____

5. Was Birth Room(s) achieved through a conversion of existing room(s)?

   _____
   Renovation of existing space? _____
   New construction? _____

III. *SERVICES:*

Which of the following services do you provide?
(Please check those that apply):
1. Parent Education   Yes   No
   a. Childbirth Preparation
   b. Infant Care Education
   c Postpartum Education
   d. Parenting Education
   For those categories checked Yes, are the Parent Educators members of the Nursing staff?   Yes _____ No _____
   If No, who offers this education?

   _____

2. Family Participation   Yes   No
   a. Sibling visitation
      (1) in Labor
      (2) in Birth
      (3) in Postpartum
   b. Unlimited Visiting after Birth for
      father or chosen companion

3. Support   Yes   No
   a. During Labor
      (1) Father   _____   _____
      (2) Other Family Members   _____   _____
      (3) Friends   _____   _____
      (4) Monitrice   _____   _____
   b. During Birth
      (1) Father   _____   _____
      (2) Other Family Members   _____   _____
      (3) Friends   _____   _____
      (4) Monitrice   _____   _____
4. Early Discharge Policy
   a. 24 hours   _____   _____
   b. Between 24-48 hours   _____   _____
   c. 72 hours or more   _____   _____
5. Follow-up Home Visits by (Please designate) _____
6. Cesarean Birth   Yes   No
   a. Fathers present at Cesarean Birth   _____   _____
   b. Fathers present in Recovery Room   _____   _____
7. Infant Care
   a. Infant Feeding
      (1) Breastfeeding:
         —within 0-15" of life   _____   _____
         —within 15-45" of life   _____   _____
         —after one hour of life   _____   _____
         —after two hours of life   _____   _____
      (2) Feeding on Demand   _____   _____
   b. Eye Prophylaxis
      (1) withheld for one hour post birth   _____   _____
   c. Parent-infant Contact
      (1) immediately after birth   _____   _____
      (2) within one hour after birth   _____   _____
      (3) 2 hours after birth   _____   _____
   d. Newborn Evaluation at Mother's Bed   _____   _____
8. High-Risk Care (if applicable)   _____   _____
   a. Please indicate approximate percent
      of obstetrical population defined
      as "high risk" _____
   b. Has your facility been designated, or does it anticipate perinatal level designation as a:
      Level III facility? _____
      Level II facility? _____
      Level I   facility? _____
   c. For the obstetrical population defined as "high risk", do visitation policies in antepartum
      hospitalization include:
                                Yes   No
      (1) Father may visit   _____   _____
      (2) Family members may visit   _____   _____
      (3) Friends may visit   _____   _____
      (4) Children may visit   _____   _____

	Yes	No
visitation policies in NICU include:		
(1) Father may visit	____	____
(2) Family members may visit	____	____
(3) Friends may visit	____	____
(4) Children may visit	____	____

(5) Are there any restrictions on who may hold the newborn in the NICU?

If Yes, please clarify _____

IV. *NURSING STAFF:*

	Yes	No
1. How do you staff?		
a. R.N.s	____	____
b. C.N.M.s	____	____
c. L.V.N./L.P.N.	____	____
d. Nursing Assistants	____	____
e. Clinical Nurse Specialists	____	____
f. Other (Please specify)	____	____

_____

2. Education
Do you provide?

	Yes	No
a. Staff Orientation to FCM/NC Practice	____	____
b. In-service education in FCM/NC	____	____

3. Apparel
Do nursing personnel wear:

	Yes	No
a. Scrub gowns	____	____
b. Nursing uniforms	____	____
c. Street Clothes	____	____

d. Other (designate) _____

V. *INFECTION CONTROL:*

	Yes	No
1. Do you have an infection control committee?	____	____
2. Do you have follow-up to detect morbidity for mothers and babies?		
a. by one month post delivery	____	____
b. by three months post delivery	____	____
3. Is there a separate housekeeping protocol for the birth room(s)?	____	____
4. Has infection rate for the obstetrical department been impacted upon since implementation of birth room(s)?		
a. Increase	____	____
b. Decrease	____	____
c. No change	____	____

VI. *PROTOCOL:*

If available, please provide us with a copy of your:
    (1) written protocols for FCM/NC
    (2) written policies for FCM/NC implementation
    (3) charges for services

Thank you for expending the time and energy to complete this survey. Would you like to receive a copy of the Manual on Implementation Strategies for Family-Centered Maternity/Newborn Care? _____ Yes _____ No
Are you willing to have an on site visit? _____ Yes _____ No
Contact person for visit _____

Thank you.

Questionnaire Respondents

ALABAMA
*Brookwood Hospital
Box 5891
Birmingham, Alabama 35209

Caraway Methodist Medical Center
1615 N. 25th Street
Birmingham, Alabama 35234

*University of Alabama Midwifery Program
University of Alabama Hospital
619 S. 19th Street
Birmingham, Alabama 35233

ALASKA
Alternative Birthing Center (ABC)
3300 Providence Drive, Suite 212
Anchorage, Alaska 99504

ARIZONA
Health Science Center
University of Arizona Hospital
8 East 1501 N. Campbell
Tucson, Arizona 85724

*Phoenix Memorial Hospital Birthing Center
1201 S. 7th Avenue
Phoenix, Arizona 85007

*St. Joseph's Hospital and Medical Center
P.O. Box 2071
Phoenix, Arizona 85001

Tucson Medical Center
Grant and Beverly
(Box 42195)
Tucson, Arizona 86712

ARKANSAS
Johnson County Hospital
1100 Poplar
Clarksville, Arkansas 72830

CALIFORNIA
Mendocino Coast Hospital
700 River Drive
Fort Bragg, California 95437

Merced Community Medical Center
301 East 13th Street
Merced, California 94530

Mercy Hospital and Medical Center
4077 Fifth Avenue
San Diego, California 92103

*Perinatal Center
Sutter Memorial Hospital
52nd and F Streets
Sacramento, California 95819

---

*Facility selected for site visit.

221

*Santa Cruz Community Hospital
600 Frederick Street
Santa Cruz, California 95060

Stanford University Hospital
300 Pasteur Drive
Stanford, California 94305

CANADA
Victoria Hospital
London, Ontario

COLORADO
*The Denver Birth Center
1601 Milwaukee Street, Suite 307
Denver, Colorado 80111

*Rose Medical Center
4567 E. Ninth Avenue
Denver, Colorado 80220

CONNECTICUT
*Manchester Memorial Hospital
Manchester, Connecticut 06040

FLORIDA
Baptist Hospital of Miami
8900 N. Kendall Drive
Miami, Florida 33176

Birth Place
635 North East 1st Street
Gainesville, Florida 32601

HAWAII
*Queens Medical Center
1301 Punchbowl Street
Honolulu, Hawaii 96813

IDAHO
The Family Medical Center
8th and Sherman
Pocatello, Idaho 83201

St. Luke's Regional Medical Center
190 East Bannock Street
Boise, Idaho 83702

ILLINOIS
Doctors Hospital
17 Country Club Court
Harrisburg, Illinois 62946

*Hinsdale Sanitarium and Hospital
120 North Oak Street
Hinsdale, Illinois 60521

*Illinois Masonic Hospital
836 W. Wellington Ave.
Chicago, Illinois 60657

Michael Reese Hospital and Medical Center
26th and Ellis Streets
Chicago, Illinois 60616

Ottawa Community Hospital
1100 East Norris Drive
Ottawa, Illinois 61350

*Prentice Women's Hospital and Maternity
  Center
333 E. Superior
Chicago, Illinois 60611

IOWA
St. Luke's Methodist Hospital
1026 A. Avenue, N.E.
Cedar Rapids, Iowa 52402

University of Iowa
Newton Road
Iowa City, Iowa 52242

KANSAS
Hadley Regional Medical Center
201 East Seventh
Hays, Kansas 67601

Suburban Medical Center
P.O. Box 5959
10500 Quivira Road
Overland Park, Kansas 66215

KENTUCKY
Baptist Hospital East
4000 Kresge Way
Louisville, Kentucky 40207

Saint Anthony Hospital
113 Saint Anthony Place
Louisville, Kentucky 40204

Woodford Memorial Hospital
360 Amsden Avenue
Versailles, Kentucky 40383

MARYLAND
St. Joseph Hospital
7620 York Road
Towson, Maryland 21204

Washington Adventist Hospital
7600 Carroll Ave.
Takoma Park, Maryland 20012

MASSACHUSETTS
Cape Cod Hospital
Park St.
Hyannis, Massachusetts 02601

Family Health Center
1 West Street
Barre, Massachusetts 01005

St. Vincent's Hospital
Winthrop Street
Worcester, Massachusetts 01604

*Newton-Wellesley Hospital
2014 Washington Street
Newton Lower Falls, Massachusetts 02162

*Worcester Hahnemann Hospital
Lincoln Street
Worcester, Massachusetts 01605

MICHIGAN
Family Birth Center
Providence Hospital
16001 West Nine Mile Road
Southfield, Michigan 48075

Iron County General Hospital
Iron River, Michigan 49935

*Providence Hospital and Family Birth Center
16001 West Nine Mile Road
Southfield, Michigan 48075

*St. Lawrence Hospital
1210 W. Saginaw Street
Lansing, Michigan 48914

*Lansing General Hospital, Osteopathic
2800 Devonshire
Lansing, Michigan 48909

MINNESOTA
*Fairview Community Hospital
2312 South Sixth Street
Minneapolis, Minnesota 55454

*Hennepin County Medical Center
701 Park Avenue South
Minneapolis, Minnesota 55415

MISSISSIPPI
Mississippi Baptist Hospital
1190 N. State Street
Jackson, Mississippi 39201

MONTANA
Missoula Community Hospital
2827 Ft. Missoula Road
Missoula, Montana 59081

NEW JERSEY
The Childbirth Center
291 S. Van Brunt Street
Englewood, New Jersey 07631

Family Born, A Center for Birth and
 Women's Health
2688 State Highway 27
New Brunswick, New Jersey 08902

NEW MEXICO
Southwest Maternity Center
321 Sandia Road, N.W.
Albuquerque, New Mexico 87107

NEW YORK
Bellevue Maternity Hospital
P.O. Box 1030
2210 Troy Road
Schenectady, New York 12301

*Maternity Center Association
48 E. 92nd Street
New York, New York 10028

NORTH DAKOTA
St. Joseph's Hospital
3rd Street, S.E. & Burdick Expressway
Minot, North Dakota 58701

OHIO
Clinton Memorial Hospital
610 West Main Street
Wilmington, Ohio 45177

*Home-like Birth Center
Booth Memorial Hospital
1881 Torbenson Drive
Cleveland, Ohio 44112

Toledo Hospital
2142 N. Cove Boulevard
Toledo, Ohio

OKLAHOMA
Birth Center
1117 N. Shartel #200
Oklahoma City, Oklahoma 73103

*Hillcrest Medical Center
1120 S. Utica Avenue
Tulsa, Oklahoma 74104

OREGON
Forest Grove Community Hospital
1809 Maple Street
Forest Grove, Oregon 97116

Good Samaritan Hospital
1015 N.W. 22nd
Portland, Oregon 97210

Rogue Valley Memorial Hospital
2825 Barnett Road
Medford, Oregon 97501

PENNSYLVANIA
Conemaugh Valley Memorial Hospital
1086 Franklin Street
Johnstown, Pennsylvania 15905

*Booth Maternity Center
6051 Overbrook Drive
Philadelphia, Pennsylvania 19131

RHODE ISLAND
*New Beginnings, Inc.
Toll Gate Road
Warwick, Rhode Island 02886

TENNESSEE
Nashville General Hospital
72 Hermitage Avenue
Nashville, Tennessee 37210

TEXAS
Maternity Center
1119 E. San Antonio
El Paso, Texas 79901

*Woman's Hospital of Texas
7600 Fannin Street
Houston, Texas 79901

UTAH
*University Hospital Medical Center
50 North Medical Drive
Salt Lake City, Utah 84132

VIRGINIA
Alexandria Hospital
4320 Seminary Road
Alexandria, Virginia 22304

Community Hospital of Roanoke Valley
101 Elm Avenue, S.E.
Roanoke, Virginia 24013

*Hampton General Hospital
3120 Victoria Boulevard
Hampton, Virginia 23669

Henrico Doctor's Hospital
1602 Skipwith Road
Richmond, Virginia 23229

*Riverside Hospital
J. Clyde Morris Boulevard
Newport News, Virginia 23601

WASHINGTON
Birth Place
4708 Aurora Avenue, North
Seattle, Washington 98103

WEST VIRGINIA
Birth Center—Woman's Health Center of
  West VA
3418 Staunton Avenue, S.E.
Charleston, West Virginia 25304

West Virginia University Medical Center
Morgantown, West Virginia 26505

Responses from 64 Hospitals to Questionnaire on Family-Centered Maternity Care

SUMMARY

Although 58% of the facilities had a planning committee for maternal and infant care services, only 12% had consumer representatives on their planning committees. Few had representatives on an ongoing basis.

In 77% of facilities, there were no early labor lounges.

Fifty-six facilities (88%) had at least one birthing room (most located in labor and delivery units), and 72% of these birthing rooms were conversions of existing space.

Although 86% reported sibling visitation, only 34% reported sibling visitation during labor; 23%, at birth. The largest percentage of sibling visitation occurred postpartum (86%).

All the respondents had the father as support person for labor and birth. Family and friends could be support persons during labor in 81%, but this percentage dropped to 73% during birth.

Early discharge (under 48 hours) is permitted in 73%; home follow-up visits are made in 14%.

Newborn evaluation at mother's bedside was reported by 72%.

In neonatal intensive care units, 40% of facilities reported children's visits; 31% friends' visits. Fathers may visit in the neonatal intensive care unit in 73%; family members, in 63%.

Clothing worn in birthing rooms was 92% scrub clothes, 36% uniforms, and 11% street clothes (percentages don't add up to 100 percent because some people marked more than one item).

Follow-up to detect morbidity in mothers and babies was reported in 55% of hospitals, although all had an infection control committee. Most of those without formalized follow-up cited "medical checks" or "routine physician visits."

All the respondents noted that their facility infection rate had not increased since implementation of birthing rooms.

QUESTIONNAIRE RESPONSES

I.   PHILOSOPHY
1.   What is your Family-Centered Care philosophy statement?

     to provide "alternatives"
     to provide "individualized care"
     to provide "holistic care"
     to provide "home-like" environment
         Birth is a "normal" process. There was frequent mention of "positive experience," the "team," "support," shared experience, involving family members, a unique and safe birth, normal healthy process, family unit, family as basic unit of society,

and nonseparation of mother and baby.

2. Does your facility have a planning committee for maternal and infant care services?

Yes   37   (58%)
No   27   (42%)

II. PHYSICAL FACILITIES
1. Total number of facility beds:

Range = 4 to 800 –900
Average number of facility beds = 330
Distribution:

0– 29	7	230–259	2
30– 59	6	260–289	2
60– 89	2	290–319	2
90–119	1	320–349	0
120–149	3	350–369	5
150–169	1	370–399	1
170–199	2	400–450	11
200–229	2	over 450	17

2. Annual birth census:

Range = 48 to 5,000
Average birth census = 1,939

No answer	3
0– 250	5
251– 500	5
501– 750	6
751–1,000	4
1,001–1,250	4
1,251–1,500	4
1,501–1,750	4
1,751–2,000	5
2,251–2,500	8
2,501–2,750	2
2,751–3,000	4
over 3,000	10

3. Number of obstetrical beds:

Range = 8 to 96
Average = 31
Distribution:

No answer	2
0– 10	12
11– 20	8
21– 30	13
31– 40	12
41– 50	6
51– 60	5
61– 70	4

71– 80	1
81– 90	0
91–100	1

4. Types of accommodations?

a. Diagnostic-Admitting Room for Labor

Yes   28   (44%)
No   36   (56%)

(Only three respondents gave cost per day figures. Average cost was $29.00 per use.)

b. Conventional Delivery Rooms

Yes   61   (95%)
No   3   (5%)

(22 respondents gave cost per day figures. Average cost was $222.06.)

c. Newborn Intensive Care Nursery

Yes   39   (61%)
No   25   (39%)

(11 respondents gave cost per day figures. Average cost was $250.00.)

d. Newborn Nursery

Yes   64   (100%)
No   0   (0%)

(18 respondents gave cost per day figures. Average cost was $84.51.)

e. Individual Labor Rooms

Yes   56   (88%)
No   8   (12%)

f. Individual Labor Rooms with Windows

Yes   38   (59%)
No   26   (41%)

g. Recovery Rooms

Yes   41   (64%)
No   23   (36%)

(9 responses to cost ranged from $7.00 per hour to $40.00 per hour or from $16.00 per usage to $135.00 per usage.)

h. Cesarean in Delivery Room

Yes   41   (64%)
No   23   (36%)

(10 responses to room cost. Average cost was $274.82.)

i. Cesarean in Operating Room

Yes   28   (44%)
No   36   (56%)

j. Family Waiting Room

Yes   60   (94%)
No   4   (6%)

k. Early Labor Lounge

Yes   15   (23%)
No   49   (77%)

l. Birth Room

Yes   56   (88%)
No   8   (12%)

Description of Birth Rooms:

Located on postpartum
  unit: 6   (9%)
Located in Labor and
  Delivery unit: 32   (60%)
Did not identify location: 16   (30%)
Used words "home-
  like" in description: 20   (38%)
Facility with one
  Birth Room: 30
Facility with two
  Birth Rooms: 8

Facility with three
  Birth Rooms: 3
Facility with four
  Birth Rooms: 1

Sizes of rooms given:

9 × 9	1	12 × 17	1	182 sq ft	1	250 sq ft	1
8 × 11	1	14 × 17	1	196 sq ft	1	260 sq ft	1
10 × 12	1	15 × 17	1	210 sq ft	1	337 sq ft	1
10 × 14	1	22 × 20	1	228 sq ft	1	3900 sq ft	1
12 × 14	1	150 sq ft	1	234 sq ft	1		

Responses to request for description of Birth Room included the following:

- At Hampton General Hospital, Hampton, Virginia, all labor rooms are used as birthing rooms. There are three private and two semiprivate, size is 8 × 10 ft.
- At Family Hospital, Milwaukee, Wisconsin, birthing rooms are used for all but complicated births.
- At the University of Utah, there are four labor and birth rooms for all births.
- At Rose Medical Center, Denver, Colorado, any labor room can be used for delivery (18 × 15).
- At Sutter Memorial Hospital in Sacramento, California, there can be labor room birth in any of the labor rooms.

5. Was Birth Room(s) achieved through a conversion of existing room(s)?
No answer 8
Yes   46   (72%)
No   2   (3%)
New construction?
Yes   3
Underway 2
No   29
(Average cost of 24-hour alternative birth room stay was $543.58, where $n = 17$.)
Responses to question on renovation included the following:

- "We turned our utility room into the birthing room."
- "Converted 2 bed p.p. rms. to single bed birth rooms."

- "Former O.R. and recovery rooms."
- "Remodeled old L&D room and closet space adjacent to it."
- "2 p.p. rooms converted."
- "Converted nursery space for transitional nursery."
- "Converted private size patient room."
- "Renovated D.R."
- "Used nursery space."
- "New hospital."
- "Conversion of two labor rooms to two birth rooms."
- "It was our second delivery room."
- "Redecorated and furnished existing labor room."
- "Have two suites, will expand to four suites in the future."
- "Three patient rooms were utilized—loss of seven beds to make three birth rooms."
- "Conversion of two postpartum rooms."
- "Was formerly used as an anesthesiologists' sleeping room."
- "Converted semi-private room on post partum."
- "Birth room is a converted two bathroom labor room."

III. SERVICES
1. Parent Education
   a. Childbirth Preparation
      Yes   52   (81%)
      No   12   (19%)
   b. Infant Care Education
      Yes   56   (88%)
      No   8   (12%)
   c. Postpartum Education
      Yes   56   (88%)
      No   8   (12%)
   d. Parenting Education
      Yes   36   (56%)
      No   28   (44%)

For those categories checked "Yes," are the Parent Educators members of the nursing staff?
      Yes   60   (94%)
      No   4   (6%)
(Yes *and* No were checked 60% of the time.)

In response to who offers this education:

- "CEA." [Childbirth Education Association]
- "Also there are Lamaze and Bradley childbirth educators who are not employed by the hospital."
- "City Health Dept. P.H.N.'s."
- "Most are OB nurses, one RN Lamaze instructor is employed by Education Dept."
- "Community offers parenting classes."
- "ASPO certified."
- "Nursing staff and contracted individuals. (We have 19 childbirth educators. Most are ASPO certified.)"
- "Lamaze Instructors are ASPO or ICEA certified. Staff is involved in teaching some classes."
- "A childbirth ed. group sponsors classes. I teach and have two 'lay' teachers."
- "Three are staff nurses, Bradley educator, one is a 'lay' instructor."
- "Supplemented by some additional persons: MD's, developmental psychologists on certain occasions."
- "RN's, social worker, dietician."
- "Nurse-midwives, instructor from School of Nursing (CEA prepared), and part time nurse for patient education only in outpatient clinic."
- "Some are individually hired instructors who do nothing but teach prenatal classes."

2. Family Participation
   a. Sibling Visitation
         Yes   55   (86%)
         No   9   (14%)
      1) In labor
         Yes   22   (34%)
         No   42   (66%)
      2) In birth
         Yes   15   (23%)
         No   44   (69%)
         No answer 5   (8%)
            (5 only in ABC)

3) In postpartum
    Yes 55 (86%)
    No   9 (14%)
b. Unlimited Visiting after Birth for Father
   or Chosen Companion
    Yes 64 (100%)
    No   0 (0%)

3. Support
  a. During Labor
    1) Father
      Yes 64 (100%)
      No   0 (0%)
    2) Other Family Members
      Yes 52 (81%)
      No 12 (19%)
    3) Friends
      Yes 52 (81%)
      No 12 (19%)
    4) Monitrices
      Yes 39 (61%)
      No 14 (22%)
      No answer 11 (17%)
  b. During Birth
    1) Father
      Yes 64 (100%)
      No   0 (0%)
    2) Other Family Members
      Yes 47 (73%)
      No 17 (27%)
    3) Friends
      Yes 47 (73%)
      No 17 (27%)
    4) Monitrice
      Yes 39 (61%)
      No 17 (27%)
      No answer 8 (12%)

4. Early Discharge Policy
  a. 24 hours
    Yes 47 (73%)
    No 17 (27%)
  b. Between 24 and 48 Hours
    Yes 47 (73%)
    No 17 (27%)
  c. 72 Hours or More
    Yes 59 (92%)
    No   5 (8%)

5. Follow-up Home Visits
    Yes   9 (14%)
    No 39 (61%)
    No answer 16 (25%)
  Please designate by whom (home visits): Public Health Nurses primarily and then hospital nurses.

6. Cesarean Birth
  a. Fathers Present at Cesarean Birth
    Yes 58 (91%)
    No   6 (9%)
  b. Fathers Present in Recovery Room
    Yes 52 (81%)
    No 12 (19%)

7. Infant Care
  a. Infant Feeding
    1) Breastfeeding:
      —within 0 to 15 minutes of life:
      Yes, 58 (91%); No, 6 (9%)
      —within 15 to 45 minutes of life: Yes 100%
      —after one hour of life: Yes, 100%
      —after two hours of life: Yes, 100%
    2) Feeding on demand: Yes, 100%
  b. Eye Prophylaxis withheld for one hour post birth
    Yes 54 (84%)
    No 10 (16%)

  Reasons given for not withholding eye prophylaxis included ''State law'' and ''Regulations.''
  c. Parent-Infant Contact
    1) Immediately after birth
      Yes 63 (98%)
      No   1 (2%)
    2) Within one hour after birth
      Yes 36 (56%)
      No   2 (3)
    3) Two hours after birth
      Yes 30 (47%)
      No   4 (6%)
  d. Newborn Evaluation at Mother's Bed
    Yes 46 (72%)
    No 18 (28%)

8. High-Risk Care (if applicable)
   a. Please indicate approximate percent of obstetrical population defined as "high risk".

Percent	No. of Facilities	Percent	No. of Facilities
5–10	4	40.6	1
15	1	50	11
20	3	60	11
24	6	69	11
29	1	76	11
30	3	80	11
35	1		

   b. Has your facility been designated, or does it anticipate perinatal level designation as:

Level	Yes	
III	19	(30%)
II	29	(45%)
I	12	(19%)
No answer	4	(6%)

   c. For the obstetrical population defined as "high risk," do visitation policies in antepartum hospitalization include:
   1) Father may visit
      Yes 58 (100%)
      No   0 (0%)
   2) Family members may visit
      Yes 58 (100%)
      No   0 (0%)
   3) Friends may visit
      Yes 53 (91%)
      No   5 (9%)
   4) Children may visit
      Yes 46 (79%)
      No   12 (21%)
   Visitation policies in NICU include:
   1) Father may visit
      Yes 43 (73%)
      No   16 (27%)
   2) Family members may visit
      Yes 27 (63%)
      No   16 (37%)
   3) Friends may visit
      Yes 14 (31%)
      No   31 (69%)
   4) Children may visit
      Yes 17 (40%)
      No   26 (60%)
   5) Are there any restrictions on who may hold the newborn in the NICU?

Yes 34 (81%)
No   8 (19%)
If yes, please clarify:
   1. Parents and grandparents
   2. Parents only

IV. NURSING STAFF
1. How do you staff?
   a. RNs
      Yes 64 (100%)
      No   0 (0%)
   b. CNMs
      Yes 16 (25%)
      No   48 (75%)
   c. LVN/LPN
      Yes 53 (83%)
      No   11 (17%)
   d. Nursing Assistants
      Yes 43 (67%)
      No   21 (33%)
   e. Clinical Nurse Specialists
      Yes 23 (36%)
      No   41 (64%)
   f. Other: Scrub Techs., OB Techs.

2. Education
   a. Staff Orientation to FCM/NC Practice?
      Yes 62 (97%)
      No   2 (3%)
   b. In-Service Education in FCM/NC?
      Yes 62 (97%)
      No   2 (3%)

3. Apparel
   a. Scrub Gowns
      Yes 59 (92%)
      No   3 (8%)
   b. Nursing Uniforms
      Yes 23 (36%)
      No   24 (38%)
   c. Street Clothes
      Yes   7 (11%)
      No   35 (55%)

V. INFECTION CONTROL
1. Do you have an infection control committee?
      Yes 64 (100%)
      No   0 (0%)

2. Do you have follow-up to detect morbidity for mothers and babies?

> Yes   35   (55%)
> No   29   (45%)

a. By One Month Post Delivery

> Yes   21   (33%)
> No   20   (31%)
> No answer   23   (36%)

b. By Three Months Post Delivery

> Yes   18   (28%)
> No   23   (36%)
> No answer   23   (36%)

3. Is there a separate housekeeping protocol for the birth room(s)?

> Yes   33   (52%)
> No   23   (36%)

4. Has infection rate for the obstetrical department been impacted upon since implementation of birth room(s)?

a. Increase

> Yes   0   (0%)
> No   56   (88%)

b. Decrease

> Yes   3   (5%)
> No   53   (83%)

c. No change

> Yes   46   (72%)
> No   5   (8%)

d. No answer   5   (8%)

Family Birthing Center, Providence Hospital, Southfield, Michigan, reported 0 newborn infections and 1 maternal infection in 500 births.

Birth Centers' Answers to Questionnaire on Family-Centered Maternity Care

SUMMARY

All but three of the birth centers utilized the services of certified nurse-midwives (79%).

Service "packages" were offered; they included prenatal care, education (classes), labor and birth care, postpartum stay averaging 12 to 24 hours, two home visits after birth, and two visits back to the center. Costs of these service "packages" averaged $1,000.

There were no restrictions on visitors and activities. There was no change in the infection rate; in fact, there were two reported "possible decreases" in infection in the birth centers.

It is interesting to note that most of the birth centers (free-standing) have opened within the past 5 years.

QUESTIONNAIRE RESPONSES

I. PHILOSOPHY
1. The philosophies spoke of the birth centers' offering safe, comfortable, and homelike places for birth. They emphasized families having control over their birth experiences.
2. Does your facility have a planning committee for maternal and infant care services?

Yes	6	(43%)
No	8	(57%)

3. Are consumer representatives on this committee?

Yes	6	(43%)
No	8	(57%)

II. PHYSICAL FACILITIES
1. Total number of facility beds?

Average = 3

2. Annual birth census?

Average = 210

(The Maternity Center at El Paso reported 1,980 as annual census. This number was not included in averaging.)

3. Number of obstetrical beds?

Average = 3

4. Most of the questions about accommodations did not pertain to the out-of-hospital birth centers.

Birth centers were all described as "homelike" and were located in

- "Three-bedroom home with attached apartment which is our clinic."

- "Unused wing of our affiliate hospital (leased from the hospital)."
- "Renovated part of a medical office building."
- "Free-standing birth center."
- "A professional building."
- "A medical office building."
- "A renovated townhouse."

- "An old house."
- "A three-bedroom house."
- "A large apartment."
- "An older home (1920 vintage)."
- "Leased professional offices adjacent to Women's Health Center."
- "An old house."
- "A two-bedroom house."

Joint Position Statement on the Development of Family-Centered Maternity/Newborn Care in Hospitals

Preamble

The Interprofessional Task Force on Health Care of Women and Children endorses the concept of family-centered maternity care as an acceptable approach to maternal/newborn care. The Task Force believes it would be beneficial to offer further comment and guidance to facilitate the implementation of such care. To this end, the organizations constituting the Task Force have participated in a multidisciplinary effort to develop a joint statement regarding the rationale behind and the practical implementation of family-centered maternity/newborn care. The effort has resulted in the development of this document, which the parent organizations believe can be helpful to those institutions considering or already implementing such programs. A description of potential components of family-centered maternity/newborn care is presented to assist implementation as judged appropriate at the local level.

Definition: Family-Centered Maternity/ Newborn Care

Family-centered maternity/newborn care can be defined as the delivery of safe, quality health care while recognizing, focusing on, and adapting to both the physical and psychosocial needs of the client-patient, the family, and the newly born. The emphasis is on the provision of maternity/newborn health care which fosters family unity while maintaining physical safety.

Position Statement

The Task Force organizations, The American College of Obstetricians and Gynecologists, the American College of Nurse-Midwives, The Nurses Association of The American College of Obstetricians and Gynecologists, the American Academy of Pediatrics, and the American Nurses' Association, endorse the philosophy of family-centered maternity/newborn care. The development of this conviction is based upon a recognition that health includes not only physical dimensions, but social, economic and psychologic dimensions as well. Therefore, health care delivery, to be effective and satisfying for providers and the community alike, does well to acknowledge all these dimensions by adhering to the following philosophy:

- That the family is the basic unit of society;
- That the family is viewed as a whole unit within which each member is an individual enjoying recognition and entitled to consideration;
- That childbearing and childrearing are unique and important functions of the family;

235

- That childbearing is an experience that is appropriate and beneficial for the family to share as a unit;
- That childbearing is a developmental opportunity and/or a situational crisis, during which the family members benefit from the supporting solidarity of the family unit.

To this end, the family-centered philosophy and delivery of maternal and newborn care is important in assisting families to cope with the childbearing experience and to achieve their own goals within the concept of a high level of wellness, and within the context of the cultural atmosphere of their choosing.

The implementation of family-centered care includes recognition that the provision of maternity/newborn care requires a team effort of the woman and her family, health care providers, and the community. The composition of the team may vary from setting to setting and include obstetricians, pediatricians, family physicians, certified nurse-midwives, nurse practitioners, and other nurses. While physicians are responsible for providing direction for medical management, other team members share appropriately in managing the health care of the family, and each team member must be individually accountable for the performance of his/her facet of care. The team concept includes the cooperative interrelationships of hospitals, health care providers, and the community in an organized system of care so as to provide for the total spectrum of maternity/newborn care within a particular geographic region.[1]

As programs are planned, it is the joint responsibility of all health professionals and their organizations involved with maternity/newborn care, through their assumptions and with input from the community, to establish guidelines for family-centered maternal and newborn care and to assure that such care will be made available to the community regardless of economic status. It is the joint concern and responsibility of the professional organizations to commit themselves to the delivery of maternal and newborn health care in settings where maximum physical safety and psychological well-being for mother and child can be assured. With these requirements met, the hospital setting provides the maximum opportunity for physical safety and for psychological well-being. The development of a family-centered philosophy and implementation of the full range of this family-centered care within innovative and safe hospital settings provides the community/family with the optimum services they desire, request and need.

In view of these insights and convictions, it is recommended that each hospital obstetric, pediatric, and family practice department choosing this approach designate a joint committee on family-centered maternity/newborn care encompassing all recognized and previously stated available team members, including the community. The mission of this committee would be to develop, implement, and regularly evaluate a positive and comprehensive plan for family-centered maternity/newborn care in that hospital.

In addition, it is recommended that all of this be accomplished in the context of joint support for:

—The published standards as presented by The American College of Obstetricians and Gynecologists, The American College of Nurse-Midwives, The Nurses Association of The American College of Obstetricians and Gynecologists, The American Academy of Pediatrics, and the American Nurses' Association.[2,3,4,5,6,7]

[1]Committee on Perinatal Health, The National Foundation-March of Dimes. *Toward Improving the Outcome of Pregnancy: Recommendations for the Regional Development of Maternal and Perinatal Health Services*, 1976.

[2]The American College of Obstetricians and Gynecologists. *Standards for Obstetric-Gynecologic Services*, 1974.

[3]American College of Nurse-Midwives. *Functions, Standards, and Qualifications*, 1975.

[4]The Nurses Association of The American College of Obstetricians and Gynecologists. *Obstetric, Gynecologic and Neonatal Nursing Functions and Standards*, 1975.

—The implementation of the recommendations for the regional planning of maternal and perinatal health services, as appropriate for each region.[1]

—The availability of a family-centered maternity/newborn service at all levels of maternity care within the regional perinatal network.

Potential Components of Family-Centered Maternity/Newborn Care

No specific or detailed plan for implementation of family-centered maternity/newborn care is uniformly applicable, although general guidance as to the potential components of such care is commonly sought. The following description is intended to help those who seek such guidance and is not meant to be uniformly recommended for all maternity/newborn hospital units. The attitudes and needs of the community and the providers vary from geographic area to geographic area, and economic constraints may substantially modify the utilization of each component. The detailed implementation in each hospital unit should be left to that hospital's multidisciplinary committee established to deal with such development. In addition to the maternal/newborn health care team, community and hospital administrative input should be assured. In this manner, each hospital unit can best balance community needs within economic reality.

The major change in maternity/newborn units needed in order to make family-centered care work is attitudinal. Nevertheless, a description of the potential physical and functional components of family-centered care is useful. It remains for each hospital unit to implement those components judged feasible for that unit.

I. Preparation of Families: The unit should provide preparation for childbirth classes taught by appropriately prepared health professionals. Whenever possible, physicians and hospital maternity nurses should participate in such programs so as to maximize cohesion of the team providing education and care. All class approaches should include a bibliography of reading materials. The objectives of these classes are as follows:

A. To increase the community's awareness of their responsibility toward ensuring a healthy outcome for mother and child.
B. To serve as opportunities for the community and providers to match expectations and achieve mutual goals from the childbirth experience.
C. To serve to assist the community to be eligible for participation in the full family-centered program.
D. To include a tour of the hospital's maternity and newborn units. The tour should be offered as an integral part of the preparation for childbirth programs and be available to the community by appointment. The public should be informed of a mechanism for emergency communication with the maternity/newborn unit.

II. Preparation of Hospital Staff: A continuing education program should be conducted on an ongoing basis to educate all levels of hospital personnel who either directly or indirectly come in contact with the family-centered program. This education program may include:

• Content of local preparation for childbirth classes.

[5] American Academy of Pediatrics. *Standards and Recommendations for Hospital Care of Newborn Infants*, 1977.
[6] American Nurses' Association. *Standards of Maternal-Child Health Nursing Practice*, 1973.
[7](a). The American College of Obstetricians and Gynecologists, the American College of Nurse-Midwives, and The Nurses Association of The American College of

Obstetricians and Gynecologists. *Joint Statement on Maternity Care*, 1971.
(b). The American College of Obstetricians and Gynecologists, the American College of Nurse-Midwives, and The Nurses Association of The American College of Obstetricians and Gynecologists. *Supplement to Joint Statement on Maternity Care, 1975*.

- Current trends in childbirth practices.
- Alternative childbirth practices: safe and unsafe, as they are being practiced.
- Needs of childbearing families to share the total experience.
- Ways to support those families experiencing less than optimal outcome of pregnancy.
- Explanation of term "family" so that it includes any "significant" or "supporting other" individual to the expectant mother.
- The advantages to families and to the larger society of establishing the parenting bond immediately after birth.
- The responsibilities of the patients toward ensuring a healthy outcome of the childbirth experience.
- The potential long-term economic advantage to the hospital for initiating the program and how this could benefit each employee.
- The satisfaction to be gained by each employee while assisting families to adjust to the new family member.
- How the family-centered program is to function and the role each employee is to perform to ensure its success.

III. Family-Centered Program within the Maternity/Newborn Unit:
The husband or "supporting other" can remain with the patient throughout the childbirth process as much as possible. Family-newborn interaction immediately after birth is encouraged.

A. *Family Waiting Room* and Early Labor Lounge, attractively painted and furnished, should be available in or near the obstetrical suite where:
   1. Patients in early labor could walk and visit with children, husbands, and others.
   2. The husband or "supporting other" person could go for a "rest break" if necessary.
   3. Access to light nourishment should be available for the husband or "supporting other."
   4. Reading materials are available.
   5. Telephone/intercom connections with the labor area are available.

B. *A Diagnostic-Admitting Room* should be adjacent to or near the Family Waiting Room where:
   1. Women could be examined to ascertain their status in labor without being formally admitted if they are in early labor.
   2. Any woman patient past 20 weeks gestation could be evaluated for emergency health problems during pregnancy.

C. *"Birthing Room":*
   1. A combination labor and delivery room for patient and the husband or "supporting other" during a normal labor and delivery.
   2. A brightly and attractively decorated and furnished room designed to enhance a home-like atmosphere. A comfortable lounge chair is useful.
   3. Stocked for medical emergencies for mother and infant with equipment concealed behind wall cabinets or drapes, but readily available when needed.
   4. Wired for music or intercom as desired.
   5. Equipped with a modern labor-delivery bed which can be:
      (a). raised and lowered.
      (b). adjustable to semi-sitting position.
      (c). moved to the delivery room if the need arises.
   6. Equipped with a cribbette with warmer and have the capacity for infant resuscitation.
   7. Appropriately supplied for a normal spontaneous vaginal delivery and the immediate care of a normal newborn.
   8. An environment in which breastfeeding and handling of the baby are encouraged immediately after delivery with due consideration given to maintaining the baby's normal temperature.

D. *Labor Rooms:*
  1. The husband or "supporting other" can be with a laboring patient whether progress in labor is normal or abnormal.
  2. Regulation hospital equipment is available.
  3. An emergency delivery can be performed.
  4. Attention is given to the surroundings which are attractively furnished and include a comfortable lounge chair.
E. *Delivery Rooms:* Should be properly equipped with standard items but, in addition, should have delivery tables with adjustable backrests. An overhead mirror should be available. The delivery rooms should accommodate breastfeeding and handling of the baby after delivery with due consideration to maintaining the baby's normal temperature.
F. *Recovery Room:* Patients may be returned from the delivery room to their original labor rooms, depending upon the demand, or to a recovery room. Such a recovery room should have all the standard equipment but also allow for the following options:
  1. The infant to be allowed to be with the mother and father or "supporting other" for a time period after delivery with due consideration given to the infant's physiologic adjustment to extrauterine life. Where feasible, post-caesarean section patients may be allowed the same option.
  2. The husband or "supporting other" to be allowed to visit with the new mother and baby with some provision for privacy.
  3. A "pass" to be given to the father or "supporting other" of the baby to allow for extended visiting privileges on the "new family unit."
G. The Postpartum *"new Family Unit"* should:

  1. Contain flexible rooming-in with a central nursery to allow:
     (a). Optional "rooming in."
     (b). Babies to be returned to the central nursery for professional nursing care when desired by the mother.
     (c). Maximum desired maternal/infant contact especially during the first 24 hours.
  2. Have extended visiting hours for the father or "supporting other" to provide the opportunity to assist with the care and feeding of the baby.
  3. Have limited visiting hours for friends since the emphasis of the family-centered approach is on the family.
  4. Contain a family room where:
     (a). Children can visit with their mothers and fathers.
     (b). Professional staff are available to answer questions about parenting and issues regarding adjustments to the enlarged family.
     (c). Cafeteria-like meals can be served and eaten restaurant-style by the mothers.
  5. Have group and individual instruction provided by appropriately prepared personnel on postpartum care, family planning, infant feeding, infant care and parenting.
  6. Allow visiting and feeding by the mothers in the special nurseries such as:
     (a). Newborn, intensive care nursery.
     (b). Isolation nursery.
  7. Allow for breastfeeding/bottle feeding on demand with professional personnel available for assistance.
H. Discharge planning should include options for early discharge. If this option is desired, careful attention to continuing medical and/or nursing contact after discharge to ensure maternal and newborn health is important. Potential for utilization of appropriate referral systems should be available.

Resource Organizations

MATERNITY CARE

Alternative Birth Crisis Coalition
P.O. Box 48731
Chicago, Illinois 60648

*American Academy of Husband-Coached
   Childbirth
P.O. Box 5224
Sherman Oaks, California 91413

American Academy of Pediatrics
1801 Hinman Avenue
Evanston, Illinois 60204

American College of Home Obstetrics
664 North Michigan Avenue, Suite 600
Chicago, Illinois 60611

American College of Nurse-Midwives
1012 14th Street, N.W., Suite 801
Washington, D.C. 20005

American College of Obstetricians and
   Gynecologists
600 Maryland Avenue, S.W.
Washington, D.C. 20024

American National Red Cross
17 & D. Street, N.W.
Washington, D.C. 20006

*American Society for Psychoprophylaxis in
   Obstetrics, Inc. (ASPO)
P.O. Box 33429
Farragut Station
Washington, D.C. 20033

*Association for Childbirth at Home,
   International (ACHI)
P.O. Box 39498
Los Angeles, California 90039

Cesarean Birth Council
1402 Nilde Avenue
Mt. View, California 94040

Childbirth Without Pain Education
   Association
20134 Snowden
Detroit, Michigan 48235

Cooperative Birth Center Network
Box 1, Route 1
Perkiomenville, Pennsylvania 18074

*Council of Childbirth Education Specialists,
   Inc.
168 West 86th Street
New York, New York 10024

---

*Organizations which have or are developing
certification programs for childbirth educators.

Cybele Society
Suite 414
Peyton Building
Spokane, Washington 99201

Home Oriented Maternity Experience
(HOME)
511 New York Avenue
Takoma Park, Maryland 20012

*International Childbirth Education
Association (ICEA)
P.O. Box 20048
Minneapolis, Minnesota 55420

LaLeche League International, Inc.
9616 Minneapolis Avenue
Franklin Park, Illinois 60131

Maternity Center Association
48 West 92nd Street
New York, New York 10028

*Midwest Parentcraft Center
627 Beaver Road
Glenview, Illinois 60015

*National Association of Childbirth Education,
Inc. (NACE)
3940 Eleventh Street
Riverside, California 92501

National Association of Parents and
Professionals for Safe Alternatives in
Childbirth (NAPSAC)
P.O. Box 1307
Chapel Hill, North Carolina 27514

The National Foundation—March of Dimes
1275 Mamaroneck Avenue
White Plains, New York 10605

Nurses Association, American College of
Obstetricians and Gynecologists
600 Maryland Avenue, S.W., Suite 300
Washington, D.C. 20024

Society for Nutrition Education
2140 Shattuck Avenue, Suite 1110
Berkeley, California 94704

ADOLESCENT PREGNANCY

American Home Economics Association
Foundation
Center for the Family
2010 Massachusetts Avenue
Washington, D.C. 20036

Future Homemakers of America
2010 Massachusetts Avenue, N.W.
Washington, D.C. 20036

The American College of Obstetricians and
Gynecologists
Resource Center
600 Maryland Avenue, S.W.
Washington, D.C. 20024

New Futures, Inc.
2120 Louisiana, N.E.
Albuquerque, New Mexico 87110

The Prepared Childbirth Association of Nova
Scotia (PCANS)
P.O. Box 5052 Armdale
Halifax
Nova Scotia, B3L 4M6
Canada

MONITRICES

Manchester Monitrice Associates
31 Bette Drive
Manchester, Connecticut 06040

Monitrices of Maryland, P.A.
307 Dunkirk Road
Baltimore, Maryland 21212

GROUPS FOR GRIEF HELP

AMEND
% Maureen Connelly
4324 Berrywich Terrace
St. Louis, Missouri 63128

Compassionate Friends
P.O. Box 1347
Oak Brook, Illinois 60521

Index

Note: Page numbers in italics indicate entry will be found in an exhibit, figure, or table.